Pope and Devil

Pope and Devil

The Vatican's Archives and the Third Reich

Hubert Wolf

Translated by Kenneth Kronenberg

The Belknap Press of Harvard University Press

Cambridge, Massachusetts, and London, England   2010

This book was originally published in German as *Papst und Teufel: Die Archive des Vatikan und das Dritte Reich,* copyright © 2008 by Verlag C. H. Beck oHG, Munich.

Publication of this volume has been aided by grants from Geisteswissenschaften International (Börsenverein des Deutschen Buchhandels) and the Robert Bosch Stiftung.

Library of Congress Cataloging-in-Publication Data

Wolf, Hubert.
    [Papst & Teufel. English]
    Pope and Devil : the Vatican's archives and the Third Reich / Hubert Wolf ; translated by Kenneth Kronenberg.
        p.   cm.
    Includes bibliographical references (p.   ) and index.
    ISBN 978-0-674-05081-5 (alk. paper)
    1. Catholic Church—Foreign relations—Germany.   2. Germany—Foreign relations—Catholic Church.   3. Catholic Church—History—20th century.   4. Germany—Foreign relations—1918–1933.   5. Germany—Foreign relations—1933–1945.   6. National socialism and religion.   I. Title.
    BX1536.W64 2010
    327.45634043089'924—dc22   2010008029

Contents

Pope and Devil

Introduction

"If it were possible to save even a single soul, to shield souls from greater harm, we would find the courage to deal even with the devil himself."[1] Pope Pius XI, who made this statement in May 1929, did in fact have the courage during his papacy (1922–1939) to negotiate with people commonly considered to be evil incarnate: Benito Mussolini, Adolf Hitler, and Joseph Stalin. The "representative of Christ on earth" was primarily motivated by concern for the salvation of the faithful and guarantees that the Catholic Church could continue its mission to provide pastoral care. To ensure the eternal life of the lambs entrusted to him, the chief shepherd of the Church was even prepared to make diplomatic concessions to the devil in the guise of totalitarian ideologies and those who spawned them. In exchange for a promise of spiritual freedom, the Church was willing to renounce worldly engagement in politics and public affairs, and literally withdraw to the sacristy.

Pius XI gave this speech on May 16, 1929. At first glance, his words seem to relate exclusively to the Lateran Pacts concluded on February 11, 1929, between Fascist Italy and the Holy See. The agreements had finally resolved the "Roman question" after a half-century of fierce conflict between the Kingdom of Italy and the Holy See. Ever since 1870, when Italian troops occupied the Papal States and the city of Rome during the *Risorgimento,* the founding of the Italian state, the popes had viewed themselves as captives in the Vatican. The traditional papal blessing "Urbi et Orbi" ("for the city of Rome and for the whole world") was no longer imparted from the outer loggia of St. Peter's on liturgical celebrations such as Christmas and Easter, but only within the inner loggia of the basilica—so that the Italian "plunderers of the Papal States" should not benefit from it. It was simply unthinkable to prominent members of the Roman Curia and to the pope himself that the leader of untold millions of Catholic faithful the world over should be a common citizen of Italy and a subject of its king. In order to practice his universal spiritual office, the pope, so they believed, required the sovereignty afforded by his own state, which would guarantee complete independence from worldly powers. Conversely, in the interest of its newly achieved national unity, the Kingdom of Italy could not return to the pope any part of the Papal States, let alone a section of the capital city of Rome. And so state and Church were at loggerheads for decades. During World War I, the Church even considered moving the Holy See from Rome to Liechtenstein or Mallorca. The *Conciliazione,* the agreement between the Roman Curia and the Italian National State, which had never been approved by parliamentary Italy, was finally signed in 1929 between the totalitarian regime of Mussolini and Pius XI. Fascism and Catholicism came to an understanding. The Lateran Pacts, which consisted of an international treaty, a concordat, and a financial agreement, established the independent State of Vatican City, which gave the pope at least a diminutive papal state. Moreover, in exchange for the depoliticization of clergy and Church, Catholic doctrines and moral principles were now specifically protected under Italian church law. At the same time, the pope reined in the Fascists' unwelcome political opposition of Catholic provenance, the People's Party. The Lateran Pacts with Mussolini's Italy may well be interpreted as an agreement between the pope and "evil," in the interest of pastoral care.

Even though Pius XI stressed the Italian aspects of his statements in his address during a private audience with Catholic professors and students, the context makes clear that he was referring not just to the negotiations recently concluded with Mussolini and Italian Fascists but also to the

Church's role more generally in meeting the challenges of modernity. Ever since the nineteenth century, the pope and the Curia had increasingly confronted efforts by the various states to limit or even eliminate completely the influence of the Church in central functions such as the education of young people. The pope viewed parochial education as a divine mission of the Church to save the souls of young people. In his eyes, the Catholic Church as "mater et magistra," mother and teacher, had not only the inalienable right but also the sacred duty to provide educational assistance to parents who, in turn, had an absolute right according to divine law to education within the folds of the Church. Individual families would otherwise be unduly burdened in attempting to educate their children properly. The state, meanwhile, must not under any circumstances arrogate to itself the right to educate. That, according to the pope, would be "absurd" and "against nature." Pius XI believed that the complete control of education sought by the various states, regardless of their ideology, imperiled not only the temporal well-being of children and young people but their eternal salvation as well.

This situation posed a fundamental challenge to the Church: eternal values were at stake. To meet this challenge, the Church must be willing to deal even with the devil himself. In his address, the pope stressed that he had already negotiated several times with nation states, and that he had carried these negotiations as far as possible "when the fate of our beloved Catholics depended on it." However, wherever natural right and divine right were at stake, the Church must, Pius XI insisted, remain adamant because these rights were "incontestable, indisputable, unopposable." In other words, neither humans nor even the Church itself could ignore them.

According to the pope and the Curia, the modern state, regardless of its underlying ideology, tried hard to make wide-ranging, even total, claims on its citizens that conflicted with the Catholic Church's claims on the faithful. Over the course of the twentieth century, Catholicism increasingly confronted totalitarian ideologies that, as quasi-political religions, posed a life-and-death challenge to Christianity and its claims to absolute truth. Certain ideologies in particular called for total appropriation of state, society, and the individual. They deified themselves, perverting the biblical injunction, "Thou shalt have no other gods before Me." The Catholic Church, with its absolute self-evident claim to truth based in God, and with the pope as the representative of Jesus Christ, felt challenged by these all-encompassing conceptions of salvation and alternative "political religions." "However, the concept of totalitarianism," according to an internal paper issued by the papal Secretariat of State in the fall of 1933, "may not under any circumstances be abused to achieve political and worldly goals. The Church itself strives for totality in order to win the entire person and all of humanity for God."[2]

The term "totalitarianism" is used here for largely pragmatic reasons and refers to no particular theory; in fact, it might refer to two very different political systems such as Communism and Fascism. The intention is merely to reduce to a single term the all-inclusive claims of various political ideologies and religious communities of faith. During the 1930s, the Curia tended to use the terms "total" and "totalitarian" interchangeably, so we cannot assume that they conceived of totalitarianism as it would come to be known.

The dualistic worldview of Catholics must be taken seriously because it was a constant touchstone in their battle against the new ideologies. In 1938, Eric Voegelin (1901–1985), who coined the term "political religion," wrote from exile in the United States that "a religious view of National Socialism must proceed from the assumption that there is evil in the world. To be sure, evil not only as a deficient mode of being, something negative, but rather as a genuine, effective substance and force in the world." He added that it "can only be opposed by an equally strong, religiously good force of resistance." In the final analysis, only "great religious personalities" were capable of resisting evil; only they could direct the battle against the compelling power of malevolent elements.[3] If anyone were capable of organizing the campaign against evil, then, according to the Church, the pope, as the representative of Christ on earth, would be the one called to perform that service.

Catholic teachings painted the battle between good and evil in vivid colors, and for the popes and many Catholics this battle was very real. The pope, consequently, was expected to meet this challenge, and the faithful, if they were papal loyalists, had a choice between truth and error, between eternal salvation and eternal damnation—between the pope and the devil. All their actions had to be determined by this fundamental choice. Just as Christ had three times been tempted by the devil in the desert and had three times rejected him (Matthew 4:1–11), the pope as the chief shepherd of the Church saw himself as called upon to confront evil in order to lead his flock through dark valleys to the heavenly pastures of eternity, losing none of his lambs during the perilous journey.

Pius XI viewed himself as the defender of eternal truths and, ultimately, of the Catholic Church's mission of salvation in this world. This responsibility allowed the pope to engage with people he considered the embodiment of evil. His address on May 16 extended beyond the various totalitarianisms of the twentieth century, the "evil" anti-Christian ideologies of Communism, National Socialism, Fascism, Franquism, and radical anticlerical liberalism, and it moved well beyond the current dark princes, Stalin, Hitler, Mussolini, and Franco. Nor did the total claims made by modern states upon the souls of their citizens exhaust Satan's arsenal. Rather, the devil functioned as a sort of stand-in for all modern temptations and for all questioning of divine eternal truth as revealed by Jesus Christ. The Catholic Church—and the pope himself as direct successor of Peter, the Prince of Apostles—was the worldly guarantor of this truth. The "evil" spirit of the times attempted by material or idealistic maneuverings to deflect the faithful from the true way. As a result, believers veered from the path of life that God had chosen for them, thereby forfeiting eternal salvation. At issue was nothing less than whether the pope as head of the *ecclesia militans,* the Church militant in this world, would succeed in holding open the gates of heaven for Catholics and sealing the gates of hell.

At the time of Pius XI, trained theologians and lay Catholics alike were well aware both of the existence of hell as a place of eternal damnation and of the works of the devil in this world. "Christ's revelations about the devil are very serious," wrote Archbishop of Freiburg Conrad Gröber in 1937 in his frequently reprinted *Handbuch der religiösen Gegenwartsfragen* [Handbook of religious questions of the day]. In the Gospel of John, Christ three times calls Satan the "prince of this world" (John 12:31, 14:30, and 16:11), and Paul even calls him the "god of this world" (2 Corinthians 4:4). For Gröber, the devil was quite simply "the foe" who, according to the unambiguous words of Holy Scripture, "sows weeds in the fields of God's kingdom. . . . The devil is the ringleader of evildoers who, whether from within the visible Church or from outside, seek the downfall of the Kingdom of Christ. He will, however, fail to overpower the Church built on the rock of Peter."[4]

But the Church had always rejected the dualism implied by two eternal principles of equal rank, that is, God on one side and the devil on the other. Rather, Lucifer had always been viewed as a fallen angel, as the Fourth Lateran Council had held in 1215: "The devil and other demons were created by God naturally good, but they became evil by their own doing. Man, however, sinned at the prompting of the devil."[5] The original sin of the angels who fell from heaven to earth is therefore an extension of the fall of man in Paradise. Since then the serpent, the devil, has existed in the world and has in one form or another always seduced humans into evil. "This power of Satan must be taken very seriously," according to an article in *Lexikon für Theologie und Kirche* [Lexicon of theology and Church] published in 1938, the standard work for Catholic theologians and pastors. Christ, who called him a "murderer from the beginning" (John 8:44), viewed the devil as the "enemy of his entire redemptive work."[6] Although Christ's death on the cross gave the Church an effective means for fighting the devil, this did not mean that evil had "simply been banished from the world," as Gröber put it. Rather, the "power of Satan is visible in the weeds 'up to the harvest,'" but his power would finally be broken for good at the Last Judgment. "In times of persecution," Gröber continued, "the Church sets its sights on Christ's final victory in this regard."[7] Until the Lord returns at the Last Judgment, individuals will be subject to the devil's temptations, and the battle between good and evil will rage relentlessly.

The pope's own understanding of his role—and of the faithful's expectations of him—was that he be the natural adversary of evil, regardless of the form it took. Like Jesus Christ himself, the "Bishop of Rome, Representative of Jesus Christ, Successor of the Prince of Apostles, Supreme Pontifex of the Universal Church, Patriarch of the Occident, Primate of Italy, Archbishop and Metropolitan of the Ecclesiastical Province of Rome, and Sovereign of the State of Vatican City"—as the pope was formally addressed in the *Annuario Pontificio*,[8] the official annual papal hand-book—was called to confront the tempter and prince of the world be-cause, according to the tenets of Catholicism, "the pope represents the figure of Jesus Christ on earth."[9] In their fierce conflicts with the absolut-ist church governments of the mostly Protestant states of the nineteenth century, many Catholics directed their hopes *ultra montes,* beyond the mountains, toward Rome and the pope as the rock of Peter, rooted in eternity. In the raging storms of modern life, they promised safety and security, something to hold onto amid the flood tide of evil. In the pope, according to an Italian bishop at the First Vatican Council in 1870, Catho-lics saw "simultaneously an incarnation of supernatural order," in which they recognized Christ, "who is therefore in all and for all in the pope and with the pope and through the pope."[10] Popular piety took this formula-tion a step further: "When the pope meditates, it is God who thinks in him."[11] In the end, the Church advanced a triple incarnation of the Son of God: through the birth of the eternal Logos in the infant Jesus in the man-ger in Bethlehem; through the transformation of bread and wine into the body and blood of Christ in Holy Communion; and finally through the secret selection in conclave of a cardinal to be pope.

At the First Vatican Council, these notions led to the dogmas of papal infallibility and of the pope's universal primacy of jurisdiction. These dog-mas were binding on all Catholics. Because he is infallible, the pope is the guarantor of revealed divine truths, according to which "God directed hu-man beings to a supernatural end, that is to sharing in the good things of God that utterly surpasses the understanding of the human mind."[12] The pope is thus indispensable "for the salvation of the Christian people." His "supreme apostolic authority," which Christ, "by the divine assistance promised to him in blessed Peter" and through Peter to all his successors to the Apostolic See, ensures the "strength and coherence of the whole Church," especially in times when "the gates of hell trying, if they can, to overthrow the Church, make their assault with a hatred that increases day by day against its divinely laid foundation." Whenever the pope speaks as supreme shepherd and teacher of the Church, his decisions in matters of belief and morals are "of themselves, and not by the consent of the church, irreformable."[13]

Whenever Pius XI was borne through a crowd of the faithful in St. Peter's, seated under a canopy on the *sedia gestatoria,* or portable throne, attired in his pontifical vestments, and crowned with the tiara, he was symbolically enacting his role as representative of the goodness of God and adversary of the devil in all his guises. The throne and the vestments, which derive from ancient Roman imperial ceremony, symbolize the sweeping authority laid claim to by the bishop of Rome in the Church and in the world. The triple crown symbolizes the pope's all-encompassing authority and his universal power as "father of princes and kings, ruler of the world, and representative of Christ on earth," as the 1596 *Pontificale*

Pius XI on the *sedia gestatoria.*
(akg-images, London)

Romanum, the papal book of ceremony, so aptly phrases it.[14] During the Corpus Christi procession, the priests generally bear the *sanctum sanctorum* within a magnificent monstrance beneath the canopy, representing the transformed host in which Christ himself is present as sacrament. The pope here assumes the role of the Eucharistic bread as a manifestation of Jesus Christ in this world.

The challenges confronting Pius XI were many and great. The period between the two world wars, which largely coincided with his pontificate, was marked by social and political upheaval. Communism was established in Russia after the October Revolution and was accompanied by thoroughgoing persecution of the Church. In Germany, the November Revolution brought an end to the monarchy; the Weimar Republic was followed by Nazi dictatorship, the annexation of Austria, and the Sudeten crisis. The Popular Front government was defeated in the Spanish Civil War and was replaced by Franco and his authoritarian regime. Mussolini, the leader of the Fascist movement, became dictator in Italy. New and old nationalisms turned radical throughout Europe, and Social Darwinian racial theories and biological anti-Semitism gained ground. The anticlerical Zeitgeist questioned all Christian values and convictions.

No fewer than three times during the 1920s the pope had offered to establish diplomatic relations with the Soviet Union under Stalin. The Church offered to recognize the legitimacy of the Communist regime in the Soviet Union provided that Stalin stopped persecuting Christians and guaranteed Catholics at least the basic sacraments, the Church's means of grace. At the same time, the pope and the Curia hoped for an upgrading of Catholicism in relation to the persecuted Orthodox state church. Achille Ratti, the apostolic visitor to Poland and nuncio to Warsaw, had seen firsthand the effects of Communist anticlerical terror after the October Revolution of 1917 and at the end of World War I, between 1918 and 1921. Russian Bolshevism has since represented the embodiment of evil for later popes and most of the Roman Curia, a danger from which the Church and the world must be protected, but one that nevertheless must be dealt with in the interest of the salvation of souls.

Many observers believe that the Reichskonkordat, the treaty signed between the Holy See and the German Reich in 1933, a few months after Hitler's seizure of power, was nothing less than a pact with the devil. Even though Pius XI had in the spring of 1933 praised Hitler as the only statesman—apart from the pope himself—who had publicly and unambiguously spoken out against Communism, neither the pope nor his cardinal secretary of state, Eugenio Pacelli, the future Pope Pius XII, harbored any illusions about the antihuman and anticlerical nature of the National Socialist regime in Germany. In the 1940s, Pius XII seems even to have characterized Hitler as "possessed by the devil." According to the Jesuit Peter Gumpel, a member of the Congregation for the Causes of Saints charged with pursuing the beatification of Pius XII, the pope had several times attempted "long-distance exorcisms" to drive the devil out of Hitler and to "free him from Satan," but without success.[15] The pact with Hitler was basically a forward defensive measure for the Curia made in anticipation of the persecution the Church would experience under Nazi rule. The Reichskonkordat was intended to erect a high wall behind which the Catholic Church would at least in part be able to make good on its responsibility to ensure the eternal salvation of the faithful and to combat the absolutism of National Socialism.

From a pastoral perspective, this calculation seems to have borne fruit. In fact, the Catholic Church remained the only institution in the Third Reich that was largely successful in resisting the Nazi policy of forced coordination (Gleichschaltung) and retaining the independence of its liturgy and its capacity to proclaim the faith. In contrast to the Protestant churches, in which so-called German Christians were installed as National Socialist bridgeheads, the "brownshirts" barely penetrated the interior space of the Catholic Church. The Reichskonkordat prevented the sort of pastoral disaster that had occurred in Germany during the Kulturkampf of the 1870s and 1880s, when thousands of parishes and numerous bishoprics could not be staffed because of the conflict between the Catholic Church and the new German state of Otto von Bismarck, which meant that countless faithful were denied the consolation of the holy sacraments. In many cases, baptism, confirmation, marriage, and the celebration of Holy Eucharist were not possible. Even last rites were often denied, so that Catholics were forced to present themselves before God without the benefit of confession and forgiveness of sins, and without pastoral support and extreme unction.

But did the Church not pay too high a price for this pastoral victory during the Third Reich? By concentrating on the eternal salvation of Catholics, did the pope not neglect the temporal well-being of all human beings? How did he come to terms with the two competing demands: first, as supreme shepherd, to lead his flock to green pastures, and second, to fulfill the duty to advocate for all human beings formed in God's likeness? How did Pius XI and his cardinal secretary of state, Eugenio Pacelli, view developments in Germany? How did they judge the political constellations in the Weimar Republic? What did they make of the ascent of the National Socialists? Had members of the Curia prepared themselves adequately for Hitler and his totalitarian regime? Did they believe that they could deal with National Socialism much as they had with Italian Fascism—with which they had come to an understanding in the 1929 Lateran Pacts? Did they underestimate Hitler because of their "positive" experience with Mussolini? In the final analysis, was the pact with the devil, which was motivated primarily by concern for the salvation of the faithful, responsible for Rome's "silence" in the face of the persecution and systematic murder of millions of Jews? Was there not, in fact, at least an indirect unholy alliance between the traditional anti-Judaism of the Church and modern racial anti-Semitism? Or did Pius XI conclude an agreement with Nazi rulers in Berlin in order to erect a bulwark to protect Europe from Russian Communism? And more specifically, what did Cardinal Secretary of State Pacelli's experiences in Germany during the crucial years between 1917 and 1929 mean for his assessment of the situation in the Reich, and for the Vatican's policies regarding Germany? What was the nature of the personal networks that he developed during his nunciature in Germany? Can we trace particular patterns of behavior on the part of the future Pius XII back to experiences he had there? And is there a connection between those experiences and his alleged silence about the Holocaust?

For many years, such questions could not be adequately answered because researchers were denied access to the Vatican archives. Although public texts and the actions of the pope and the Curia provided important insights, and state and private archives yielded interesting material, the central records containing reports by the nuncios, minutes of the deliberations of "Vatican ministries," the files of the Holy Office as Supreme Congregation of the Faith, and deliberations between the cardinal secretary of state and the pope remained closed for this period. As a result, we could only speculate about discussions within the Curia. The Vatican Secret Archives again lived up to their name.

In the Vatican Secret Archives

Could Dan Brown have been right when in his thriller *Angels and Demons* he described what the Vatican Secret Archives look like, who gets in, and who is barred from entrance?

> [Robert] Langdon had never met a single non-Catholic American scholar who had been given access to the Secret Vatican Archives.
> Archivio Vaticano. One of his life dreams. . . . The images he had held for so many years of this room could not have been more inaccurate. He had imagined dusty bookshelves piled high with tattered volumes, priests cataloging by the light of candles and stained glass windows, monks poring over scrolls. . . .
> Not even close.
> At first glance the room appeared to be a darkened airline hangar in which someone had built a dozen free-standing racquetball courts. Langdon knew of course what the glass-walled enclosures were. . . . humidity and heat eroded ancient developments and parchments, and proper preservation required hermetic vaults like these—airtight cubicles that kept out humidity and natural acids in the air.[16]

In Brown's account, entering these vaults is perilous because atmospheric pressure and oxygen levels are kept low. Indeed, "the oxygen was regulated by a reference librarian."

Brown certainly provided the perfect backdrop for a thriller. Unfortunately, the picture he painted of the Vatican Secret Archives was not even close. The only truth in his depiction is that any historian privileged to work in this unique collection considers it a dream come true. The archives resemble an airplane hangar as little as they do a Gothic crypt. Most of the rooms are filled with filing cabinets—a good thirty-five miles of them in all. Access is by no means limited to faithful Catholics. On the contrary, parish registers play no role whatsoever in admittance. One need only prove the ability to do research. Anyone with a letter of recommendation from a university or other research facility, anyone who can demonstrate research done in major archives, anyone who has good knowledge of Latin and Italian and can decipher old handwriting will be granted unlimited access.

The fact that the Vatican archives are "secret" does not mean that the Church is attempting to conceal or suppress their contents. Rather, the term is used in the sense of "private." The Archivio Segreto Vaticano is not a public archive in the usual sense but rather the archive of a sovereign, the pope, who therefore has the full and sole right of disposition over all its holdings. Originally, the secret archives functioned solely as an administrative register for the popes and the Curia. Such collections were common throughout Europe; the Prussian Secret State Archive, in Berlin, or the Secret Archive of the House of Wittelsbach, in Munich, are good examples.

No one wishing to do research in the Vatican archives need present a baptismal certificate, but a day visa is required at least for the first visit because Vatican City is an independent state. Each visit also requires a border crossing between the Republic of Italy and Vatican City. Visitors can obtain a visa by filling out a form after describing their business to the Swiss Guard, who mans the only official border crossing between Italy and the Vatican, the Porta Santa Anna, located to the right of St. Peter's Square. The street leading to the archive, the Via del Belvedere, passes by the towering walls of the Vatican Palace. The Vatican Supermarket, Vatican Post Office, and the Bank of the Vatican are located on this street. A wide gateway leads to the courtyard of the building complex, which also includes the Vatican museums and the Vatican Library. The entrance to the archive is on the right side of this courtyard, the Cortile del Belvedere. At 8:30 A.M. on the dot, the friendly clerk behind the reception desk takes the researcher's reader pass, or *tessera,* and distributes locker keys in return. (The pass is issued by another clerk next door.) A first-time researcher in the archive must present a letter of recommendation to the archivist and historian Bishop Sergio Pagano, along with personal information and the purpose of the research. A digital photograph is then taken for the *tessera*. And that's about it.

The modern reading room is located on the third floor and has seating for about seventy researchers, most of whom bring their laptops. Although appropriate clothing is requested, some of the younger historians wear running shoes and blue jeans with their sports coats. A large window and a door that is only half closed provide a view onto a green yard, the Cortile della Pigna, which is at the same level as the reading room on the third floor, evidence that the Vatican is a hill. Visitors can hear the splashing of a small fountain in the yard; the friendly staff serve a first-class cappuccino in a small cafeteria, where they also sell sandwiches. The

The reading room of the Vatican Secret Archives with its old seating arrangement. Today there are modern desk chairs, reading lamps, and electrical outlets at each seat. The lecterns have remained; the archival material is placed on them. A door at the back of the reading room leads directly to the Vatican Library.

(Copyright © Archivio Segreto Vaticano)

murderous monk in Dan Brown's thriller would presumably have taken little inspiration from this scene. But this is where historians from all over the world gather and trade stories. More than a few research projects and international symposia have been hatched here.

It goes without saying that no serious researcher harbors the notion that the Catholic Church is hiding the Holy Grail behind the high walls of the Vatican, nor, for that matter, any other secrets that might imperil the existence of the Church. Mystical conspiracy theories and tales of horror are the stuff of novelists, not historians. Nonetheless, some historians suspect that the Vatican is withholding uncomfortable material, or at the very least shows scant interest in digging around too deeply in its own past. More to the point, some researchers contend that though the Vatican does provide all the files from an entire papacy simultaneously, it does not follow any established release schedule. Unlike German state archives, for example, the Vatican does not release particular types of files such as personnel records or case files at regularly scheduled times. Rather, the decision to open particular holdings belongs to each pope. For example, in the early 1990s John Paul II (1978–2005) directed that the files relating to Benedict XV, who was pope from 1914 to 1922, be opened. This was followed in 1998 by the opening of the archives of the Holy Roman and Universal Inquisition and of the Congregation of the Index, which are among the most secret Church archives. These archives, which were made available in preparation for the Jubilee year 2000 and the pope's prayer for forgiveness for the sins of the Church, were considered sensational by many. They are not, however, in the Vatican Secret Archives, but are controlled by the Congregation for the Doctrine of the Faith, which is located in the Palazzo del Sant'Ufficio, to the left of St. Peter's Square.

The fact that the Vatican files from the National Socialist period were not accessible led to wild speculation. Matters became particularly heated when the Vatican took up the beatification process of Pius XII, who was pope from 1939 to 1958 and was certainly among the most controversial figures of the twentieth century. To some he was "Hitler's pope" (John Cornwell), to others, "the greatest benefactor of the Jewish people" (Pinchas Lapide). Was Pius XII really the pope who was silent in the face of the Holocaust, as many charge? Did he perhaps secretly sympathize with National Socialism? Perhaps he was even an anti-Semite? To answer such questions, Pope John Paul II in 1999 formed a commission consisting of three Catholic and three Jewish historians. Their task was to work through the voluminous Vatican files from World War II that had already been made public at the instruction of Paul VI (1963–1978), and to reevaluate them with regard to the role of Pius XII. Most of the members of the commission, however, were not satisfied with the files they received and demanded unimpeded and unlimited access to the Vatican Secret Archives, which was denied on the grounds that the holdings had not yet been properly archived. Before the files could be made accessible, the pages would have to be bundled, inventoried, paginated, and stamped. This impasse led to increasing discord, and the commission was dissolved.

In large part because of the criticism that ensued, Pope John Paul II decided to break with convention. In 2003, he made four series from the papacy of Pius XI, that is, from the years 1922 to 1939, available separately. These included the archives of the nunciatures, the diplomatic representations of the Vatican in Munich and Berlin, which had been transferred to Rome. In addition, he released the Vatican responses to these German holdings in the archives of the papal Secretariat of State and of the Congregation for Extraordinary Ecclesiastical Affairs—the nerve centers of international relations. They bear the descriptive titles "Baviera" and "Germania." With this, the nuncial reports from Germany and the instructions to the nuncios in Germany for the period up to 1939 were made available for the first time.

These sources are informative, particularly as they relate to the person of Eugenio Pacelli. During his time in Germany Pacelli wrote to Rome daily, sometimes several times a day; thus far almost five thousand of his detailed reports have been identified in the Vatican Secret Archives. In addition, Pacelli was named cardinal secretary of state by Pius XI in 1930 after he left Germany, which meant that he received the reports sent by his successor, Cesare Orsenigo (1873–1946). Now he analyzed the situation in Germany with the pope and developed his policies accordingly. These roughly one thousand archival units, consisting of boxes, fascicles, omnibus volumes, and file bundles, represent a quantum leap in our understanding of the Vatican view of Germany, even though evaluation of the sources has only just begun. However, internal curial discussions, minutes of the various congregations, the pope's conversations with his cardinal secretary of state, and records of audiences with emissaries to the Holy See remained unavailable at that time, as did the reports from nuncios throughout the world, their instructions from Rome, and the corresponding nuncial archives. These papers were needed to shed light on what information Rome had about particular questions, and especially on how the Vatican developed positions internally. As a result, in February 2006 Pope Benedict XVI made available to researchers all files in the Vatican Secret Archives relating to the pontificate of Pius XI from February 6, 1922, the day that Achille Ratti was elected pope, to February 10, 1939, the date of his death. This represents an enormous quantity of about one hundred thousand archival units, each containing up to a thousand pages.

Once they have been analyzed and evaluated, the sources made available between 2003 and 2006 will provide a unique opportunity to reconstruct from the Curia's point of view the confrontation between the Catholic Church with its claim to absolute truth and the totalitarian systems of the twentieth century. The holdings relating to Soviet Bolshevism, Italian Fascism, Spanish Franquism, Mexican anticlericalism, Austro-Fascism and the corporative Austrian state, and not least German National Socialism, are voluminous. These files from various country series of the Secretariat of State or of the Congregation for Extraordinary Ecclesiastical Affairs and the various nuncial archives have all been transferred to the Vatican Secret Archives.

The internal files of the secretary of state, the conversations between the cardinal secretary of state and the emissaries to the Holy See, and not least Pacelli's notes about his almost daily audiences with Pius XI contain fascinating information. In addition, the archives contain records of the various congregations, and particularly of the Holy Office, the supreme Roman congregation responsible for the doctrine of the faith.

Only international collaboration among historians can provide a comprehensive analysis of the almost apocalyptic confrontation between the *totalitarismo* of the Church and the totalitarianisms of the twentieth century. It is too early to render a judgment, given the mass of documents and the short amount of time the archives have been opened. In addition, few of the files relating to Germany and National Socialism have been analyzed or evaluated. Nonetheless, since these sources were already accessible in 2003, some initial conclusions may be advanced. For this book, I have also consulted an array of French, Italian, and German-language works based on the new Vatican sources that had already been published. These primarily include studies published by Thomas Brechenmacher, who is in the process of mounting an Internet edition of Cesare Orsenigo's nuncial reports from Berlin for the years 1930 to 1939. In addition to works by Gerhard Besier, Giovanni Sale, Andrea Tornielli, and Matteo Napolitano, two biographies deserve special mention: Emma Fattorini's *Pio XI, Hitler e Mussolini*, which incorporates a few of the documents available since 2006, and Philippe Chenaux's comprehensive biography of Pius XII, published in 2003. I have, however, consciously refrained from commenting on their various positions.

It is not yet possible to write a comprehensive history of the relations between the Vatican and Germany during the period between 1917 and 1945. For one thing, we do not have the archival documents relating to the crucial years of World War II because they fall completely within the pontificate of Pius XII. We have no way of knowing when Rome will see fit to make these files available. Furthermore, the Vatican sources generally allow only a reconstruction of Rome's view of Germany and conditions in that country. They contain the perspectives of the pope, the cardinal secretary of state, and the nuncios in Berlin and Munich. The new sources document the Vatican's assessment of developments in the Reich as well as internal curial discussions about how the Church should respond to the German challenge. This double perspective—the view from Rome and the consultations within the Vatican about German affairs—is the focus of this book.

One

Neutralizing Evil?

Vatican Prescriptions for Germany (1917–1929)

In spite of its many efforts, the Catholic press in Bavaria has not made much headway. . . . Bavarian Catholics still do not understand the need to collect funds to establish a newspaper capable of neutralizing the evil spread by the Münchner Neueste Nachrichten, *the most widely read German newspaper. This paper is popular because of its low price and abundance of news and advertising. The evil that it inflicts is incalculable. Before the war, news and articles attacking not only the Church but Christianity itself and religion in general were commonplace. This newspaper may be viewed as the mouthpiece of free thought and monism.*[1]

With these harsh words, in November 1916 Cardinal Secretary of State Pietro Gasparri (1852–1934) described for the newly selected nuncio to Munich, Giuseppe Aversa (1862–1917), the difficult situation of the Catholic Church in Bavaria and Germany as he saw it. His instruction simply glossed over the fact that though the *Münchner Neueste Nachrichten* was a liberal newspaper, it opened its columns to progressive Catholics. In any case, from the perspective of Rome, liberal Catholics who were infected by the spirit of the age were merely "half" Catholic. What was lacking was a well-executed ultramontane Catholic daily that could successfully stand up to the mass-circulation liberal and Socialist papers, which at the time were key opponents of the Catholic Church and its worldview. And so the instructions to the representatives of the Holy See in Germany were unambiguous: "As His Eminence the Nuncio is well aware of the enormous influence that the press exerts on public opinion, and of its immense advantages, but also of the tremendous damage it does to the Holy See, to the Church, and to religion, He will therefore make every effort to support and propagate the good press."

Each nuncio dispatched by Rome to represent the diplomatic interests of the Holy See and to oversee the Catholic Church in a given country received from the cardinal secretary of state, to whom all papal emissaries were subordinated, two important documents to tuck into his briefcase. The first contained his credentials, which he presented to a head of state in the process of formal accreditation. The other was the so-called general instruction, which gave the new nuncio, who was not infrequently traveling to the country of his posting for the first time, an overview of the political and religious situation into which he was walking. Whereas these instructions had usually been limited to a few pages in the early nineteenth century, the Secretariat of State, in Rome, had by the turn of the century begun to put considerably more effort into drafting these texts. As a result, they now occasionally went on for more than a hundred pages. These nuanced situation analyses were based on reports of the previous nuncio. It is important to recognize, however, that reality and the representation thereof were not, strictly speaking, congruent; rather, matters were always viewed from the perspective of the papal nuncio or the Roman Secretariat of State. After this overview of conditions in his country of posting, the nuncio then received a catalogue of tasks to be dealt with during his term.

Like any secular diplomat, the nuncio had to submit regular reports to his superior, in this case, the cardinal secretary of state, about the progress of his efforts. At the same time he kept the Holy See informed of political and religious developments in his host country. These nuncial reports, which were usually sent to Rome weekly and sometimes even daily, contained not only a list of facts and their evaluation by the nuncio but also numerous enclosures. These included interesting newspaper clippings, expert opinions that the nunciature had solicited, and also letters of denunciation or complaint from a myriad of sources. This is where the nuncio's crucial network of personal informants comes into view. Generally, the secretary of state received the nuncial reports without further comment. However, whenever the pope or the Curia deemed the subject matter to be important, he would respond with specific instructions to the nuncio.

The appraisal and to-do list that were included in the general instruction signed by the secretary of state at the beginning of a nunciature were followed by the so-called final report at the end of his term. In this generally voluminous summation, a nuncio looked back over the scope of his activities. He gave an accounting both to himself and to his superiors in Rome of which items on his list he had brought to a successful conclusion during his nunciature. In addition, he noted any new problems or issues that had emerged which might be of particular concern to his successor. The general instruction and the final report provide a unique opportunity to reconstruct the Roman perspective on the political and religious situation in the country to which the nuncio was posted. This "view from Rome" uniquely reveals what the Curia knew, and from whom, as well as which information the nuncio chose to pass on to Rome. These documents permit us to draw conclusions about what the cardinal secretary of state—as political head of the Curia—knew, and thus also what information was available to the pope. The evaluations contained in the instructions and reports also reveal the strength and tint of the spectacles worn by the "Roman" observers—the nuncio in a particular country and the secretary of state and his staff in Rome. They bring into clear focus the criteria on which they based their judgments and the theological categories that determined their guiding principles. A dualistic worldview in which a phenomenon, a person, or an event was seen as either "good" or "evil" often set the tone—as was evident in their assessment of the German press. Such entities served either the pope and Church or their enemies, the devil and his agents.

In many respects, the sources recently made available in the Vatican Secret Archives for the period between the end of the Second German Reich and the crisis of the Weimar Republic provide an especially dramatic view from Rome, focusing in particular on the years 1916–1917 and 1929–1930.

A new nuncio, Eugenio Pacelli, assumed office in Munich in the spring of 1917. Pacelli would remain nuncio to Germany for more than twelve years, until the summer of 1929. He, too, was bound by the general instruction, which was more than 110 pages long and based on the exceedingly nuanced reports submitted by Andreas Frühwirth (1845–1933), Pacelli's predecessor in Munich from 1907 to 1916. At the end of his nunciature, Pacelli himself submitted a final report that was a good 100 pages in length. Between 1917 and 1929, he sent more than 5,000 reports to Rome. Many of these have not yet been found in the archives, much less recorded and evaluated. Nonetheless, the general instruction and the final report, supplemented by an array of pertinent individual reports, provide an opportunity to learn more about Rome's perspective on Germany on two historically arbitrary occasions, the beginning and the end of Pacelli's nunciature.

The year 1917 was a pivotal one in European and Church history, and it therefore provides a particularly interesting window on the view from Rome. The October Revolution in Russia and the emergence of Bolshevism, the failed attempts to end World War I, including Woodrow Wilson's Fourteen Point Plan, and the imminent collapse of the German Reich and the end of the monarchy were crucial events. Another development inside the Church itself stands out, namely, the enactment of a new centralist canon law, the *Codex Iuris Canonici* (CIC), which would fundamentally determine the relationship between Church and state. At the same time, the ascension of Benedict XV had put an end to the furor over modernist persecution under his predecessor Pius X (1903–1914). Although the reformist forces within the Catholic Church, which sought a fundamental reconciliation between the Church and modernity, faith and knowledge, and the natural sciences and revelation, continued to be viewed with suspicion by Rome, they were no longer subject to exclusion from the Church as a matter of course. The Catholic Church also became more receptive to the youth movement, for which words like "community" and "experience" were of central importance. By contrast, 1929, Pacelli's final year, marked the end of the Roaring Twenties and the onset of the worldwide economic crisis, with rapidly increasing unemployment. It also marked the beginning of the end of the Weimar Republic and the ascendancy of the National Socialist German Workers' Party (Nationalsozialistische Deutsche Arbeiterpartei, or NSDAP). In terms of Church politics, Pacelli's successful negotiation of a concordat with Prussia in this year represented his greatest political triumph as nuncio to Germany.

Instructions to a Nuncio

The very first sentence of the general instruction of November 1916 addressed to Giuseppe Aversa, the new nuncio to Munich, spelled out a double mission. In addition to the "diplomatic mission" to the king of Bavaria, the papal emissary was also vested with "the delicate and important authority to manage religious matters throughout the entire German Reich." Along with other ambassadors, he became part of the diplomatic corps at the Munich court. It is noteworthy that the Holy See's only nuncio in Germany was based not in the capital city of Berlin but in Munich—as his accreditation with the Bavarian king shows. This unusual posting was the result of a complicated history of papal diplomacy and the delayed formation of a German national state.

Historically, the Church did not have permanent nunciatures. Rather, Rome had dispatched traveling legates to the various courts as the need arose. Since the development of formal papal diplomacy in the early modern period, the nuncio to the imperial court in Vienna was, after about 1513, entrusted with representing the interests of the Holy See throughout the empire. Two additional permanent nunciatures were eventually established in other German-speaking areas, in Cologne (1584) and Lucerne (1579), to represent the political and diplomatic interests of the pope with the emperor and princes. In addition, these nuncios, in their capacity as archbishops, supervised and provided spiritual leadership to the bishops of the diocese. In 1785, an independent Bavarian nunciature was established in Munich to serve as an instrument of the Bavarian state church. Because there was no independent bishopric in the territory of the electorate of Bavaria, whose subjects fell under the jurisdiction of several "foreign" prince bishops in Freising, Regensburg, Salzburg, Passau, Eichstätt, Augsburg, and Bamberg, efforts were made with the help of the pope to install a nuncio as supreme bishop and state supervisor over these bishops. These steps led to fierce opposition by the so-called Febronians, members of a reform movement in Germany that advocated episcopal independence from the pope and restrictions on papal power. The German archbishops, however, were unable to move Rome and Munich to dissolve this nunciature, which would prove to be of crucial importance for all of Germany after the secularization of 1803. Indeed, the nunciature in Cologne disbanded during that revolutionary period, and though the nunciature in Lucerne continued to function until 1873, it concentrated primarily on Switzerland.

Meanwhile, the nuncio to Vienna was responsible only for the Austrian double monarchy. Although the authority of the nuncio to Munich continued to extend solely over Bavaria in a formal juristic sense, in fact Munich increasingly came to function as a German "Reich nunciature" throughout the nineteenth century. Roman doctrine eventually trailed after this actual expansion of authority, as the main instructions and the nuncial archive in Munich clearly demonstrate. The nuncio's political function as diplomatic representative of the Holy See in Catholic Germany was generally recognized, but his attempts at strict supervision of the local German churches often came under fierce criticism. For example, liberal Catholics during the nineteenth century came up with the equation "nuncio = denuncio," black humor with a sharp edge. In fact, numerous denunciations of enlightened and progressive German Catholics found their way via the Munich nunciature to the Holy Office in Rome, where proceedings against them were not infrequently initiated.

Although Prussia had its own embassy at the Vatican, there was at first no papal equivalent in Berlin. Only in 1920 after the end of World War I were diplomatic relations established between the Holy See and the German Reich. However, the Munich nunciature remained in place until 1934, shortly after the political coordination of the German states. As a result, Pacelli was nuncio in Munich alone from 1917 to 1920, received double accreditation for both Munich and Berlin between 1920 and 1925, and was active only in Berlin from 1925 to 1929. During this period, the nunciatures in Munich, and later in Berlin, became pivotal to the Vatican's policies toward Europe. Because diplomatic relations had been broken between the

Holy See and numerous European governments, including those of Italy, Spain, and France, Brienner Strasse 15 in Munich, the residence of the nunciature, took on critical importance, particularly after the outbreak of World War I.

The general instruction of 1916 largely followed the classic pattern for such directives as they had developed during the nineteenth century. At their core was an assessment of the political, social, and religious life in the individual states of the German Reich, followed by a list of deficiencies as well as initial, generally vague, prescriptions for dealing with them. After a glance at Bavaria, the perspective of the instruction widened to include all of Germany. In addition to the fundamental reorganization of the relationship between Church and state, Rome focused primarily on interconfessional collaboration between Catholics and Protestants, retaining laypeople, and particularly recruiting and training clergy and seating bishops.

Rome was at least partially comfortable with the ruling Bavarian Wit-

The nunciature at Brienner Strasse 15 in Munich.
(Pascalina Lehnert, *Ich durfte ihm dienen. Erinnerungen an Papst Pius XII* [Würzburg: Naumann, 1982])

telsbach dynasty. Ludwig III (1845–1921) "is deeply Catholic" was the succinct assessment. And though Crown Prince Rupprecht (1869–1955) was respected for his intelligence, Rome counted him among the anticlerics. Recently, however, he had "modified many of his old ideas." With regard to religion, "he is now less liberal than earlier and less critical of the Catholic clergy." The Vatican viewed the early death of his wife, Marie Gabriele (1878–1912), who had been a model of "virtue" and "piety," as largely responsible for this change for the better.

Yet Rome continued to view the political position of the Church in Bavaria as dominated by "regalism and liberalism." The cardinal secretary of state saw the relationship between Church and state as particularly thorny. The government had unilaterally annulled the Bavarian concordat of 1817 by issuing a religious edict based on the false premise of the "sovereignty of the state and its superiority to the Church." This legal concept of the relationship between Church and state was diametrically opposed to the new Roman canon law elaborated by Gasparri and Pacelli, which sought to eliminate the influence of the state in Church matters. Nuncio Pacelli was instructed to use all means to ensure the freedom of the Church. He must make every effort to attenuate the application of this rigid Bavarian body of law as it related to Catholicism.

According to the Secretariat of State in its instruction to Pacelli, "The bourgeoisie and the aristocracy are largely liberal. Although they observe their religious duties, they seek to be completely independent of the Church in their politics, and they tolerate no restraints on their private lives. It matters little what kind of book or newspaper is published; they will read it, and they enter into relationships with Protestants and persons of every other religion so that mixed marriages have markedly increased in Bavaria, resulting in extreme harm to the Catholic Church." In order to limit the damage, the nuncio was urged to give greater support to the Bavarian Center Party (Deutsche Zentrumspartei, or Zentrum), because only this party could be counted on to support the Church. He should use "all means at his disposal" for that purpose. The authors of the instruction hoped thereby to increase Roman influence over Catholic politics in Germany. To that end, Pacelli was also to utilize public opinion and media outlets throughout Germany that were consistent with Church teachings. It is evident that Rome believed in journalism controlled by the clergy.

The instruction acknowledged with remarkable openness the Church's helplessness in countering losses among the working classes, even in Bavaria: "The number of Socialist workers in Munich is much larger than that of Catholic ones. No one knows how to remedy this unfortunate reality: greater involvement on the part of the episcopate and clergy might perhaps arrest it somehow; however, one must take into account that the workers are easily attracted by very active Socialist propagandizing, and either join the Socialist Party or elect its members to the parliaments without joining themselves." Pacelli received no guidance for resolving the worker question. Rome simply had none to give.

If the relationship between Church and state in Catholic Bavaria was a thorn in Gasparri's side, legal relations between Church and state in most of the other German states were even less reconcilable with the Church's concept of total autonomy, as it had been elaborated in the CIC. Nuncio Pacelli's primary task was consequently to effect a change in German constitutional law as it related to the Church. In filling Church leadership positions, specifically when naming bishops and pastors, the Church must shake off all state influence. Concretely, this meant both a total assertion of the papal right to name bishops and limitations on patronage rights. In fact, bishops in numerous German dioceses such as Württemberg could fill very few pastoral positions because royal patronage placed that right almost exclusively with the government, which frequently used this power to advance liberal and "ecumenical" clergy to important and well-funded positions while denying permanent pastoral positions to "ultramontane" firebrands loyal to the pope. The individual German states had in various ways sharpened these methods for influencing Church personnel during the Kulturkampf of the 1870s and 1880s.

The complete revocation of Kulturkampf-era laws and the satisfactory resolution of the general situation are recurrent themes in the instruction. The degree to which Bismarck's "persecution of the Christians"— the wording referenced the anti-Christian policies of the Roman emperors Nero and Decius—had been scaled back in the individual German states was the criterion for evaluating the progress of the Church. The instruction underscored that the nuncio was to negotiate satisfactory solutions to the legal position of the Church. It is uncertain whether Gasparri had been considering new concordats as early as 1917. However, in 1914,

Pacelli had successfully negotiated an agreement between the Church and Serbia. This made him the ideal person to smooth the relationship between the Catholic Church and the German state; moreover, like the cardinal secretary of state himself, he was also a product of Sant' Apollinare, the school for canon law in Rome.

Although it was possible in the nineteenth century to negotiate a concordat with the Catholic king of Bavaria on the basis of the old Roman doctrine of concordats, the Holy See felt compelled to reject this path when negotiating with Protestant potentates such as the kings of Prussia and Württemberg. The pope felt that concluding a concordat at least implicitly entailed recognizing the government's negotiator and the form of government that he represented. But at the beginning of the twentieth century, the theory of concordat advanced by Adolfo Giobbio (1868–1932) at Sant' Apollinare gained increasing acceptance in the Roman Curia. According to this theory, the primary purpose of a concordat was to ensure Catholic autonomy, particularly freedom of pastoral care. From that point on, a concordat related simply to the content of the agreement between the Church and a state but did not extend to recognition in principle of the government negotiating the agreement. This meant that the state's official denomination, its form of government, or the worldview that animated it was for the Church of no importance when concluding a concordat. This new doctrine not only paved the way for treaties with Protestant kings and parliamentary democracies but would also make possible agreements with Fascist Italy and Nazi Germany.

Nonetheless, the cardinal secretary of state understood very well that not everything in Germany could be negotiated. According to the instruction, the Church was confronted with ideological opponents in all the German states—in particular liberalism, Socialism, and Protestantism. To combat these enemies, Rome planned to bundle all Catholic social and political assets into "Catholic Action," which was understood in the instruction to mean an as yet unspecified union of all existing Catholic associations and parties. At that time, the Vatican appears not to have considered a united Catholic bloc under the leadership of the bishops. This model became standard only under Pius XI.

Ecumenism, or at least an accommodation with the Protestants, received scant mention in the instruction. In Gasparri's opinion, it was not necessary to deal with German "heretics." In fact, he surmised that "the national Lutheran Church is undoubtedly on the verge of collapse." The "only engine keeping it alive is the massive support it receives from the Prussian government." Protestantism in Germany, so Rome thought, would eventually have the rug pulled out from under it because the Socialists advocated a "mass exodus" from the official church—primarily to evade church taxes—and because its "dogmatic basis" was increasingly disintegrating. Pastors, and Protestant professors of theology in particular, were increasingly corrupted by pantheistic and liberal ideas, and they spread these dangerous ideas to their parishioners. And though Protestantism in other European countries had become more "tolerant" of Catholicism, the old animosity of the sixteenth century persisted in Germany.

The question of collaboration between Catholics and Protestants around the issue of Christian labor unions became particularly problematic. Two different tendencies had developed under the bishops within German Catholicism at the turn of the century. Whereas the approach taken in Cologne was to foster cooperation between the two churches in interconfessional unions, the so-called Berlin approach forbade such "ecumenical" mixing and permitted Catholic workers to join Catholic labor unions only. Pius X and the hardliners in Rome had de facto subscribed to this approach, which would not have been viable in Germany because Catholics could develop the necessary strength to form effective trade unions only if they banded together with Protestants. Moderate forces within the Roman Curia saw interconfessional labor unions as the lesser evil, given that Catholics might otherwise join Socialist unions. The 1916 instruction to Nuncio Aversa in effect advocated this approach to unions but nonetheless labeled the state of affairs in Germany as *difficilissima*. At least between the lines, Gasparri criticized Pope Pius X for contributing in his statements to a worsening of the interconfessional conflict.

In addition to organizing at the political and social level the battle against the evil that might be lurking behind any of the novelties of the modern era, Pacelli was also charged with supervising conditions within the Church and the religious life of Catholics in Germany. The instruction largely characterized the situation in this area as "not bad," noting that "the Germans' great sense of practicality, their submissiveness to authority and law, and the earnestness of their education . . . make them reverent toward religion and those who serve it. Catholics, particularly in the countryside, are deeply religious, and large numbers of them attend the sacraments." In addition, they were especially generous at collection time. In the large cities and industrial sectors, by contrast, "Socialism is perpetrating a bloodbath among the workers, while religious indifference and monism condemn the educated classes to perdition." The clergy, whom the faithful loved dearly, were firm in their conviction, without a trace of modernism. The instruction here shows the moderating influence of Nuncio Andreas Frühwirth, who frequently took the wind out of the sails of the firebrands in Pius X's Curia. He had been unable to uncover any modernistic contamination of the clergy on his visitations; by contrast, those close to the pope in Rome viewed Germany as the "reservoir of all heresies."[2] Frühwirth's more moderate perspective fit well with the policies of the new pope, Benedict XV, who ended his predecessor's pursuit of modernists and rehabilitated priests and professors who had been unjustly persecuted.

Although pastoral conditions in the larger cities, and particularly in the Diaspora, were judged deficient, the instruction was not broadly prescriptive but paid tribute to the efforts of the German Church. Pacelli was, however, to direct his attention in particular toward the preservation of Catholic lower schools. He must oppose any attempts to set up so-called simultaneous schools or Christian community schools, in which pupils of all Christian denominations would be taught by teachers of all denominations. Catholic children were to be taught exclusively by Catholic teachers, and not only in religious education but in language classes, mathematics, and the sciences as well. Rome held to the belief that only Catholic education was capable of barring the dangers of "ecumenical" influences.

The instruction also implied that the nuncio must on occasion press the bishops to greater zeal in furthering Catholic interests. Rome demanded of the German bishops not only the human virtues of intelligence and talent but also a childlike submission to the Holy See. In terms of the German episcopate, the Vatican was concerned with the way the seating of bishops in Germany deviated from common Church practice. In particular, the Prussian government constantly undermined chapter election rights in the larger dioceses such as Cologne and Breslau. Rather than permit an adequate number of candidates to remain on the lists submitted by the cathedral chapters, the government in Berlin not infrequently presented the cathedral chapter with a single name for which they were forced to cast their votes. This was tantamount to Protestant rulers naming Catholic bishops. This "abuse" had last occurred when Berlin permitted only Bishop Adolf Bertram (1859–1945) of Hildesheim to run for election in 1914. The nuncio was expressly instructed to observe all episcopal elections in Germany and to ensure that all provisions of the Holy See were strictly followed. Any transgressions were to be reported immediately to the secretary of state.

But from a Roman perspective, the education of priests in Germany was the most pressing issue, especially the fact that they studied in Catholic theological faculties within state-run universities. Receiving their salaries from the state made professors too independent of Church authority. Because of this situation, the bishops were called upon to investigate carefully the teachings, moral conduct, and comportment of candidates for professorships. However, a denial of *nihil obstat* by the Church could result in conflicts with the state, which is why some held that state faculties should be completely abolished. The instruction was especially critical of university faculties for their lack of attention to the disciplines of scholastic philosophy and theology and for neglecting the teachings of St. Thomas Aquinas, whom Leo XIII (1878–1903) had declared the patron of all Catholic institutions of education:

> The young clergy are thirsty for knowledge and . . . more gifted in analysis and experimentation than in abstraction and synthesis, so that they are more fervent in their historical and critical studies, without having an appropriate foundation because philosophical and theological training in the theological faculties . . . is not any better than that which is to be had at a mediocre Italian seminary. . . . Those who wish

to devote themselves to the difficult path of biblical scholarship and the history of dogmatic theology . . . are largely forced to consult the works of Protestant scholars, which are permeated by Kantian philosophy and impertinent and arbitrary theories. . . . One cannot, however, conclude from this that the German clergy is poisoned by modernism, as some pessimists claim.

That assessment notwithstanding, Pacelli was instructed to be more vigilant in countering reformist Catholic tendencies, which Rome considered to be little more than German variants on modernism. Poorly trained young priests, that is, priests not inculcated in neoscholasticism, were the prime instrument by which the modern Zeitgeist, and evil with it, insinuated itself into the Church.

In conclusion, Cardinal Secretary of State Gasparri stressed to the new nuncio the need to "inform the Holy See regularly and immediately" if there were new developments in the areas discussed, particularly if intervention by the Holy See might prove necessary. As much as possible, the nuncial reports should be based exclusively on well-researched, verified, and accurate information so that the Holy See could make informed decisions. A report may not treat more than a single subject, which should be clearly noted in the title. If Pacelli felt the need to enter into discussions with other congregations of the Roman Curia, he must prepare a copy for the secretary of state so that the central political office of the Vatican was kept apprised of all matters. Armed with these instructions, Eugenio Pacelli set out to serve the Holy See in Germany.

These 1916 instructions to the nuncio to Munich at least indirectly anticipated one of the important provisions of curial reform initiated by Paul VI in 1967. Up until then, all congregations of the Curia, particularly the Holy Office, had been able to consult with other officials of the Church such as bishops or nuncios without engaging the office of the secretary of state. This meant that numerous activities bypassed the central political office of the Vatican. Sometimes the right hand of the Curia had no idea what the left hand was doing. For example, during the papacy of Benedict XV, the secretary of state was considering conferring the title of prelate on a particular professor in recognition of his services to the

Church. At the same time, however, his teachings were in the process of being sanctioned by the Congregation for the Doctrine of the Faith. Gasparri was understandably keen to avoid such contradictions. The secretary of state's office was to be the de facto superagency through which all correspondence was funneled, and it would therefore be informed of everything. In 1967, under Pope Paul VI, the secretary of state's office legally assumed this responsibility. This development foreshadowed a competition between the office of the secretary of state and the Holy Office—between diplomacy and dogma—which was to assume greater importance during the Nazi period.

A Roman in Germany: Eugenio Pacelli

On May 29, 1917, Eugenio Pacelli presented his credentials to King Ludwig III of Bavaria at his Munich residence. With this, he officially became the papal nuncio to Bavaria, after having been elevated to titular bishop of Sardes by Benedict XV several days earlier. Through this action, the pope had expressed his esteem for the man who was perhaps the most talented diplomat in the Curia in those years. The new nuncio placed his efforts to bring peace, and to end World War I, at the center of his inaugural speech: "Never has the need to rebuild human society on the secure foundation of Christian wisdom been as clear as in this heavy hour, or the fact that a just and lasting peace can exist only if it is based on the rock of public Christian law. I, with my meager powers, have been entrusted with the mission of collaborating on this work of peace at a time that is perhaps unprecedented in history."[3]

Who was the man to whom Benedict XV entrusted the Vatican's most important foreign diplomatic posting in the fateful year 1917? What qualified him to take on this delicate diplomatic mission? What theological beliefs and Church policies did he bring with him to Germany?

Eugenio Pacelli was born on March 2, 1876, in Rome, the son of Filippo Pacelli (1837–1916) and Virginia (née Graziosi) Pacelli (1844–1920). Ever since the unification of Italy in 1870, the population of the capital city had been split into supporters of the modern national liberal state and followers of the pope, whom they viewed as a "prisoner in the Vatican." The

Pacellis were decidedly "black" in their loyalties, having for generations produced lay jurists who had made their careers in the Curia. The children were raised in an atmosphere of strict and protective traditional Catholic piety. This did not, however, prevent Pacelli's parents from sending their son at the age of ten to the Liceo Ennio Quirino Visconti, the leading liberal secondary school in Rome, where he received a solid classical education. Pacelli was a sensitive and highly talented student, who in 1894 passed his final examination with top grades. His favorite subjects were music and the Latin classics.

He began his theology studies at the prestigious Tridentine Collegio Capranica Seminary and at the Jesuit Gregoriana University. After a few months, however, he had to interrupt his studies for health reasons, and

Eugenio Pacelli in 1920.
That year he received double accreditation as nuncio to Munich and Berlin.
(SV-Bilderdienst/Scherrl)

he spent time recuperating at his family's country estate. He later received a special dispensation to continue his studies from home, this time under the faculty of the Seminarium Romanum, located in the Palazzo Sant' Apollinare, the later Lateran University. In other words, Pacelli never lived in a seminary. Compared with other Italian educational institutions, Sant' Apollinare proved to be relatively liberal. The school had not yet been completely permeated by neo-Thomism, which was at the end of the nineteenth century propagated as the de facto theology of Catholicism. In addition to speculative subjects such as dogmatics and philosophy, the school also offered positive theology, that is, biblical exegesis and Church history. Although Pacelli, who sat for his examinations in 1899, seems to have been anti-Kantian and Thomistic—though more juridical and practical—he also seems to have developed interests that were not markedly speculative. He was ordained a priest in a private Roman chapel on April 2, 1899, in the presence of numerous cardinals and bishops. His parents were determined to use their contacts to enable him to pursue a career in the Curia. At Sant' Apollinare Pacelli continued his studies in canon law, so crucial for advancement in Church administration, with the goal of achieving a Roman doctorate in both civil and Church law. In the meantime, Cardinal Vincenzo Vannutelli (1836–1930) had recommended the young priest to the newly named secretary of the Congregation for Extraordinary Ecclesiastical Affairs, Pietro Gasparri, who in 1901 took on Pacelli as an *apprendista,* or apprentice.

His mandatory studies at the Accademia dei Nobili Ecclesiastici, the Curia's elite school for Vatican diplomats, and at the school for canon law at the Seminarium Romanum, seem to have been particularly formative. On the one hand, the Seminarium Romanum advanced the view that the Holy See, as subject to international law, did not have to possess territory of its own to ensure its existence. This position was a response to the occupation by Italian troops of the papal state and the city of Rome during reunification. Because the pope no longer possessed his own state, he would not, in accordance with the conventions of international law, have the right to accredit nuncios and diplomats from foreign courts to the Holy See. On the other hand, the seminary stressed in a remarkable fashion the doctrine of *societas perfecta,* which advanced the notion of the Church as an independent juristic entity, which above all else sought to defend against state intrusion in Church affairs.

Pacelli became a *minutante,* a sort of senior clerk in the Congregation for Extraordinary Ecclesiastical Affairs, on October 3, 1903; *sottosegretario,* or undersecretary, on March 7, 1911; and finally secretary on February 1, 1914. Since 1912 he had also been consultor of the Holy Office. This rapid ascent in the Curia of Pius X would not have been possible if Pacelli had not shared the rigid antimodernism with which the pope and Cardinal Secretary of State Raffaele Merry del Val (1865–1930) fought off all modernistic tendencies and attempts at reform within the Catholic Church. It is, however, unclear to what extent he was involved with the antimodernist network of informers, the Sodalitium Pianum associated with Umberto Benigni (1862–1934). There is at least circumstantial evidence that he might have been: for five years Pacelli had performed preliminary groundwork for Benigni in the congregation before succeeding him as undersecretary. The consensus in well-informed curial circles was that with Pacelli, a good friend and loyal collaborator of Benigni had followed in his footsteps. Moreover, in his decisions relating to Church policies, Pacelli repeatedly supported his positions with information received from "secret services" coordinated by Benigni.[4] Of course, Pacelli was clever enough not to allow himself to be discredited by too open an association with Benigni and his "secret service." Such a visible relationship could easily have caused him trouble with the new pope, Benedict XV, who ended the modernist baiting of his predecessor.

Pietro Gasparri, with whom Pacelli had worked closely on the new centralist canon law since 1904, became his most important mentor. Gasparri, who was himself professor of canon law in Paris and representative of the canon law school of the Seminarium Romanum, had since 1901, in his capacity as secretary of the Congregation for Extraordinary Ecclesiastical Affairs, been Pacelli's supervisor. Named a cardinal in 1907, he had been elevated to cardinal secretary of state by Benedict XV on September 3, 1914. Pacelli's patron was now a force in the halls of power. The 1917 Code of Canon Law, the *Codex Iuris Canonici,* which was largely the work of Gasparri and Pacelli, reflects the spirit of ultramontanism and the decisions of the First Vatican Council of 1870. The dogmas of papal infallibility and the universal primacy of jurisdiction of the pope, adopted in 1870, now became part and parcel of canon law. Roman centralism instead of local church autonomy, a Church of the pope instead of a Church of the bishops, Roman unity instead of diversity at the local level—these were the cornerstones of the new canon law. Pacelli would make it his life's work to translate the letter and the spirit of the CIC into practice, especially in Germany, which had retained a good deal of autonomy from Rome.

Rumors had been circulating in the Curia ever since the outbreak of World War I that Eugenio Pacelli, the most capable diplomat that the Vatican had at its disposal in those years, would be named nuncio to Germany. Apparently, Pacelli himself had considered it a realistic possibility, and he had prepared as well as possible for such a posting. He read widely in current events, particularly in the history of the German Reich. Among other things, he studied Bismarck's *Reflections and Reminiscences,* which had been translated into Italian in 1898, the same year it appeared in Germany. Pacelli viewed the first German chancellor as a luminous figure in Prussian-German history. Only Bismarck would have been able to control the military, which became a bedrock of Prussian Germany after the wars that culminated in German unification. He viewed the fact that Helmuth von Moltke (1800–1891) had made so little headway after the Franco-Prussian War of 1870–1871 in spite of his push for military victory as a credit to Bismarck's politically astute readiness to compromise, which had led to a quick peace with France. By contrast, World War I showed that politics had become so diluted in Germany that it could no longer hold its own against the military. The problem, Pacelli opined, was not merely the lack of "a strong political personality" but also the fact that an "incomparably greater" authority had been shifted to the military.[5]

All rumors to the contrary, Giuseppe Aversa, who had been papal emissary in Brazil, was named nuncio to Munich on January 17, 1917. Because Gasparri continued to be very skeptical of the prospects for success of a papal peace initiative, he wanted to avoid releasing his model student into the wilds too early. But when Aversa died of heart failure on April 9 after appendix surgery, the pope had free rein. After a fierce argument with

Gasparri—Carlo Monti (1851–1924), a friend of the pope's, spoke of open "opposition" on the part of the cardinal secretary of state[6]—the pope named Pacelli nuncio to Munich. However, Gasparri was still not prepared to accept the pope's position, and he told Pacelli that the general instruction prepared for Aversa in the fall of 1916 also applied to him without restriction.[7]

Intervention or Neutrality: The Papal Peace Initiative

In fact, this instruction dealt with the crucial question of the role of the Holy See in World War I, which had in those years been the subject of vigorous discussion and argument within the Curia.[8] Did not the Vatican, in its role as defender of human rights, have a moral duty through a peace initiative to put an end to the senseless murder taking place in the trenches, and to the use of poison gas? Or must the Holy See avoid all worldly involvement so as not to risk the neutrality of the pope, who stood above all parties involved in the war and was father to all the Catholic faithful—whichever side they were fighting for?

Initially the Holy See had no unified approach to this question. The pope and his secretary of state, who had radically different ideas about the political role of the papacy, first had to work out a policy between themselves. Gasparri stood for strict neutrality: as head of a universal church, the pope had to be above the parties to the conflict and avoid any actions that might, for example, be construed by French Catholics as too friendly to the Germans, or vice versa. The pope must not take sides. Because of his authority, he must either remain silent or express himself in abstract terms in his admonitions to the parties involved. Doing otherwise would imperil the Catholic Church's pastoral mission and its jurisdiction over all sides in the war.

The pope, by contrast, tended toward a policy of active mediation in the name of peace, along the lines of that adopted by Leo XIII. Although he no longer saw himself as arbitrator in the world, he felt called upon to act as defender of all suffering human beings because the new and deadly materiel with which the war was being conducted had unleashed an unprecedented level of terror. Benedict XV believed that as pope he could no longer be silent about the war; rather, he must make concrete recommendations about the path toward peace. At the same time, his actions would protect the vital political interests of the Holy See.

In spite of his disagreement with Benedict XV, Gasparri, as head of the Vatican's foreign policy arm, had made Pacelli aware of his position in November 1916. "Whereas almost the entire world is hostile to Germany," he noted, since the outbreak of the war the Holy See had "shown extreme correctness" toward the German Reich, and had, in particular, always demonstrated strict impartiality in the current conflict. The Curia was at the time suspicious of Italy because of the unresolved Roman question, of France because of its laicism and the separation of Church and state, and of Great Britain because it was a Protestant power. And so this neutrality may be seen as having tilted toward the central European powers— a policy that Gasparri viewed as the only appropriate attitude given the nature of the Catholic Church. Furthermore, quite a few Germans who may have been indifferent toward or even rejected the Church before the war had come to approve of the pope and the Church, not least because the Curia remained neutral. As the instruction indicated, the Holy See simply found it impossible to blame a single warring country for the conflict. Rather, this slaughter had, in the final analysis, been instigated by "international freemasonry," with the goal of destroying the Church of God and the only remaining Catholic dynasty, the House of Habsburg. It is easy to discern in Gasparri's position the classical stereotypes and thought structures of ultramontanism, which in the instruction was literally identified with the only "true Catholicism." Being Catholic meant being Roman—in other words, acquiescent to the Holy See. "True" Catholics knew where to hold fast amid the swells of modernism: on the eternal rock of Peter. "Liberal" Catholics were still seen as lukewarm or half-Catholic, unable to decide between good and evil.

As Gasparri made clear to Pacelli, criticism of this policy of impartiality or suprapartisanship came from various quarters. The pope, the critics held, must sharply condemn Germany's violation of international law in invading Belgium and Luxembourg, as well as the war crimes committed there by German soldiers. These objections, however, could be countered with the German chancellor's argument that Germany had acted defensively in advance of an imminent French invasion of his country. Furthermore, documents had turned up in Belgium that controverted the claim of Belgian neutrality. Moreover, Belgians had committed crimes against Germans as well. Given the confusion on the ground, however, it would have been difficult to distinguish between war propaganda and truth in these reports. For that reason, Gasparri believed it impossible to render an impartial judgment on the question of culpability: "The accusations against the Church for its strict neutrality and absolute impartiality since the beginning toward all states who are party to the conflict are known. The anti-Catholic press would gladly have seen the Holy See excommunicate and anathematize the Central Powers" and solemnly condemn "the

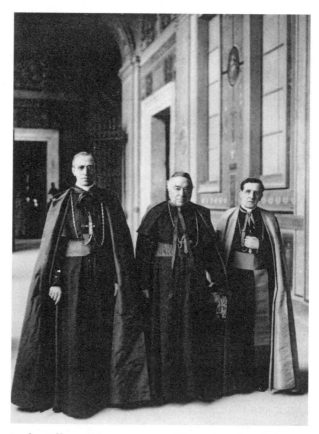

In the Office of the Secretary of State: Pacelli with his mentor Pietro Cardinal Gasparri and Undersecretary and later Cardinal Giuseppe Pizzardo.
(Pontifica Fotografia Felici, Rome)

violation of international law and the atrocities committed by German and Austro-Hungarian troops." However, Gasparri noted, the Holy See had not been moved by this "anticlerical campaign" but had "remained true to its absolute policy of impartiality" and "concentrated all its energy on the return of peace." Consequently, Pacelli was instructed to hew to this course of strict neutrality no matter what.

The instruction spent several pages on a difficult problem that was intimately connected with whether the Holy See should intervene or remain neutral in the war, a problem that had sharpened considerably as a result of Italy's entry into the conflict, namely, "imperilment of the immunity of the accredited ambassadors of the central powers to the pope" and the free exchange of correspondence between the Curia and the bishops in Germany and the Habsburg monarchy. For Pacelli, as nuncio in a country at war with Italy, this was a point of no minor concern. These issues could in the final analysis be traced back to the occupation of the Papal States and Rome by Italian troops during the *Risorgimento* in 1870 and the resultant Roman question. The pope had become a prisoner in the Vatican, and access to him had since been possible only through Italian territory. In spite of the guarantees decreed in 1871 by the Italian government, which accepted the freedom and sovereignty of the pope, the Curia apparently distrusted the peace. Rather, Gasparri, as he had written into the general instruction, believed that Italy would use the opportunity of the world war to contest the right of the Holy See to accredit its own ambassadors because the Vatican lacked statehood. He feared that Italy might expel diplomats from the hostile powers, whose offices were located not in the Vatican Palace but in the Kingdom of Italy. The pope was unable to "offer his hospitality" because, for one thing, there were not enough apartments in the apostolic palaces, and for another, he would be suspected of "being under the influence of his guests"—and as such would be considered a partisan of the central powers.

Nuncio Pacelli was directed to plead for understanding of the Vatican's difficult position and to ensure that diplomatic relations with Germany were maintained: "In order to achieve direct relations with Berlin as with Vienna and Munich," the instruction noted, "the Holy See would even be prepared to accredit one of its chargés d'affaires in Berlin." An unusual suggestion for resolving the Roman question, which German Center Party Deputy Matthias Erzberger (1875–1921) had submitted to the Roman Curia, was not addressed in the instruction. Erzberger had proposed that one way of evading the Italian stranglehold on the pope was to move the Holy See out of Rome. Specifically, he suggested the Principality of Liechtenstein or the Mediterranean islands of Mallorca and Minorca. Elba was also considered for a time, but it would not, of course, have been acceptable given its association with Napoleon. In the end, all these possible re-sitings came to nothing, even though, for example, the Vatican had conducted extensive negotiations with the prince of Liechtenstein that had resulted in the preparation of a treaty. In exchange for renouncing his sovereignty in favor of the Holy Father, the prince and his successors would have received a hereditary cardinal's hat.

By the time Pacelli took up his post in Munich in the summer of 1917, the political analyses originally formulated in November 1916 in the general instruction for Aversa were already obsolete owing to deep changes in the international political landscape. The peace feelers put out by the central powers, the German request for Vatican mediation, the fall of the Russian czars, and the failure of the American peace initiative, with the United States entering the war shortly thereafter, made papal mediation seem uniquely necessary and promising. For this reason, Gasparri fell in line with Benedict XV's thinking and directed Pacelli, in June 1917, to sound out the German government about the possibilities for peace. Pacelli entered into negotiations in Berlin with Reich Chancellor Theodor von Bethmann-Hollweg (1856–1921), from June 26 to June 28, and on June 29 he was received by Kaiser Wilhelm II (1859–1941) at his headquarters in Bad Kreuznach. The fundamental readiness of the chancellor and the kaiser to make concessions prompted Pacelli's euphoric comment that the possibility of a real peace was at hand for the first time. The nuncio wrote to Gasparri that Wilhelm II "seems not to doubt in the effectiveness of such a papal initiative."[9] As for subsequent negotiations between Nuncio Pacelli and the kaiser, evidence from the two sides is not easily reconciled. But what is certain is that Pacelli was satisfied when he returned to Munich and believed that an armistice was imminent, as was German renunciation of claims to Belgium, while the kaiser embraced the pope's peace initiative as a weapon against Socialism.

By then, Georg Michaelis (1857–1936) had become Reich chancellor. In good faith, Pacelli and the Roman Curia believed that the pledges made to them by Michaelis's predecessor, though without reassurances from the kaiser and supreme military command, would continue to guide German policies. During his second trip to Berlin, on July 24, Pacelli submitted an agenda containing seven concrete conditions for peace. Berlin objected orally, and the Roman Curia relented—though it held firm on the crucial guarantee of a German withdrawal from Belgium. The pope then made public his peace appeal to the warring powers, backdated to August 1. His primary recommendations for peace included freedom of the seas, mutual disarmament, Germany's withdrawal from France, England's withdrawal from the German colonies, and especially the complete independence of Belgium. The Vatican believed that it was acting in accord with Germany; it hoped that these advance German concessions would also move the entente, and that a pivotal breakthrough in the negotiations might be at hand.

But contrary to Roman expectations, not even the German government could bring itself to make concrete promises—particularly not to renounce Belgium, which the military viewed as a bargaining chip—and as a result gave only evasive answers. The other warring powers simply rejected the pope's offer to act as a go-between. The Vatican made no further attempts at mediation during the war after this diplomatic failure. Pacelli seems to have been so traumatized by the turn of events that he became extremely skeptical of further efforts. His first great diplomatic assignment had ended in fiasco. Gasparri's conviction that the Holy See should remain absolutely neutral in political and military conflicts had been borne out by Pacelli's own experience. Pacelli subsequently rejected all calls for intervention in such conflicts.

Servants of the Pope or Servants of the State: The German Bishops

In addition to addressing delicate political questions such as the papal peace initiative, Pacelli expended much energy from the beginning on internal Church matters, especially the recruitment of leadership personnel. Whoever installed the bishops in Germany and supervised the training of future clergy effectively had control over key elements of the Church machinery. This is why it was so important for Pacelli to prevent the state and local churches from influencing these functions. Rome alone was to decide. When Pacelli took up his post in 1917, the pope's role in seating bishops in Germany was marginal. The end of the war, and with it the end of the German Reich, gave the Curia the opportunity to reformulate its claims, and to challenge a historical system that had evolved over time.

Up until the demise of the almost thousand-year-old Imperial Church (*Reichskirche*) as a result of secularization at the beginning of the nineteenth century, the right to elect bishops in Germany had been held exclusively by the cathedral chapters, which were usually filled by the nobility, who saw themselves as the defenders of the local church. At this time, the noble dynasties such as the Wittelsbachs in Bavaria or the Habsburgs in Austria offered bribes to the capitulars whenever they wished to see one of their own princes elevated to prince bishop. In spite of frequent attempts, the pope had been unable to restrict the electoral rights of the cathedral chapters. If the chapters and the emperor—as protector of Church freedom in Germany—were united, Rome could do little more than confirm the prince bishops elected by the cathedral chapters. This was generally a mere formality.

After the collapse of the Imperial Church system, and with it the end of the double-ranking of the prince bishops in Germany as both secular rulers over a territory and spiritual bishops in a diocese, the states succeeded in gaining crucial influence over the election of bishops, power that was then codified in agreements with the Holy See. In fact, the Catholic king in Bavaria was even able to nominate bishops, whom the pope had only the power to confirm. In the remaining territory, which was generally under the control of Protestant rulers, the cathedral chapters' right of election was maintained simply because Rome was not prepared to surrender the nomination rights for Catholic bishops to Protestant sovereigns. Nonetheless, the pope did concede to Prussia, as well as to the upper Rhine states of Baden, Württemberg, and Hessen, that the cathedral chapters would not elect a candidate to bishop who was "less than agreeable" to the state. This concession essentially gave the states veto power. A Protestant king or duke could demand that any Catholic candidate whom he considered disagreeable be stricken from the electoral list of the cathedral chapter. This meant that no Catholic bishops could be seated in Germany without the consent of the state, regardless of whether it was ruled by Catholics or Protestants.

The new centralist canon law of 1917 stated succinctly, "The pope freely names the bishops."[10] Nonetheless, Pacelli was unable even once to enforce this absolutist claim in its totality. Originally, the majority of states were unwilling even to participate in new negotiations for a concordat with Rome because they were intent on retaining the agreements hammered out at the beginning of the nineteenth century. A change in form from monarchy to republic did not imply an automatic change in the substance or legal character of the state as such. Rome, by contrast, viewed agreements between the Church and the state made from the beginning of the nineteenth century as having been concluded by God's grace between the pope in Rome and the particular sovereign in question. As far as the Curia was concerned, the fall of the monarchies in Germany meant that one of the partners to the agreement no longer existed. The agreements were therefore null and void. As nuncio, Pacelli insisted on this legal position whenever a bishop's throne was to be filled. This caused many problems for the cathedral chapters and governments, but eventually the German states were forced to agree with this position. Without a doubt, this was one of the greatest diplomatic victories of Pacelli's nunciature.

Pacelli approached almost all the German states about potential negotiations for a new concordat. In the end, he was able to conclude three new concordats: with Bavaria in 1924, Prussia in 1929, and Baden in 1932. Solutions analogous to the Reichskonkordat of 1933 were later found for the states not already covered. In fact, all these provisions, which more or less accommodated Rome's push for centralism, are still applicable law in the Federal Republic. However, Pacelli's deep wish to conclude a Reichskonkordat during his nunciature fell apart because of the political situa-

The Dioceses in the German Reich in 1930

DENMARK

North Sea

Helgoland

NETHERLANDS

BELGIUM

LUX

FRANCE

SWITZERLAND

Flensburg

Schleswig

Rostock

Lübeck

Schwerin

Bremer-haven

Hamburg

Neustrelitz

Groningen

Oldenburg

Bremen

Elbe

Weser

Hannover

Potsdam

Osnabrück

Hildesheim

Magdeburg

Münster

Paderborn

Göttingen

Rhine

Dortmund

Essen

Cassel

Leipzig

Roermond

Marburg

Weimar

Liege

Aachen

Cologne

Koblenz

Limburg

Fulda

Mosel

Frankfurt am Main

Carlsbad

Trier

Mainz

Würzburg

Bamberg

Luxembourg

Verdun

Saarbrücken

Speyer

Nuremberg

Metz

Regensburg

Nancy

Stuttgart

Eichstätt

Strasbourg

Rottenburg

Dänube

Augsburg

St. Die

Rhine

Munich

Salzburg

Freiburg

Belfort

Constance

Besançon

St. Gallen

| 0 | 50 | 100 | 150 miles |

SWEDEN

Baltic Sea

Bornholm (Den.)

Rügen

● Kolberg

● Stettin

FREE CITY OF DANZIG

✝ Olivia
● Königsberg

● Tilsit

○ Frauenburg (Ermland)

Danzig

Kulm ○

● Allenstein

Vistula

Schneidemühl ○✝
Bromberg ●

● Thorn

○ Berlin

Posen ■
✝ Gnesen

Warta

● Wlockawek

✝ Płock

■ Warsaw

● Frankfurt am Oder

P O L A N D

● Cottbus

Elbe

○ Bautzen

Breslau ■

Oder

✝ Kielce

Dresden

● Czestochowa

○ Sandomierz

○ Leitmeritz

Oppeln ●

Königgrätz ○✝

Glatz ✝

○ Catowice
✝ Krakow

○ Tarnow

■ Prague

● Pilsen

Vistula

C Z E C H O S L O V A K I A

■ Olmütz

Brno ○

Budweis ○✝

✝ Passau

✝ Neutra

Linz ○✝
St. Pölten ○✝

■ Vienna

H U N G A R Y

Eisenstadt ○

✝ Raab

■ Gran

A U S T R I A

Danube

● Budapest

○ Szombathely

- - - - Borders of the German Reich	■ Archbishop's see
· · · · · · Borders of dioceses	○ Bishop's see

atholic dioceses in the German Reich, 1930.

Meridian Mapping)

tion in the Reichstag. Liberal and Protestant forces as well as sections of the Social Democratic Party (Sozialdemokratische Partei Deutschlands, or SPD) categorically rejected such an agreement.

The importance to Pacelli of seating bishops is made abundantly clear in the files from his nunciature. He was generally more than a little dissatisfied with the German bishops who had been named before 1917, when his nunciature began and the CIC came into effect. As far as he was concerned, they were little more than bishops of the state because they had achieved their positions with the support of the various governments and were therefore beholden to them. He accused them of a latent tendency to place German interests and those of their local churches above the interests of the pope and the Church as a whole.

In his final report of 1929, Pacelli described the fifteen bishops of the non-Bavarian German dioceses for which he was responsible as nuncio in Berlin. His critical opinion of the German episcopate is striking. Pacelli's clear assessments, each of which was preceded by a short biography, all revolved around three themes: training and doctrinal purity; submission to the Holy See and its representative in Germany; and personal character and conduct. Because quite a few of these bishops remained in office during Pacelli's time as cardinal secretary of state and then as pope, their relations with the nuncio are of central importance. On whom could Pacelli depend during Hitler's dictatorship? Which bishops did he trust and which did he view with suspicion? Who was reliable in terms of theology and Church policy? Simply put, who was with him and who was against him? These portrayals of the individual bishops also shed light on the criteria that were important to the nuncio in his evaluations.

The picture that Pacelli painted of Adolf Cardinal Bertram, the prince bishop of Breslau and chair of the Fulda Conference of Bishops, is especially interesting.[11] Elected bishop of Hildesheim in 1906, he had been elected prince bishop of the cathedral chapter, in Breslau, by an overwhelming majority. Before the election, however, the Prussian government had stricken as "less than agreeable" all the other potential candidates advanced by the cathedral chapter. Bertram was the sole remaining candidate, and so no real election could be said to have taken place. Pacelli viewed this election as invalid because it was based on significant "intervention by the government" and "robbed the electors of all freedom." "Therefore," he declared, it "had to be retroactively corrected by the Holy See." For Pacelli, Bertram was the quintessential old-order Prussian state bishop of the type he deeply despised, and he made no effort to conceal this opinion in his report. The cardinal, he wrote, is "not of an easy character, authoritarian and sensitive. He has not seldom shown himself inadequate to the task of defending the faith against erroneous modern teachings, possibly as a result of deficiencies in his theological training." Pacelli made his opinion even clearer: "One cannot expect from him the serious and effective reforms in the instruction and training of clergy that are necessary in Breslau because of the theological faculty. His Eminence shows outward interest and fervor for the Catholic Action. However, he . . . has in fact—may the word be forgiven—'sabotaged' all attempts and initiatives to form an organization or central committee such as exists in Italy." And there was more: "In addition, His Eminence Bertram has a pronounced tendency to do everything himself, while in the process gladly ignoring the Holy See whenever possible (except in such cases where he needs it in order to cover his own responsibility)." Pacelli was particularly irritated by Bertram's position with regard to the relationship between the German dioceses and the central authority in Rome. Here, Bertram transferred the subsidiarity principle propagated by Catholic social teachings to relations within the Church itself. The cardinal was convinced that the local dioceses had greater expertise to solve practical questions than did far-distant Rome. The nuncio was of a different opinion: the Vatican possessed greater competence than did Breslau.

Pacelli blamed Bertram's training for his unreliability—he had studied not at the Gregoriana or another Jesuit university, but rather at a German state university, which was infected by a false modern theology deriving from Protestantism. This was why he was particularly susceptible to the modernism associated with the Church historian Joseph Wittig (1879–1949), who was eventually suspended and finally excommunicated. Instead of decisively rejecting this malicious tendency, which threatened to destroy the Church from within, Bertram had, in Pacelli's opinion, coddled it for far too long. What else could one expect from a state theologian who was trained in Germany? Furthermore, Bertram secretly rejected Catholic Action, the pet project of Pius XI, while outwardly pretending to support it. In addition, he simply gave a new name to the so-called Vereins- und Laienkatholizismus, associational and lay Catholicism, deemed "dreadful" because it was too independent of the hierarchy, without changing its substance one iota. All in all, the nuncio—who was only a titular archbishop but was judging a cardinal with higher standing in the Roman hierarchy—felt that Bertram acted too independently. But more than that, he appeared far too self-reliant in relation to the Holy See and to himself, the Vatican's representative in Germany. In a word, he lacked the necessary reverence because he was bishop by the grace of Prussia. It was time, Pacelli believed, to put a stop to such Josephinian and episcopalist figures in German bishoprics. Small wonder, then, that given his portrayal of Bertram in 1929, Pacelli never really had "pull" with the chairman of the Conference of Bishops during the Nazi period and World War II, when he was cardinal secretary of state and later pope, and that he tried to replace Bertram as liaison in the Conference of Bishops. Bertram's final, fruitless petitions to Hitler to eliminate grievances and protect the freedom of the Catholic Church smacked of cabinet politics, the closed-door politicking of the nineteenth century. His fundamental loyalty to the state, mirrored among other things in his annual congratulatory birthday messages to Hitler—not to mention the requiem he ordered for the führer after his suicide in May 1945—were viewed as behavior typical of a Prussian state bishop.

In contrast to Bertram, Ludwig Maria Hugo (1871–1935), of Mainz, who was bishop from 1921 to 1935, was viewed as a shining light of the German episcopate.[12] As an "alumnus of the Collegium Germanicum et Hungaricum" he came close to Pacelli's ideal of the good bishop. At the beginning of his portrayal, the nuncio specified the crucial criteria that landed Hugo in that category: "He has good philosophical and theological training, is especially loyal to the Holy See, and extremely orthodox in his teachings. . . . He dedicates himself with great care to his seminary because it is purely episcopal and free of all state influence." In addition, he is "worried about the inadequate training" of the alumni, "especially in the Latin language." Because several tendencies of the youth movement had negatively influenced future seminarians, mainly by opening the floodgates to the evil spirit of the times, the bishop of Mainz had permitted no candidates to the priesthood who "belong to the 'Quickborn' group."

Above all, Hugo was a good bishop because he had studied the right theology (with the Jesuits) at the right place (in Rome). This meant that he was not open to the false teachings of modernism and was unquestionably loyal to Rome. Mainz was a particularly good place for him, given his orientation, because there were no state-controlled Catholic theological faculties at any of the universities at which candidate priests studied. Instead, candidates for the clergy received neoscholastic training without state interference at a Tridentine seminary under episcopal supervision. In addition, Pacelli particularly appreciated that Hugo valued Latin and rejected the youth movement with its emphasis on the experiential nature of faith and piety.

Prince bishop of Breslau and chairman of the Fulda Conference of Bishops, Adolf Cardinal Bertram, a "Prussian state bishop" in Pacelli's opinion, with an honor guard of the German military in front of the cathedral in Breslau, in 1935.
(SV-Bilderdienst/Scherrl)

Johannes Baptista Sproll (1870–1949) also became bishop during Pacelli's nunciature. His election as bishop of Rottenburg had caused no small difficulties for the Berlin nuncio in 1927. For one thing, the concordat negotiations with Württemberg had failed as a result of resistance from the government and the cathedral chapter to sacrificing the free election of bishops. Then again, once Rome and Stuttgart had, after much back and forth, agreed on Auxiliary Bishop Sproll as the candidate of choice for the cathedral chapter, rumors began to surface of personal misconduct during his time as pastor in Upper Swabia. Although these charges were refuted—the instigators were forced to retract their accusations in court—and Pacelli presented the newly elected bishop with a letter of appointment from Rome, the question remained whether the nuncio might not still harbor a hint of suspicion toward Sproll. For this reason Pacelli's portrait of this somewhat problematic figure in his final report in 1929 is of particular interest:

> He is a simple and modest prelate, beloved by the people, whereas the ruling house of Württemberg and the nobility exhibit a certain coolness toward him because he lacks the refinement in personal conduct and the fine sense of tact of his predecessor. He is without fear and without fear of men, as his steadfast opposition to female gymnastic events has proved. . . . He has shown himself to be deferential toward the apostolic nunciature, whose instructions he faithfully carries out. Educated at the Tübinger Schule he naturally cannot be expected to have the sort of understanding for the guidelines and reforms relating to the training of clergy that one might find in prelates who, for example, were trained at the Collegium Germanicum et Hungaricum, in Rome.[13]

Even though the aristocrat in Pacelli might have felt more at ease with Sproll's predecessor, Paul Wilhelm von Keppler (1852–1926), who had a native understanding of nobility, and even though the "prelato semplice" Sproll was something of a Swabian peasant to him, without proper bearing, the nuncio could find little to object to in the manner in which Sproll carried out his duties. This is somewhat surprising since Sproll had studied exclusively at what Rome deemed that "dreadful" Tübingen, with its all too anticlerical Catholic theological faculties. But Sproll carried out Pacelli's instructions without complaint, making him the epitome of a good bishop. He had even signed on to one of the issues dearest to the nuncio, the fight against women's sports with their immoral sportswear that accentuated women's curves.

In fact, Pacelli found little to criticize in the moral comportment of any of the German diocesan bishops. Piety, priestly conduct, zeal, conscientiousness, and love of order were several of the positive character traits that he mentioned. For a Roman like Pacelli, Archbishop Carl Fritz (1864–1931) of Freiburg, whose archiepiscopal archive was "in fact a model of precision and order," was nonetheless too "exaggeratedly bureaucratic"—

Nuncio Pacelli in regalia at a procession in Rottenburg.
(Pascalina Lehnert, *Ich durfte ihm dienen. Erinnerungen an Papst Pius XII* [Würzburg, 1982])

as, he noted, one might expect from a German.[14] Intelligence, proper bearing, and social sophistication were also important to him.

"Submissiveness to the Holy See," which in Pacelli's opinion apparently followed automatically from studies at the Gregoriana or other Jesuit seminary, was another factor critical to his evaluation of bishops. By the same token, doctrinal reliability and the unquestioning execution of instructions from Rome were also traceable to the one institution where "correct" Catholic theology was taught. By contrast, study at a German state Catholic theological faculty was suspect from the outset, even though the majority of German bishops and priests received their education there. Even after Pacelli had spent a dozen years in Germany, a fundamental characteristic of German Catholic theology, which was practiced in the *universitas litterarum* in dialogue with all other disciplines, remained foreign to him. Nonetheless, in spite of his fundamental skepticism, he had to admit that most of the later German bishops had, surprisingly, not been permanently damaged by studying at a German university. Quite a few had nonetheless become "good" bishops—that is, loyal to Rome and to him.

Pacelli reserved his strongest criticism for bishops like Cardinal Bertram, who had assumed their duties before World War I, when Prussian government influence was most pronounced and before Pacelli's nunciature. This further supports the notion that the replacement of the German episcopate with increased Roman control over the election and naming of bishops was one of Pacelli's most pressing concerns. Another important feature of Roman policy in the naming of bishops during the pontificate of Pius XI was a clear preference for candidates who had studied in Jesuit seminaries or had received training in Jesuit faculties.

Also evident from Pacelli's portrayal of the bishops is his rather distant relationship with most of the non-Bavarians. Almost half the German bishops had died within a few years after he wrote his final report, which meant that Pacelli's most important dealings were with bishops who were named after 1929 with considerable input from him as cardinal secretary of state. One outstanding example was Bertram's future opponent in the Fulda Conference of Bishops, Bishop Konrad Count von Preysing (1880–

1950) of Berlin, who would become Pope Pius XII's most trusted liaison to the German episcopate.

The Career of Bishop Preysing

A vacancy in the bishop's throne in Eichstätt, in June 1932, provided the first opportunity to place Preysing in the German episcopate. The occasion also marked the first time since the concordat of 1924 that the new mode of papal appointment was applied. Pacelli had come to know and appreciate Preysing during his time as nuncio in Munich. A jurist who felt the calling relatively late in life, Preysing had decided to study theology under the Jesuits in Innsbruck, which meant that he conformed to Pacelli's understanding of the ideal education for a bishop and the "correctness" of the theology imparted to him. After 1912, he gained administrative experience at the diocesan level while serving as secretary to Archbishop Franz von Bettinger (1815–1917) of Munich. In 1928, Preysing was named a member of the Munich cathedral chapter after having served as cathedral preacher there since 1921. During those years, Pacelli had called on him frequently to perform legal and diplomatic tasks in the nunciature. However, Preysing's prospective appointment to the bishopric of St. Willibald found favor with neither the local church nor the Bavarian government. Pacelli, for his part, disregarded these objections in order to implement his personnel policies.

At its meeting of June 26, the Eichstätt cathedral chapter compiled an alphabetical list of four candidates for bishop whom they considered suitable: the capitulars Ludwig Bruggaier (1882–1970), Karl Kiefer (1866–1940), and Matthias Lederer (1875–1935), and the head of the seminary and rector of the episcopal philosophical-theological university in Eichstätt, Michael Rackl (1883–1948). Rome, however, wanted Pacelli in his role as cardinal secretary of state to pull the strings, and so he gave the matter top priority. On July 27, he informed his successor in Munich, Nuncio Alberto Vassallo di Torregrossa (1865–1959), that the Holy See was focusing on three of the candidates recommended by the Bavarian Conference of Bishops and the cathedral chapters from the lists submitted in accordance with the provisions of the Bavarian concordat: first, Preysing; second, Ludwig Bruggaier, who had been nominated by the Eichstätt chapter; and third, Vicar General Johann Baptist Höcht (1870–1950). This meant that at least one of the Eichstätt candidates was under consideration.[15]

The fact that Preysing was most favored did not mean that he had come off well in the triennial lists, the recommendations for suitable candidates that all Bavarian cathedral chapters and the Bavarian Conference of Bishops submitted to Rome every three years. If anything, the opposite was the case: Preysing's name was on the list for 1926, but the outcome was disastrous. Even though his own metropolitan chapter of Munich and Freising had nominated him as a potential candidate, he received only three of ten votes. Apparently, no one considered him bishop material.[16] The same happened when he was nominated in the list submitted by the chapter of Speyer.[17] He received a majority (five of seven votes) only from the Bavarian Conference of Bishops, where he was the protégé of Cardi-

Konrad Count von Preysing, Pacelli's liaison and opponent of Cardinal Bertram in the Fulda Conference of Bishops.
(SV-Bilderdienst/Scherrl)

nal Michael von Faulhaber (1869–1952), his local bishop, who recognized his moral probity and talents as a preacher and writer. In addition to the highest respect accorded him by the "association of nobles," the Munich cardinal stressed that Preysing was "highly esteemed by Nuncio Pacelli."[18] In 1929, Preysing's name was again placed on three lists; by 1932 he managed to appear on only two.[19]

It is clear that whenever Preysing's name was mentioned as a potential candidate outside of his home diocese or the Bavarian Conference of Bishops, which was dominated by Faulhaber, he received fewer votes. Even in his own cathedral chapter, it took two attempts for him to gain the majority. Even there, he was nominated as a candidate only because of the intervention of his bishop, who regularly argued that Preysing would make an ideal candidate because he had gained the pertinent experience in Rome in 1914 (as Cardinal Bettinger's secretary he had accompanied him to the conclave at which Giacomo della Chiesa was elected Pope Benedict XV), and in addition because Pacelli held him in high esteem. He was *acceptissimus* to the cardinal secretary of state. That made clear which criterion really mattered.

Nuncio Torregrossa's inquiries at Pacelli's behest were overall quite positive. In his opinion, Preysing had all the qualities required of a future bishop. He consistently defended the rights of the Church against encroachment by the state, and he voiced the Church's positions even in social conversation. But what was most apparent was his deep reverence for the Holy Father and his "faithful devotion to the representative of the Holy See in Munich, as Your Eminence has already experienced." The candidate put forward by the Eichstätt chapter was also highly praised. Torregrossa attested to Bruggaier's immaculate record as a priest. Not only was he completely familiar with local custom in Eichstätt, but the entire bishopric loved him. In short, Bruggaier would be the ideal candidate to be bishop of Eichstätt.[20]

Given the information received, the Holy See could well have named any of the three candidates to the Eichstätt bishopric. But if its primary goal had been to foster harmony, Rome would have surely selected Bruggaier, especially since Bavarian Prime Minister Heinrich Held (1868–1938), who was close to the Church, interceded with Rome on his behalf in the summer of 1932. Held let Pacelli know that he considered Bruggaier to be "the most suitable and religiously pleasing candidate." He was also "a scholar of renown, but for that a very experienced practitioner and priest, a highly respected pastor, and a man of polish with the finest of education," who could move with self-assurance in all social circles. In a word, "I . . . know of no other priest in Bavaria who could better adorn a bishop's throne than Bruggaier."[21]

Although Held did not bring up the nomination right that the Bavarian state had relinquished in the concordat of 1924, it would have been difficult for Pacelli to reject out of hand a desire so ardently expressed by a Catholic head of state. The various drafts of his response give an indication of how problematic Held's intercession was for the cardinal secretary of state. As he formulated it in his final response, the Holy See thanked Held for his suggestion, but the Holy Father had "for quite some time had his eye on another outstanding Bavarian priest for Eichstätt." The government, Pacelli continued, would be pleased because he was one of the priests recommended by the Bavarian bishops and the chapters.[22] Pius XI named Preysing bishop of Eichstätt on September 9, 1932.

This procedure sheds light on how Pacelli intended to circumvent the participatory rights of the local churches in Germany, which had been at least indirectly guaranteed. In general, he simply ignored them in favor of his own personnel policies in order to advance his candidates and so replace as quickly as possible the established German state episcopate with bishops who were loyal to Rome. In the case of his friend Preysing, Eichstätt would be merely a waystation. Barely a year later, Pacelli brought Preysing to Berlin with the intention of making him a bishop there. In spite of opposition from the Berlin cathedral chapter and the Prussian bishops, he placed Preysing in the second spot on the Roman list of three. Nikolaus Bares (1871–1935), who was in the first spot, was actually elected.[23] But when he died unexpectedly in 1935, the process started all over again.

Yet neither the Berlin cathedral chapter nor the chairman of the Fulda Conference of Bishops was prepared to consider Preysing for the vacancy. The chapter placed Bishop Clemens August von Galen (1878–1946) of Münster in the first spot on the list, along with two capitulars. Bertram, too, favored Galen, but he had a rather deprecatory opinion of Preysing:

"I would not wager to argue whether he is as suitable in the assuredness of his judgment and the agility of his manner." Nonetheless, five Prussian bishops spoke in favor of Preysing. On April 5, 1935, the Berlin cathedral chapter received a list of three nominees from Rome that contained none of the candidates suggested by the chapter. Instead, Preysing was in the first spot, followed in the second and third spots by the cathedral capitular Paul Weber (1881–1963) from Berlin and Professor Wendelin Rauch (1885–1954) from Mainz, two completely unknown candidates. The cathedral chapter had no real choice. Amid a general gnashing of teeth they elected Preysing bishop of Berlin.[24] The bishop had de facto been named by Rome.

Pacelli immediately made clear to the new bishop that he viewed him as his liaison to the German episcopate and to the government of the Reich, with which the Church was increasingly in conflict. His seat in the capital city would allow him to "observe conditions close up" and maintain "personal contacts of a direct and indirect nature." "Under certain circumstances a particularly important function might devolve" upon Preysing. Pacelli expected him to take "initiative" and demonstrate an aggressive understanding of the political aspects of the pastoral mission. Although he well understood Preysing's hesitation in taking on this role, the unusual circumstances demanded that personal sensitivities be pushed aside "in order to preserve the Church and immortal souls from serious losses."[25]

Good Lambs and Rebellious Intellectuals: The Catholic Laity

A nuncio is not merely the diplomatic representative of the Holy See in a sovereign country. His responsibilities extend beyond the political environment in which pastoral care is dispensed, the training of pastors, and the installation of the right kind of bishops. In the final analysis, all his ecclesiastical and political activities are aimed at ensuring that the lambs entrusted to his care by Rome "are kept from poisoned pastures" and led safely to the sweet waters of eternal life.[26] From the Roman perspective, and according to the new canon law of 1917, the bleating lambs bore no responsibility of their own in churchly matters; the shepherd and his sharp-eyed herding dogs were responsible for holding the flock together, protecting the lambs from predators, and keeping them on the straight and narrow. Accordingly, Pacelli was primarily concerned with protecting the Catholic laity from the challenges of the modern world with all its supposedly satanic seductions. These included fallacious ideologies propagated by Socialism, liberalism, and freemasonry. In Germany, of course, it also included Protestantism. Small wonder that Pacelli devoted a great deal of attention in his final report of 1929 to his lambs, the Church laity in Germany.

Pacelli painted a generally sophisticated and nuanced picture of the German laity for his readers in the Secretariat of State in Rome. He first turned his attention to the religious life of German Catholics before reporting on their personal morality and public morals. "In general," he noted, "the piety and behavior of the faithful in religious services leave nothing further to be desired; the comportment of Catholics in the churches is dignified and uplifting."[27] It is unlikely that Pacelli would have found as much discipline and fervor during the liturgy in his own homeland. He was mostly satisfied with the 55 percent of Catholics who attended church each Sunday and the 75 percent who participated in the compulsory Easter communion each year. He would have liked more children to receive communion, because "in places where the children more frequently approach the Eucharistic table one sees wonders of moral improvement and steadfastness of virtue."[28] Whether this prescription could have properly served children and young people in the German metropolis is a question for another day. As it was, Pacelli struggled to come to terms with the almost 44,000 Catholics who left the Church annually during the 1920s. The general religious indifference of the populace, anticlerical Communist propaganda, and the effects of various sects all took their toll. But Pacelli assigned special blame to the "poor economic situation" and "church taxes, which are hated by all" and were often "severely enforced."[29] He did, however, make it clear that defections from the Protestant churches had been six times higher than in Catholic churches, and that Catholics had overall proved considerably more resistant to modern temptations.

Pacelli presented a split assessment of the German laity. On the one side was the "mass of the simple faithful" who were "genuinely devoted to the Holy See" and unquestioningly followed the instructions of the pope and his representatives.[30] On the other side, however, were the rebellious Catholic intellectuals who were no longer willing to trot behind in blind obedience to Rome, but wished to find their own path as independent and responsible Christians and to create a life for themselves based on their faith. As Pacelli noted in his report, the goal of these intellectuals was "as much as possible to introduce Catholics to modern culture," while in the process "establishing the limits of such a reconciliation themselves, independent of Church officials, and even in opposition to them."[31] The nuncio's position on this matter is evident.

This split is exemplified by the "two liturgical movements" that Pacelli perceived. One praiseworthy form of lay engagement with the liturgy was the project of the Benedictine monk Anselm Schott (1843–1896) from Beuron, who had published a German-Latin missal that had gone through numerous printings. This work made it possible for churchgoers who were unfamiliar with Latin to follow in German the Latin liturgy in the Roman missal of 1570. Pacelli praised the widespread practice in Germany of singing German hymns during Mass instead of Latin ones because they "contribute effectively to piety and frequent church attendance," even though this practice did not meet Roman guidelines. However, the widespread custom of allowing women to sing along in church choirs during High Mass was completely intolerable to Rome. This "abuse" was something Pacelli sought to abolish, immediately if possible.[32] He found altogether too visionary the intellectual liturgical movement of Maria Laach that developed around the Benedictine monk Odo Casel (1886–1948). He was not persuaded that the "theology of mysteries" represented a more objective and social piety in church services. The notion that the laity could possibly be endowed with the power "to consecrate the body and the blood of Christ" was simply not reconcilable with Catholic dogma.[33] Pacelli also rejected criticism of popular devotions and the rosary by educated Catholics.

For Pacelli, what was true in the area of liturgy also held true at the level of principle. Although he was pleased with the religiousness of simple Catholics, the intellectuals were another matter. Pacelli viewed them as part of the tradition of rebellion against the Church and Church authorities, which first reared its head during the Enlightenment, gaining strength once again in the "modernistic tendencies" that cropped up around the turn of the century. In this he was in complete agreement with the ultramontane Catholic restoration: "The ideas championed by them [intellectuals] are equivocal or erroneous from many points of view. Their philosophy approaches that of the Protestants. Religion becomes a completely subjective matter, an exclusively internal experience."[34] These intellectuals rejected the Church of law, instead holding forth for a Church of love. Furthermore, in times of more democratic governments, they demanded more democratic church structures and challenged the hierarchical underpinnings of the Catholic Church. Pacelli was particularly irritated by Ernst Michel (1889–1964), whose *Politik aus dem Glauben* [Politics from faith], published in 1926, criticized the naming of bishops by the pope and demanded greater inclusion of the local churches in the naming process. This notion ran counter to Pacelli's strict Rome-centered model of the Church, which he had codified in 1917 in the CIC and had for twelve years attempted to translate into policy in Germany. Catholic intellectuals in Germany dreamed of a democratic Church in which the laity shared responsibility with the clergy, whereas Pacelli wanted a centralized papal Church with compliant lay members. These conceptions were simply irreconcilable. To protect young people, the nuncio demanded strict censorship of all works by Catholic intellectuals because, "unlike in the past, they are no longer accustomed to submitting to Church authority."[35]

Pacelli believed that Pius XI's Catholic Action model, which provided for strict subordination of the laity to the pope and bishops, was the solution to this problem. But it was not a solution that the Catholic associations in Germany would endorse. These groups had a primarily lay membership, and though clergy were not excluded, they were accorded no special privileges. Pacelli had to acknowledge these associations as "beautiful evidence of the goodwill and lively involvement of Catholics," but he criticized the Volksverein für das katholische Deutschland [People's Association for Catholic Germany], for example, for being "too independent of the Church hierarchy, and overstating the importance of culture to the detriment of religion."[36] Pacelli's hopes for greater clerical oversight of the associations did not bear fruit. The Catholic Action model that had been so successful in Italy did not prove transferable to Germany.

The Catholic laity was also subject to many personal moral perils. The use of contraceptives and the increasing number of abortions, even in Catholic families, "represent perhaps the thorniest problem for religious life and pastoral care in Germany."[37] These practices not only led to a drastic decline in the birthrate but also increasingly alienated educated Catholics from the Church. The so-called intellectuals in particular erred in their assertion that the Church was not competent in questions of marital and sexual morality. The nuncio identified mixed marriages with Protestants, which the German bishops had, unfortunately, tolerated for far too long, as a primary reason that so many of their children left the faith. Sooner or later the Catholic Church would largely disappear from the lives of the children of such marriages, at least in the Diaspora. This was another reason that the battle around Catholic schools was so important to Pacelli. Catholic parents should demand that their children be instructed in all subjects only by Catholic teachers. Only then could purity of faith and morality be ensured in education. Christian community schools in which Catholic and Protestant students received common instruction were not acceptable. Thus Pacelli's attempts to negotiate concordats with the various German states were largely focused on guaranteeing denominational schools, with varying success.

The temptations and loose morals of the Roaring Twenties challenged Pacelli's asceticism. He railed not only "against the perverse propaganda of nudism" but also against the idea that sports, gymnastics, or swimming should be taught in coeducational classes, a situation that was simply unthinkable.[38] "Any gymnastics wear for girls that provocatively accentuates their shapes or that is inappropriate for the female character must be avoided," he stated. "Gymnastics for girls must take place in halls or places that are not open to the public."[39] According to the nuncio, Catholics must fight against immorality in literature, film, and theater, and must on social occasions "return to the old simplicity and to the old decency." Modern dances like the tango were of "very evil origin, which threatened good morals and shame." The creations of fashion houses that were to be seen on the runways in Berlin and elsewhere were anathema to Catholic decency. "Although Catholic morality has no objection to becoming and tasteful clothing, nor to changes in fashion, it must with disgust resolutely and unconditionally condemn and reject the currently dominant fashion with its tendentious exposures and accentuations of physical forms, because in the final analysis they emanate from a cynical and paganistic conception of life and tend to engender concupiscence. Parents, and mothers in particular, are responsible for the clothing of their daughters."[40]

Pacelli's depictions gave the authorities in Rome a relatively clear picture of the Catholic laity. While the Catholics in the countryside were still largely under Roman control, the workers, and particularly the Catholic upper classes, were increasingly becoming emancipated from the magisterium in terms of faith and morality. As far as Pacelli was concerned, this state of affairs resulted from the false attempt to reconcile Catholicism and modernity in all areas of life. There would be no dismantling of fortifications. Rather, Pacelli intended to deliver the defiant fortress of the Church intact through the tempests of modernity. Yet the nuncio was unable to go beyond an analysis of the situation to offer any convincing and timely plans for action.

Between Scylla and Charybdis: The Catholic Center Party

The political landscape in Germany had not changed much since the second half of the nineteenth century. The Center Party, which was the voice of German Catholics, played an important role in the cacophony of political tendencies that included the Communist and Socialist parties on the left, the various liberal and bourgeois groupings, and the conservative and nationalist forces on the right. While the Center advanced the interests of the Catholic Church in all religious and cultural arenas, it also functioned as a party capable of bridging the attitudes and worldviews of the various social classes. And though its organizational structure was still rather antiquated, this backwardness was largely balanced before elections by strong support from the clergy. Nonetheless, in spite of the discussions prompted by Julius Bachem's (1845–1918) influential article of 1906, "We Must Get Out of the Tower," the goal of which was to expand the Center Party's electoral base beyond its traditional Catholic supporters, and in spite of several attempts to found an interconfessional party in 1918, the Center never succeeded in expanding its base of support beyond active and faithful Catholics.[41] Ever since the end of the Kulturkampf, and even during the first decade of the Weimar Republic, the party's support had eroded in tandem with the erosion in church attendance. This was in marked contrast to the periods of external pressure on the Church, such as the Kulturkampf in Prussia and the anticlerical measures initiated in Prussia by the radical Socialist minister of culture Adolf Hoffmann (1858–1930) during the 1918 revolution, when the Center Party's integrative appeal and vote count had swelled. These successes, according to Pacelli, resulted from the Center's ability to "adapt to the new situation, while at the same time paying attention to the proletarian masses in order to prevent Catholic workers, too, from defecting to Socialism."[42] But this shift to the left also engendered splits on the more right-leaning end of the party. The Catholic nobility, large landowners, intellectuals, and industrialists felt that they were no longer represented by the Center and turned to other parties, particularly the German National People's Party (Deutschnationale, or DNVP).

Two crucial changes had occurred since those years. For one thing, during the revolution of 1918, the Bavarian People's Party (Bayerische Volkspartei, or BVP), which was more conservative and federalist than the Center Party, with a larger bourgeois and agrarian membership, split off. In addition, because of its intermediate position in the party spectrum, the Center was almost constantly part of the ruling coalition during the Weimar period, providing no fewer than four Reich chancellors. But in the process, the party was forced to make compromises with ever-changing coalition partners. These alliances led to defections on both the left and the right edges of the party but never attracted a broad pool of voters.

Even though the 1917 general instruction to Pacelli had noted that the Center Party was the only acceptable political grouping in Germany, relations between the Center and the Roman Curia were never free of tension. The pope did not favor an independent party that was controlled primarily by the laity and not directly beholden to the Church hierarchy. According to the Catholic Action model, the laity were not to act independently, but were to take their cue from the pope and the bishops. Even as the Kulturkampf of the 1880s and 1890s was being resolved, Pope Leo XIII paid little heed to the Catholic party, though the Center had been Rome's standard bearer for almost two decades after the founding of the Prussian-led German national state. Leo XIII settled matters with Reich Chancellor Bismarck by himself, essentially in the style of cabinet politics, causing the leader of the party, Ludwig Windthorst (1812–1891), to exclaim in disappointment, "Shot! Shot at the front! Shot at from the rear! I'm going home!"[43]

This issue flared up again with the fall of the monarchy in Germany in 1918 and the defeat of the Council Republic through the formation of the Weimar coalition, consisting of the Center, the SPD, and the liberals. This was because the Church had often condemned liberalism and Socialism as corrupting errors and had declared both worldviews to be irreconcilable with Catholic principles. How could the Catholic party now not only ratify the Weimar constitution in cooperation with enemies of the Church but even worse, share joint responsibility with them in the government? Although Rome had to admit that during consultation on the constitution the Center had succeeded in inserting Church-friendly articles into the Weimar constitution that for the first time ensured the autonomy and legal standing of the Church, a constitution that in principle made no reference to God was a fundamentally unfriendly instrument. A state founded exclusively on the sovereignty of the people and not on eternal divine right was inconceivable according to Roman doctrine.

Pacelli seems to have been a decided opponent of collaboration between the Center and the parties of the left. Certainly, pertinent passages from the memoirs of Heinrich Brüning (1886–1970), the Center politician who served as Reich chancellor from 1930 to 1932, have been interpreted this way. For example, he reported on an audience with Pacelli in the Vatican, in August 1931: "Pacelli raised the question of the Reichskonkordat. . . . Pacelli thought that with regard to a Reichskonkordat I must form a government with the right on the condition that a concordat be concluded immediately."[44] Even as nuncio, Pacelli had "never correctly understood the fundamentals of German politics nor the particular position of the Center Party . . . even though he had lived in Germany uninterruptedly for thirteen years. Rooted firmly in the concordat system, he believed that by concluding agreements between the Vatican and the individual states he ministered to the interests of Catholics better than did lay politicians with their powers."[45]

Pacelli's final report from 1929 and numerous nuncial reports that he had sent from Munich and Berlin to Rome since 1917 now provide more precise information about his basic attitude toward the Center, and particularly about the Catholic party's coalition with the SPD. Pacelli's assessment of the party was largely positive during the first years of his nunciature. When the Center entered Philip Scheidemann's (1865–1939) cabinet, in February 1919, Pacelli greeted this development warmly, even though any coalition with the Social Democrats seemed problematic to him. "In my opinion, the Center has very adroitly resolved the difficult question of participation in the government," Pacelli noted in one of his reports.[46] The coalition with the Social Democrats had to be entered into because of the constellation of parties; an alliance with bourgeois elements within the German Democratic Party had been rejected, and tolerance for a Socialist minority government shortly after the revolution was inadvisable. Even so, the Center insisted on fewer ministerial posts than it was entitled to given its proportion of the total vote, which enabled the party to maintain a certain distance from the government—and particularly from the party's "Socialist" coalition partner. Pacelli's understanding of the role of the Center may have been influenced by his understanding of the Kulturkampf. The notion that compromises between parties should be a normal part of democratic give-and-take seems to have escaped him completely.

Nuncial reports during the 1920s consistently addressed the relationship between the Center and the SPD. On September 12, 1924, Pacelli received instructions from the Secretariat of State in Rome to report on collaboration between the Center and the "Socialists in Germany." "I am particularly interested in knowing," wrote Cardinal Secretary of State Gasparri, "whether this collaboration developed during the preparatory and electoral phases of the elections, or only after the Socialists had managed to achieve mandates on their own."[47] Pacelli replied with a detailed report in which he made clear that the Center was in no danger of compromising with Socialism, particularly since it had always combated Socialist theories. He continued with a retrospective of previous Center alliances since the Weimar national assembly of 1919. The Center Party, said Pacelli, had always subordinated itself to the interests of the nation, and had therefore entered into coalitions with partners with whom it was less than friendly. Furthermore, the Center had ensured that the Weimar constitution was not written solely along Social Democratic lines. Of course, the Center's participation in the Weimar coalition also had a downside. The apparent leftward drift of the Center caused many conservative Catholics to defect to the DNVP. As a result, some Center politicians questioned whether the party should not ally itself with the DNVP instead of with the SPD. Although the chairman, Wilhelm Marx (1863–1946), and the left wing of the party around Joseph Wirth (1879–1956) were skeptical of such an alliance, politicians such as Adam Stegerwald (1874–1945) and Theodor von Guérard (1863–1943) were open to the alternative of a "bourgeois bloc cabinet."[48]

The concern of the Secretariat of State did not abate during the subsequent period. When Paul von Hindenburg (1847–1934) was elected Reich president in 1925, defeating the Center candidate Wilhelm Marx, Rome questioned Pacelli about whether the SPD had—as reported by the press—withheld its support from Marx.[49] The nuncio then described the facts of the election as he saw them: Hindenburg had been supported by a "right bloc," Marx by a "left bloc." But some Social Democrats, particularly in Saxony, considered the idea of running Prussian Prime Minister Otto Braun (1872–1955). It appeared that some "Socialist" voters in Saxony had in fact denied Marx their votes. Furthermore, the "intolerant Protestant press" had attacked the Catholic candidate in the run-up to the election.[50] Pacelli felt it best to conceal from Rome that the Bavarian People's Party and even Cardinal Faulhaber had spoken in favor of Hindenburg—and presumably voted against Marx.

The Secretariat of State then immediately sent Pacelli a note that was crystal clear in its intent. Referencing the wordings of Pius XI in consistory in December 1924, Gasparri wrote, "The Holy Father, who knows well the openly antireligious content of the Socialist program . . . is very concerned about the fact that the heads of the Catholic parties seek opportunities to form alliances with Socialists in order to follow behaviors that they claim are necessary for the defense of political and economic advantage. . . . The Holy Father continues to be concerned about Germany because he sees that the Catholics of the Center have for many years all too frequently allied with the Socialists to defend their so-called economic achievements and their independence."[51] Gasparri subsequently instructed the nuncio to "carefully remind the German bishops of the will of the Holy Father that those Catholics who actively take part in the political life of this country earnestly scrutinize in light of the eternal principles of the Church whether the alliances entered into with Socialists, who have always opposed Catholic ideas and denigrated them as reactionary and antiprogressive, may not in the long term represent a serious danger to the authority of the Church."[52]

Pacelli followed through immediately. After consulting Cardinal Bertram, the chairman of the Fulda Conference of Bishops, he decided to talk to Wilhelm Marx, the chairman of the Center Party. Marx asserted that he had already presented his point of view to the Holy See and had received papal consent for his position—a claim that Gasparri later vehemently denied: "His Holiness remembers well that in his audience with Mr. Marx last May they had spoken only about the assent telegrammed to the Protestants, and that he had expressed his astonishment at this way of doing things. In addition, he had listened to the representations made about the goal of preventing a civil war pursued by the Center after the revolution; however, not a single word was uttered about the problem of collaboration with the Socialists."[53] Fundamentally, Pacelli reported, the Reichstag faction that had joined a coalition under Hans Luther (1879–1962) in January without Social Democratic involvement was tending rightward. Nonetheless, there were also influential circles, including partisans of ex-Chancellor Joseph Wirth, who advocated collaboration with the political left. Pacelli felt distinctly uncomfortable in his role. He made clear that he would have to proceed very carefully because the position of the Berlin nunciature could be "irreparably compromised if it leaked to the public that the nuncio had involved himself in party questions, for whatever reason, or intended to influence the domestic politics of German Catholics."[54]

This did not mean that political influence was subsequently reined in. After the German nationalists had withdrawn their ministers from the government in protest against the Locarno treaties, which aimed at international reconciliation and understanding, and spoken in favor of a renewed coalition with the Social Democrats at the Center Party's congress in Kassel, Pacelli sharpened his position on December 9, 1925. A coalition government with the SPD was necessary at the moment to overcome the economic crisis and to avoid saddling the bourgeois parties with the sole responsibility for foreign policy. Not entering into such a coalition would boost the radicals and Communists. He noted, "It would be dangerous, however . . . if the coalition with the Socialists were to become a permanent method."[55]

Pacelli had already touched on this sensitive issue in a report to Gasparri dated December 1, 1925, titled "On Collaboration between Socialists and Catholics in Germany."[56] First, he gave the cardinal secretary of state a brief overview of the partisan landscape in Germany. "In spite of its weaknesses and errors," the Center remained the only party that represented Catholic interests in the Reichstag. To the left were the Communists and Social Democrats, who, in spite of tactical statements to the contrary, were "in fundamental opposition to Christianity," and the liberal democrats, whose "notorious anticlerical tendencies" were known. To the right were Erich Ludendorff's (1865–1937) ultranationalist German Völkisch Freedom Party (Deutsch-Völkische Freiheitspartei); the German People's Party (DVP), which was still caught up in the anti-Catholic mentality of the Kulturkampf; and the DNVP, which represented the majority of German Protestants. The DNVP, for its part, had developed an abiding hatred of Rome. Faced with this unpalatable choice between Scylla and Charybdis, the Center opted for collaboration with the left for reasons of "necessity and opportunity." "I admit that with regard to the interests of the Church, this constant tendency of the Center to ally with the Socialists displeases me," wrote Pacelli to Gasparri, and he let it be known that he could well imagine collaboration between the Catholics and Ludendorff's party because it would represent a far-reaching convergence of interests between Catholics and Protestants with regard to concordats and agreements between Church and state and safeguard the Catholic schools. After the DNVP had rejected the Locarno treaties and the center-right coalition had broken apart, Pacelli considered it extremely unwise for the pope to condemn outright a coalition with the Socialists. Given the situation on the ground, the Center had no choice but to revive the center-left coalition, including the SPD. Between the lines, the nuncio urged Cardinal Secretary of State Gasparri to convey these concerns to Pius XI, and to prevent him from taking such a "catastrophic" step.

When in January 1927 Pacelli was again asked to submit a report on the relationship between the Center Party and the SPD (consistently referred to as "Socialists"), he expressed his views about the Center's ideal ally even more categorically:

> It is correct that the parties of the right, a large majority of which (though not all) consist of Protestants, are frequently hostile to the Catholic Church, and that they ply their *furor protestanticus* even to the detriment of their own interests for the sole purpose of fighting their detested Rome, nonetheless the atheistic and materialistic Socialists, who have temporarily moderated their attacks for primarily tactical reasons, are no less rejecting of Catholic principles. It appears from experience that though fraught with difficulties, the probability of a good concordat (think of the one earlier concluded with Bavaria) and school laws that favor confessional schools—currently the two most important religious questions—is greater through an alliance with the German National People's Party than with the Socialists.[57]

This assessment of the situation led Pacelli to criticize harshly the left wing of the Center Party. Although he had to admit that the Christian unions "were the most moderate and reasonable of the German unions," he accused them of being "too partisan" in defending "the economic interests of the workers (wages)" without adequately taking into account the other social classes, and of advocating social legislation that "was too close to Socialist ideas and made the workers completely dependent on assistance from the state."[58] The left wing of the Center had ceded all claims to representing religious positions in favor of foreign policy and social legislation. As an article in *Germania* made clear, the former Prussian prime minister and minister for social welfare Adam Stegerwald claimed that the school question was not the linchpin of Center Party policies.[59] Large sections of the party operated out of an aversion to the old regime that was only partially understandable, and many still found warm words to describe the "Socialist" enemy. However, in so doing they overlooked large areas of common interest with the DNVP, which was even prepared to shelve potential points of conflict such as the reintroduction of the monarchy. Pacelli's reports are fairly scathing in their criticism of the behavior of leading Center politicians, particularly of Marx, the party's chairman, who simply ignored directives from Rome.[60]

But despite serious misgivings, neither Pacelli nor the Curia could ignore the Center Party. The nuncio thus felt compelled to repeat almost verbatim in his final report of 1929 the largely positive assessment in the general instruction of 1917: "To be sure, the Center was not free of deficiencies and errors, but it nonetheless remains (together with the Bavarian People's Party) the only party that one can count on when it comes to defending the interests of the Catholic religion in Parliament."[61] The election of Ludwig Kaas (1881–1952) as chairman of the Center Party in 1928 further strengthened this positive assessment. Prelate Kaas had been a

Prelate Ludwig Kaas, the chairman of the Center Party.
(SV-Bilderdienst/S.M.)

longtime liaison and coworker of Pacelli's. By clericalizing the party, the nuncio hoped that its policies would increasingly mirror the interests of the Roman Curia. It is no accident that Pacelli heaped high praise on the new chairman in his final report: "Extremely praiseworthy is the canon, Monsignore Dr. Ludwig Kaas, also a former student of the Collegium Germanicum et Hungaricum, a clergyman of extraordinary gifts and education, exceedingly loyal to the Holy See and the nunciature. After the resignation of Mr. Marx, he was, despite his opposition, elected leader of the Center Party, on which he will be able to exert a very positive influence, especially in the area of religion."[62] But the crucial question was whether Pacelli would finally be able, through Kaas, to exert control over the Center, which had been Rome's dream ever since the party was founded. This issue would become particularly venomous after Adolf Hitler was named Reich chancellor.

The Return to Rome as a "German": Lasting Effects?

"My German mission has come to an end," Pacelli declared. "A larger, more wide-ranging one is about to commence at the spiritual and supernatural center of the universal Church. I return from whence I came. To the grave of the rock under the dome of Michelangelo to the living Peter in the Vatican. Standing close to Peter means being close to Christ."[63] With these words Nuncio Pacelli bid farewell to the Catholics of Berlin on December 10, 1929, looking back on the efforts of twelve years in Germany. Shortly thereafter he left for Rome to assume the post of papal secretary of state and receive the rank of cardinal. His speech disclosed very little about the effect that his experience of German culture had had on him or about the peculiarities of German Catholicism. Pacelli himself viewed his unusually long nunciature in Germany as something of a transition in which he applied what he had learned in Rome but which contributed only little to the development of new "German" convictions and modes of action.

At first glance, one would have to concur with Pacelli's assessment: Germany was little more than a way station between Rome and Rome. The clear theological and canonical premises that Pacelli brought with him to Germany in 1917 remained immutable to the day he left. It could not have been otherwise because the eternal truths for which the Roman Catholic stood were not changeable or even adaptable to changing situations. If his instructions were to neutralize evil, this task could be accomplished only from a secure, immovable foundation based upon the principles taught by an infallible pope. Pacelli had encountered evil not only in the modern ideologies of liberalism, Socialism, and Communism, but especially in the "modernists" and Church reformers who based themselves on the German tradition of an alternative non-Roman Catholicism, which they believed was reconcilable with modernism.

Numerous peculiarities of the German Church, particularly the involvement of the local churches in installing bishops, and the independence of German lay Catholicism with its numerous associations operating independent of the Church hierarchy, remained deeply alien to him. He propounded a radical program of Church centralism that in the final analysis equated the Catholic Church with the papal Church. He rejected all centrifugal tendencies within Catholicism that would result in greater local independence and that drew on centuries of tradition in Germany. Pacelli also opposed episcopalist tendencies that insisted on the intrinsic importance of the bishops as successors of the apostles. For Pacelli, the bishops were little more than papal head altar boys, called on to act only on the instructions of the pope. The Church was not looking for autonomous personalities equipped with independent views and judgment, open to the immense economic and social challenges and trends of the postwar period. Rome wanted yes-men with childlike devotion to the Holy Father. This was Pacelli's crucial criterion for a good bishop, and he bent every effort to install just such men and to stamp out the independence of the German Church.

Pacelli left the Germany of the Weimar Republic as a stranger in other respects as well. He had been unable to come to terms with German culture as it developed during the Roaring Twenties, or even with the German university, which at the time was still the flagship of German intellectual achievement throughout the world. He found repugnant the critical and original thinking that a liberal course of studies unleashed, particularly in candidates for the ministry. This kind of education was completely antithetical to his image of the world and of human beings because he firmly believed that all correct interpretation of reality (and not only of faith) could be based only in the Roman magisterium. Academic learning had no place in this worldview.

It could be argued that this rigid adherence to Roman principles was the result of a peculiarity in Pacelli's personality. In that case, he would have to be characterized as a narrow-minded, rigid Roman prelate, completely incapable of adapting to new situations. Recent research into nunciatures indicates, however, that this narrowness in fact characterized all too many nuncios of the early modern period. They seem to have been unable to understand anything outside their frame of reference because "their own horizon of meaning as curial representatives and as Italians" was "the only possible one." The notion that "the beliefs of heretics could have meaning, or that the German way of life might possibly be superior to the Italian, was not even thinkable."[64] Wolfgang Reinhard has in this connection spoken of an "illusory empiricism." If such limits on perspective or even blind spots apply to the nuncios of the twentieth century as well, then we are faced not just with a simple personality trait but with a fundamental attribute of the Roman nuncios per se.

But despite the fact that Pacelli's Roman perspective was irreconcilable with the German reality, evidence suggests that his experiences in Germany did have an effect on him. For example, he seems to have been extremely impressed by what are sometimes characterized as typical German virtues. He frequently praised German punctuality, order, and reliability. He apparently internalized German industriousness and even the Protestant work ethic, as many of his contemporaries have attested. He very much approved of the "decent" comportment of German Catholics during Mass, so different from the tumultuous country-fair atmosphere to which he had become accustomed in Italy.

He was also fascinated by German technology, even though he never overcame his fear of flying.[65] His reports contain passionate descriptions of his official car, a Mercedes-Benz. The vehicle was sitting at the door of the Munich nunciature when Pacelli arrived in May 1917 after a long train trip from Rome. It was paid for by none other than the Center Party politician Matthias Erzberger, whom Pacelli probably got to know in 1915, and with whom he continued to stay in close contact. Erzberger often visited Rome to negotiate with the pope and the secretary of state about potential resolutions to the Roman question. The nuncio showed real enthusiasm for his particular model of car, which had only been in production since 1916. Luxury cars were a rarity at the time in economically backward Rome. He lovingly described all the details of the car: "It is a beautiful Benz 18/45 HP, powerful and elegant. It has all the modern features that the automobile industry has to offer, from an automatic starter to an electric cigar lighter, from a device to measure speed and gradient to automatic fuses. It is an automobile that is truly worthy of a papal representative." His enthusiasm for his official vehicle with its papal coats of arms on the door mountings moved the nuncio to send a letter to the Secretariat of State in Rome. In it, Pacelli requested that a special letter of thanks be sent to Erzberger in the name of the Holy Father. This gift, he noted, was not only for him as apostolic nuncio but was meant to demonstrate Erzberger's reverence for the pope.[66]

Pacelli's enthusiasm for automobiles never waned. One time, when

Pacelli had a custom-built Benz 18/45. This photograph shows the standard model.

(DaimlerChrysler AG Corporate Archive, Stuttgart-Untertürkheim)

Erzberger accompanied him to a discussion with representatives of the Reich government, he was unable to contain himself and remarked in a later report about the "captivating military vehicle" that had been placed at his disposal during his entire visit to Berlin.[67] Whatever contributed to his enthusiasm, whether enjoyment of the ride, naïve pride in ownership, or even an interest in the potential of technological progress, Pacelli's official vehicle probably enhanced his understanding of his function as papal representative.

His status symbol would undergo harsh treatment two years later, on April 29, 1919, when, under the Council Republic, the nunciature was occupied by Communist revolutionaries. The grounds were cleared a few hours later on orders from the new political leadership. Pacelli was forced to surrender his garage, and though his chauffeur had the presence of mind to remove an essential part of the vehicle, the revolutionaries were eventually able to get the car rolling. Pacelli immediately lodged a protest with the military, at first to no avail. Only the next day, after numerous protests to various ministries, was the vehicle brought back. On returning it, the government claimed that the car had been "confiscated out of military necessity." But the car was now in rough shape, and though the garage performed the most important repairs, the rubber attachments for the wheels were delivered as parts.[68] Pacelli's next report to the Secretariat of State should have dealt primarily with the occupation of the nunciature. However, the sad story of his luxury coach was a recurrent theme throughout the multiple-page document, even though the nuncio made every effort to focus his condemnation on the violation of the building.

But were enthusiasm for German luxury cars and German virtues really all that Pacelli took back with him to Rome? More recent research shows that two other experiences in Germany appear to have had such a lasting effect on him that they might, at least in part, explain Pius XII's "silence" about the Holocaust. One frequently mentioned event is the failure of his peace initiative. The lesson he learned from this was that the Holy See must remain strictly neutral in international conflicts, particularly in military disputes, because the pope must as *padre comune* of all Catholics remain above the parties to the conflict. This experience taught him that political involvement could only redound to the detriment of the

Church. The other issue that is frequently raised is the trauma of the Kulturkampf, from which many leading men of the Church suffered and which Pacelli internalized as well. The fact that thousands of parishes remained without pastors because of political disagreements between the Catholic Church and the Prussian state, and that as a result countless Catholics died without the benefit of the means of grace, the holy sacrament of final unction, the Eucharistic viaticum, and absolution of all sins through confession, and might as a result be consigned to purgatory or even to hell, was nothing short of a pastoral catastrophe. If the supreme purpose of the Church was to ensure the salvation of the lambs entrusted to it, the lessons to be learned from the German Kulturkampf included no political involvement, no unnecessary battles with the state, and, if need be, complete withdrawal from society into the sacristy—as long as the state guaranteed the Church's right to administer the sacraments and pastoral care. If these theses are correct, and if these experiences in fact crystallized into modes of action, this would go a long way toward clarifying the motives behind Pacelli's silence about the persecution of the Jews.

The research to date indicates that anti-Semitism played only a minor role in Pacelli's nuncial reports. In 1920, the nuncio noted that the Protestant theologian Karl Dunkmann (1868–1932) intended to publish an interconfessional Christian journal. Pacelli advised the Secretariat of State not to support the project, citing both the potential damage that exclusively theoretical collaboration might inflict on the Catholic cause, and the difficulty in separating religious goals from everyday politics. Yet he also pointed out that as early as World War I there had been a concrete reason for Dunkmann's openness to interconfessional understanding: "His recurrent assertion of the necessity for peace among Christians could lead one to conclude that he was driven by anti-Semitic motives, which are very widespread at present among the old conservatives and German nationalists."[69]

Pacelli expended far more energy on the machinations of German Protestantism than on observing the Jewish congregations. He was well aware and suspicious of the anti-Semitism emanating from the German right, particularly from the *völkisch*-nationalist wing. In March 1923, he reported on an anonymous letter published in the *Bayerische Kurier,* which supposedly issued from Church circles and was addressed to Kaiser Wilhelm II. It concerned "a vulgar polemic against the Jesuits, who were accused of working together with the Jews and Jewish freemasonry in the war against Germany in order to return the Christian world to Rome, and to break the Protestant domination of Prussia once and for all."[70] As Pacelli immediately noted, the purpose of the letter had been to damage German Catholicism. The nuncio then argued at length about "Protestant circles in Germany" that attacked the Catholic Church "out of jealousy over the growing prestige of the Holy See." Pacelli wasted not a single word on the defamation of the Jews, who in the letter were also accused of working with the "Jewish Soviet government." His mandate was solely to defend Catholicism. A year later, Pacelli again reported on an article in the *völkisch*-nationalist press that struck the same chord, claiming that "non-German powers, the Jew and Rome," had taken control in Germany.[71] It should come as no surprise that Pacelli generally opposed such propaganda, which was not at all rare in Germany at the time. A connection between anti-Semitism and anti-Roman agitation had been widespread in *völkisch*-nationalist circles since the turn of the century.

But this does not mean that Pacelli's distaste for German anti-Semitism had any basis in a general openness toward Judaism or Jewry. Pacelli's reports also contain anti-Semitic stereotypes. Disparaging remarks about Jews are particularly frequent in his reports about the Council Republic in Munich. For example, the nuncio railed against the "grim Russian-Jewish-Revolutionary tyranny."[72] Moreover, his descriptions of the revolutionaries frequently betrayed ideological stereotypes: "An army of staff who go, who come, who give orders, who spread news, and among them a swarm of young women who do not look particularly trustworthy, and Jewish like the first. . . . At the head of this group is Levien's lover, a young Russian, Jewish, divorced, who gives orders like an overlord. The nunciature was forced too frequently to bow to her for permission to pass freely. Levien is a young man, also Russian and Jewish, approximately thirty or thirty-five years old. Pale, dirty, with lifeless eyes and a rough and vulgar voice: a truly disgusting type, but intelligent and crafty nonetheless."[73]

Pacelli constantly mentioned the Jewish backgrounds of the revolutionaries. Without hesitation, he garnished the connections he made between

Jewry, Communism, and Russian nationality with remarks about the un-attractive appearance of the revolutionaries, which included more than a little misogyny. Although the notion of a "Jewish-Bolshevik world conspiracy" played a much more virulent role in the propaganda of the German right, the nuncio was not wholly free of such sloganeering.

These quotations demonstrate that Pacelli's tendency to disparage Jews and his simultaneous distancing from the *völkisch*-nationalist right wing cannot be easily categorized or reconciled. Apparent digressions and side references often reveal glimpses of his attitude toward Jews. The numerous other nuncial reports, which are being studied as part of a long-term project financed by the German Research Foundation (DFG), may help to further complete this puzzle.

Two

Perfidious Jews?

The Battle in the Vatican over Anti-Semitism (1928)

Racial anti-Semitism, which during the Nazi era led to the murder of more than six million Jews, represents the defining evil of the first half of the twentieth century. The Catholic Church and its leader, Pope Pius XII, are frequently accused of having remained silent during the Holocaust and, in the final analysis, of having been indifferent to the fate of the Jews. Instead of protesting publicly and defending without reservation the human rights of the persecuted, the Church had been concerned solely with its survival as an institution and with the salvation of its members. It had, in addition, disregarded, or at least repressed, knowledge of the gas chambers. In 1933, it had even concluded a pact, the Reichskonkordat, with the devil in the form of Adolf Hitler—in order to protect its "flock." If we give credence to Daniel Goldhagen's argument, which he rightly admits is "not a historiographic exercise," this pact with the devil had been an easy choice for both the pope and the Vatican.[1] In Goldhagen's view, all Catholics were equally anti-Semitic: the pope and his secretary of state, the cardinals and the bishops, the clergy and the laity. In fact, according to Goldhagen, Nazism and Catholicism had one thing in common: a deep hatred of Jews.

Defenders of the Catholic Church have made every effort to counter these blanket accusations. After all, the Church had explicitly condemned the doctrine of modern racial anti-Semitism five years before Hitler's seizure of power in 1933, an event that marked the onset of official persecution, and more than ten years before Kristallnacht, in 1938. On March 22, 1928, Pope Pius XI had approved a decree of the Holy Office, the supreme office for Catholic doctrine, which stated, "The Catholic Church has always been accustomed to praying for the Jewish people, the recipients of a divine promise up to the coming of Jesus Christ, in spite of this people's blindness. More than that, it has done so on account of that very blindness. Ruled by the same charity, the Apostolic See has protected this people against unjust vexations, and just as it reproves all hatred between peoples, so it condemns hatred against the people formerly chosen by God, the hatred that today customarily goes by the name of anti-Semitism."[2]

It should be noted that before the opening of the archives it was not possible to analyze the reasons the pope condemned anti-Semitism. We were able to interpret only what was stated in the text of the decree. The text itself does make clear that the Holy Office's attention to the subject of anti-Semitism was related to proceedings to place on the Index of Forbidden Books a pamphlet titled *Pax super Israel* published by a group of priests calling themselves the Amici Israel (Friends of Israel). After a thorough investigation, the Roman Inquisition decided to dissolve this group. Although the Holy Office praised the group's intention to pray for the conversion of the Jews, it nonetheless had come to its attention that the priests had in the two years since the group's founding "assumed a manner of acting and thinking that was contrary to the *sensus ecclesiae,* that is, contrary to the thinking of the Holy Father and to the sacred liturgy."

It is not clear from reading the decree exactly how banning a decidedly philo-Semitic association of priests with more than three thousand members, among them cardinals and bishops of high standing, could be reconciled with the Church's simultaneous condemnation of racial anti-Semitism. The reasons for the judgment cited in the text remain rather vague as well. For one thing, the violations against the sacred liturgy were formulated in very general terms. Even before the archive was opened, scholars had theorized that the ban may have occurred in the context of a reform of the Good Friday liturgy then under way. This effort was strongly supported by elements of the Church who were critical of the Jews. Of particular importance here was not only the Passion according to St. John, in which the guilt of the Jewish people for the crucifixion and death of Jesus is far more pronounced than in the passions of the synoptic Gospels; the so-called Improperia, or Reproaches, and the Good Friday prayer deserve mention as well. The Reproaches were chanted during the adoration of the cross, when Jesus lamented to his faithless people, *"O my people,* what is it I have done unto thee? How have I grieved thee? Answer thou me! It was I who brought thee out of Egypt . . . and thou hast dragged me before Pilate's judgment seat. . . . It was I who drew from the rock the water of salvation for thee to drink: and thou hast brought me gall and vinegar in my thirst. . . . and thou hast set upon my head a crown of thorns."[3] In addition, the eighth prayer of the Good Friday liturgy included a prayer for the "perfidious Jews" or, more specifically in the prescribed Latin liturgy, "pro perfidis judaeis."

A file that turned up in 2003 in the archive of the Congregation for the Doctrine of the Faith under "Rerum Variarum," bearing the signature "1928 No. 2," allows us to reconstruct in minute detail how the redefinition of the Chosen People of God as "perfidious Jews" became the starting point for a fierce controversy within the Curia, not only about the Good Friday liturgy, but also about the fundamental relationship between the Catholic Church and the Jewish people, and the Church's understanding of anti-Semitism. Pius XI was just as engaged in this controversy as were the Holy Office and the Congregation of Rites, which was responsible for the liturgy. The full spectrum of possible attitudes toward Jews would come to the fore in this conflict, from hardcore anti-Semitism to outright philo-Semitism, from support of Theodor Herzl (1860–1904) to anti-Zionism. The crucial question was how this pope would deal with these tensions within the Roman Curia. Where did he stand personally? What official line of approach did he lay out? What was the precise background of the pope's condemnation of anti-Semitism in 1928? Had this condemnation really distanced the Catholic Church from all forms of anti-Semitism? Or did these formulations conceal an entirely different set of intentions?

"Let Us Pray for the Perfidious Jews"

The eighth of nine prayer intentions in the Good Friday liturgy according to the Roman Missal of 1570, the prescribed text for masses throughout the world, begins: "Oremus et pro perfidis Judaeis: ut Deus et Dominus noster auferat velamen de cordibus eorum; ut et ipsi agnoscant Jesum Christum Dominum nostrum." ["Let us pray also for the faithless Jews: that Almighty God may remove the veil from their hearts; so that they, too, may acknowledge Jesus Christ our Lord."] Before the oration itself, the celebrant was made aware of the following in a rubric: "By exception . . . in this place *Flectamus genua* [Let us kneel.] and *Levate* [Arise.] are omitted and the celebrant straightaway chants the Collect: 'Almighty and everlasting God, from whose mercy not even the treachery of the Jews is shut out: pitifully listen to us who plead for that blinded nation, that opening at last their eyes to the true light, which is Christ, he may dispel the darkness in which they are shrouded.'"[4] A decision was made during the nineteenth century to publish bilingual missals so that celebrants not familiar with Latin could follow the Tridentine liturgy. In Germany, the German-Latin missal published in 1884 by Anselm Schott became a bestseller, going through multiple editions. Most serious believers brought a copy of "Schott" to Mass, along with the hymnal used by the particular diocese.

The English translation of the Good Friday prayer for the Jews (in this case from the 1925 edition of the Latin and English missal) stated, "Let us pray even for the treacherous Jews, begging the Lord our God to take away the veil from their hearts so that they, too, may believe in Jesus Christ our Lord." In the translation and in the margin of the rubric was the following explanation: "By exception, in the supplication for the Jews, the early Christians neither knelt nor paused for private prayer, in abhorrence, it is said, of the Jews having in mockery knelt before and jeered the suffering Saviour." This explanation was followed by the actual oration: "Almighty and everlasting God, from whose mercy not even the treachery of the Jews is shut out: pitifully listen to us who plead for that blinded nation, that opening at last their eyes to the true light, which is Christ, he may dispel the darkness in which they are shrouded . . . Amen."[5]

The Good Friday prayer according to the Tridentine Missal of Pius V

(1566–1572) consisted of nine prayer intentions. Prayers were said for Church, pope, clergy, monarch, catechumens, and all those who found themselves in need or danger, as well as for heretics (primarily Protestants), Jews, and pagans. All the prayers, even those for the unfaithful, were accompanied by the oration, introduced with "Let us pray"; "Let us kneel"; "Arise"; along with a silent prayer—except in the case of the Jews, where it was omitted for the reason cited in the rubric. In addition to the omission of kneeling, the formulations "pro perfidis judaeis" (for the perfidious Jews) and "judaicam perfidiam" (Jewish perfidy) are also striking. It is certainly understandable that a group of priests intent on reconciliation between Judaism and Catholicism would have been particularly sensitive to these elements of the Good Friday liturgy at a time when racial anti-Semitism was increasing in Europe. Members of the Amici Israel understood that talk of "perfidious Jews" could easily be co-opted by racial ideologues, providing them with an anti-Semitism based in liturgy.

This was why they appealed to Pius XI in early January 1928. In a letter written in Latin, the group requested a reform in the Good Friday prayer for the Jews. The letter was signed in the name of the central committee of the priests' association of the Friends of Israel, which had been founded on February 24, 1926, that is, two years before the reform initiative. Benedict Gariador (1859–1936), the abbot general of the Benedictine Congregation of Monte Cassino, served as its president. Another priest from a religious order, Knight of the Cross Anton van Asseldonk (1892–1973), served as its secretary.

As it happened, the founding of the Amici Israel was not the idea of a priest, which is somewhat surprising given that only clergy could join. The idea actually came from a Jewish convert named Sophie Franziska van Leer (1892–1953). Cardinal Michael von Faulhaber and the Franciscan priest Laetus Himmelreich (1886–1957) had played an important role in her conversion to Catholicism. Himmelreich also introduced van Leer to van Asseldonk, who soon became one of the early theoreticians of the Amici Israel.

By 1928, the association already counted 19 cardinals, 278 bishops and archbishops, and approximately 3,000 priests among its members. They included very prominent figures like Cardinal Pietro Gasparri of the

Roman Curia, secretary of state to Pius XI; Cardinal Raffaele Merry del Val, the secretary, and therefore head, of the Holy Office; and Willem van Rossum (1854–1932), prefect of the all-important Congregation of Propaganda. Other members included the general of the Dominican order and former Munich nuncio Andreas Frühwirth and the archbishop of Munich and Freising, Michael von Faulhaber, both high-profile German-speaking cardinals. In addition, Faulhaber had assumed the role of confessor and spiritual mentor to van Leer. He had even entrusted her with a canonical mission to hold Bible classes for other Jewish converts in Munich.[6] From here, she actively publicized the cause of the Amici Israel.

We do not know whether all members of the Amici Israel were com-

The president of the Amici Israel, Abbot Benedict Gariador.

(Buckfast Abbey, Buckfastleigh, Devon)

pletely aware when they joined in 1926 or 1927 of the implications for theology and Church politics of the association's overall program, parts of which were explosive. The cardinals of the Roman Curia specifically seem, at least at first, to have viewed the Amici Israel as a sort of prayer brotherhood for the purpose of converting as many Jews as possible to the "true" Catholic faith. The first publicity efforts by this association, in 1926, can certainly be read this way. They spoke of "a more rapid and merciful conversion of the Jews," and of the "institution of constant prayer" for this purpose. The main theme in this publicity letter was the "more rapid return" of Israel to the true Church.[7] Only in its sixty-seven-page *Pax super Israel,* which bears the incorrect publication date 1925, but which appeared in early 1928 under the imprimatur of the Roman Vicegerent Giuseppe Palica (1869–1936), and therefore had official Church authorization, did the group actually make public in any cohesive way its theological and political agenda.[8] It made clear that the goal of the association was not primarily to function as a prayer brotherhood for the conversion of Jews. Rather, it intended to bring about fundamental Jewish-Catholic reconciliation, as the title of its pamphlet had already signaled. The priests in the association should turn with special love toward the people of Israel, who were God's first chosen people. Proceeding from a theology of the Catholic sacrament of ordination, according to which priests act in the person of Christ, the Amici Israel postulated that the Jewish origin and identity of the Savior created a special kinship between each member of the clergy and the Jews because "Christus est primogenitus et veritas et caput Israel" ["Christ is the firstborn, the Truth, and the King of Israel"]. In addition to praying for Israel and its conversion, the Church should also foster an understanding of the Jewish people and their religion, the history of their relationship with God, and their witness to the faith.

But above all, the transition of the Jews into the Catholic Church would be made easier by the specific practices advocated by the Friends of Israel, in particular, by refraining from elements in the Catholic liturgy that could be interpreted as anti-Semitic. The members had agreed to avoid all anti-Semitic formulations and practices both during religious services and in everyday life. In the Catholic context, this meant no longer referring to the Jews as the "people who killed God" or Jerusalem as the "city of God killers," or proclaiming that the Jews are "fundamentally unconvertible and unteachable." In addition, "the unbelievable things" of which the Jews stood accused, especially ritual murder, the myth that had Jews abducting and killing Christian children for religious purposes, was to be rejected. The Amici Israel also recommended avoiding the term "conversion" for the Jews because it was so offensive to them. They suggested that the formulation "transition from the Kingdom of the Father to the Kingdom of the Son" was more appropriate. Because the Jews shared with Christians a belief in the God of the Old Testament, whom Jesus Christ had also proclaimed as his Father, there would be no conversion in the usual sense of turning one's back on one religious community of faith and professing one's faith in another. Rather, Jews would merely reorient themselves in relation to a faith that they already held in common with Christians. In addition, the Friends of Israel would renounce all gen-

The symbol of the Amici Israel makes clear its goal of reconciliation between Judaism and Christianity. The star of David is combined with the cross with the inscription INRI. This symbol is framed by the Hebrew "Shalom al-yisrael" and the Latin "Pax super Israel."
(Erzbischöfliches Archiv München, NL Faulhaber 6284)

eralizations about the Jews such as the canard that "their only God is money." To the contrary, Jewish ways of life, ceremonies, and religious customs should be accorded unqualified respect. The concluding collection of prayers and actions culminated in the challenge, "All types of anti-Semitism must be avoided; in fact, they must be explicitly combated and rooted out."

In its pamphlet the Amici Israel held that the Catholic liturgy was the culmination of the Mosaic ritual. As a result, members believed that they had a special calling to study and meditate on the Old Testament as an integral part of Holy Scripture. In so doing, they expressly rejected anti-Semitic tendencies that sought to eliminate everything Jewish from the Christian religion, including the Old Testament. Member priests were also urged to identify with the frame of mind of their Jewish contemporaries whenever they celebrated Holy Mass. All too frequently, sermons larded with anti-Semitic invectives made it clear that the priests who gave them had no understanding of the Jewish people and were completely ignorant of Jewish religion and culture. Without reservation, *Pax super Israel* recognized as justified the complaints of many Jews about harassment at the hands of Christians. The Jews had for more than nineteen centuries been forced to bear heavy crosses every day—not just once, as Jesus had.

German members of the group included the bishops Eduard Count O'Rourke (1876–1943) of Danzig, Johannes Leo von Mergel (1847–1932) of Eichstätt, Ludwig Maria Hugo of Mainz, and Hermann Wilhelm Berning (1877–1955) of Osnabrück. Cardinal Archbishop Karl Joseph Schulte (1871–1941) of Cologne was also a member. Cardinal Faulhaber was a supporter of the Amici Israel, and he created an institutional link for it in Munich to an association called the Ludwig-Missionsverein.[9] As a former professor of Old Testament exegesis at the Catholic Theological Faculty of the Reichsuniversität, in Strasburg, Faulhaber defended the Jews of the Bible, even though he himself was somewhat tainted by anti-Semitic stereotypes that placed Jews in the same category as freemasons and Socialists. Nonetheless, he immediately assured van Asseldonk, secretary of the Amici Israel, that he would publicize the association by distributing more than 100 flyers, and, more important, he promised to place greater emphasis on the Old Testament in the homiletic training of clergy in Munich. He also pledged to admonish pastors in his diocese to avoid careless formulations in their sermons that might be interpreted as anti-Semitic.[10]

The cardinal immediately made good on his promise in the Munich *Homiletischer Kurs* [Homiletics course] of October 1927, which was also adapted in print. The Amici Israel prepared a Latin summary of his theses, thereby ensuring their wide distribution.[11] Among other things, Faulhaber stated that preachers were to avoid anything that "might sound in any way anti-Semitic." He also made it clear that the synagogue was indispensable to the Church because without Judaism, there could historically be no Catholicism. True, the prophets of Israel had often scolded their people for their idolatry, their wanton behavior toward God and man, their profiteering, their corrupt religious practices, and not least the deficiencies of their priests. But the prophets' words referred expressly and exclusively to the Jewish people of that time. Faulhaber held that it was inadmissible to take prophetic admonitions aimed at moving the Jews to repent in a specific historical situation as statements about the eternal nature of Jews.

Here we see the Old Testament scholar warning preachers that by identifying a historically determined prophecy with the present-day people of Israel, they risked eliciting in the congregation only images of Pharisaism. The Catholic Church had derived core beliefs crucial to its own faith from the Old Covenant between God and Israel, in particular the Ten Commandments, the psalter, and messianic prophecies, so that "we as Christians are in debt to [the Old Covenant]." It was all too easy to say in a sermon that the Jews had crucified the Lord. But no one should forget that Christ, the Lamb of God, had taken on himself not only the sins of the entire world but also those of his own people. Referencing the Epistle of St. Paul to the Romans, Faulhaber held that Israel would be saved and would gain salvation as a fact of revelation. There was a reason that Jesus Christ had at the moment of redemption on the cross professed himself to be the King of the Jews. Faulhaber expressly supported the program of the Amici Israel at the conclusion of the homiletics course, stating that "we prepare for this hour of mercy through prayer, and for this reason we must ensure wide distribution of the writings of the Amici Israel."

In the context of these many efforts by the Amici Israel to reconcile Catholicism and Judaism, Abbot Gariador also sent a letter to the pope on January 2, 1928, pleading that the words *perfidis* and *perfidiam* be removed from the Good Friday prayer for the Jews because they represent to them something "hateful," which is not consistent with the original intention of the prayer. In addition, the formula "Let us pray. Let us kneel. Arise," which had been omitted only since the sixteenth century "for anti-Semitic reasons," should be restored to the prayer for the Jews as it is said for the other eight prayers.[12] The plea included a sample prayer without these objectionable wordings.[13]

The Votum of the Congregation of Rites

Pius XI passed this submission on to the Congregation of Rites, probably without examining it too closely himself; the congregation, in turn, sent it on to its liturgical committee. As was customary in the congregations of the Curia, before the cardinals of the dicastery took up a particular matter, they sought advice from an expert from the circle of consultors, who would then write a usually lengthy opinion, or votum. Only after this was done would the congregation decide in session. Ildefons Schuster (1880–1954), abbot of the Benedictine Monastery of Saint Paul Outside the Walls, in Rome, was entrusted with the matter. He was an extremely well qualified expert in the field of liturgical history and had, since 1914, been a consultor to the liturgical committee of the Congregation of Rites —in other words, he was an old hand. His instructions from the Congregation of Rites would have been to render an expert opinion on the Amici Israel's submission. Whether he actually wrote such an opinion or merely limited himself to brief remarks in letters is unclear from the files, at least at first glance. Although the pertinent documents contain a detailed memorandum that supported the Amici Israel's recommendations for reform with arguments based on liturgical history, this opinion is not signed.[14]

This memorandum may have been a written opinion by Schuster, which he had enclosed in his letter of response to the prefect of the congregation. The author's profound understanding of liturgical history speaks for this interpretation. Ildefons Schuster was a well-respected historian of the liturgy who had published widely in the field. Furthermore, his explicit brief as expert had been assigned to him "pro studio et voto."[15] However, the letters written by Schuster on January 16 and 20, 1928, to the secretary of the Congregation of Rites, which were only a few lines long, seem much too short for a votum based on extensive research. It should be noted that Schuster was never again expressly connected with this memorandum during the proceedings. The actual arguments it contained were never rebuked by the Inquisition, which undertook the proceedings later. At issue here was a tough formulation in his letter of January 20 in which he spoke of a "superstitious custom" in connection with the Good Friday prayer for the Jews. He may also have signaled to the congregation, in his letter of January 16, that his opinion was so brief because he felt constrained to append his own "modest opinion," which largely concurred with the "detailed arguments" advanced by others. But this formulation can only apply to the memorandum, which cannot have come from Schuster because the "detailed arguments" had already been presented by "others."

Abbot Ildefons Schuster spoke in favor of reform of the Good Friday prayer for the Jews but was later forced to repudiate his "error" before the Holy Office.
(Abbazia di Viboldone, *Il Cardinale Ildefonso Schuster*, Cenni Biogafici [Milan: Viboldone, Milano, 1958])

Another interpretation is that the document may have been an addendum to the submission from the Amici Israel itself. Dutch publications
about Sophie Franziska van Leer and Laetus Himmelreich report, on the
basis of non-Vatican sources, that the Franciscan Himmelreich had together with van Asseldonk written "een 'Pro Memoria' voor de Congre-
gatie der Riten."[16] Unfortunately, no copy of this memorandum has been
found in the documents used by the Dutch authors. In addition, Himmelreich had prepared for the journal *Pax super Israel* an extensive article with
arguments drawn from liturgical history in favor of reform of the Good
Friday prayer for the Jews. He was due to lecture on this topic on the occasion of the second anniversary of the founding of the Amici Israel in
Rome on February 24, 1928. Because of this, it seems likely that the memorandum that was slipped anonymously into the files of the Holy Office
is none other than the memorandum written by Himmelreich and van
Asseldonk.

This memorandum again sums up precisely the basic concerns advanced by the Amici Israel: "In these days, now that the number of Friends
of Israel is growing, and the urgent prayer for the return of Israel from all
parts of the world ascends unto God, and signs are growing that the moment of the glorious return of this people is no longer distant, voices are
also multiplying to demand that everything that may appear harsh or less
than pleasant toward Israel be removed from learned disputation and in
principle from every type of speech and prayer."[17] The authors demonstrated that a specific intention for the Jews had in fact been customary in
the General Prayer of the Church as far back as could be documented.
The Good Friday prayer was the last remnant of this all-inclusive General
Prayer. A specific prayer intention for the Jews on Good Friday was documented back to about the year 500. Himmelreich and van Asseldonk were
also clear that, "by praying for the Jews, the Church is not praying for
them as if they were far removed. Israel merely fails to see that a veil
hangs before its eyes, but that Israel itself cannot lift this veil because, as
St. Paul says, this is specifically reserved for the grace of God" (Romans
11:25–36). This introductory section of the memorandum concluded wist-
fully: "O that God may soon hear these prayers."

The first main section of the memorandum dealt with the two troubling elements of the Good Friday prayer for the Jews, "which, if they are

declared false, would give the entire prayer an appearance of falseness." The first was the word *perfidus*. Here, the authors were forced to concede that this formulation, which "sounds so harsh to us," had been in consistent use from the oldest liturgical codices up to the present. A reform could not be justified on the basis of liturgical history. They would not be able to use the tried-and-true argument that this abuse had not existed in the old Church but had crept in over the course of centuries, particularly during the "dark" medieval period; in other words, they could not simply reform this deformation and return to the purity of the old liturgy. Because they could not play the historical card, they were forced further afield. They then tried the philological card, dusting off linguistic arguments about how the meaning of the word *perfidus* had changed. They posed the following question: "Could it be that this expression, which seems so injurious to our ears, did not at the beginning possess this harshness?" According to the *Lexicon Totius Latinitatis,* the word *perfidiosus* differs from *perfidus* just as *ebriosus* differs from *ebrius;* that is, as "intemperate" differs from "drunk."[18] The petitioners attempted to illustrate their subtle interpretation using a concrete example that some of the cardinals and consultors might well have appreciated: getting drunk once or twice is very different from being an alcoholic. Applying this logic to religion, they argued that "someone who breaks the faith now and again is *perfidus,* whereas someone who is completely faithless would be *perfidiosus.* According to this explanation, we must conclude that the meaning of this word has been significantly transformed because the word *perfidus,* which has entered almost all modern languages as a loan word, now seems to some extent to express complete corruptness."

From this the authors concluded, "It does not seem likely that the Mother Church would have wished to attach such a corrosive meaning to this term when it introduced it into the holy liturgy. Now, however, experience clearly teaches that whenever Christians seek arguments for anti-Semitism they almost always cite this formulation. And because the Church had not intended this harshness, and because the prayer has taken on its element of harshness only because of the transformation in the meaning of the words *perfidus* and *perfidia,* these words should either be replaced or changed for the better." As a possible solution, they suggested replacing *perfidiam Judaicam* with *plebem Judaicam,* the Jewish people, as it had appeared in the eleventh-century Codex Z of the *Manuale Ambrosianum.*[19] Of central importance was that the formulation "perfidious Jews" in the Good Friday liturgy was used as a strong argument for a specifically Catholic anti-Semitism, an anti-Semitism that the Catholic Church itself propagated in its religious services as a matter of course. Significantly, the petitioners were not merely talking about Catholic anti-Semitism in general terms or a more attenuated traditional anti-Judaism; rather, they were expressly accusing the Church of liturgical anti-Semitism.

The second main section of the memorandum examined the lack of the formula "Oremus—Flectamus genua—Levate" (Let us pray. Let us kneel. Arise.), which had, at least until the year 800, been contained in all the Good Friday prayers, including that for the Jews. However, a change had been in the air since the Carolingian period, the reasons for which are no longer completely clear. The wording disappeared definitively from the Tridentine Missal only in 1570: "Since then, liturgists have tried to explain the mysterious reason for the difference in the prayer for the Jews in comparison to the other Good Friday prayers by saying that the Jews had disgracefully mocked the Lord Jesus on the evening of the Passion by kneeling before him, and because of this shameful act we have been warned not to kneel when praying for the Jews. This, however, contradicts the truth of the Gospel. The Jews cannot in any way be accused of having mocked Jesus by kneeling on that evening. This story is told exclusively of the Roman soldiers who had guarded the Lord Jesus in prison." It would be hard to find more absurd reasoning for not kneeling for the Jews. The memorandum concluded with prayerlike wording: "O, may this rubric, which was introduced because of hatred for the people and is based on a mere fiction, be changed in our liturgy so that the return of Israel to Jesus and the Savior be made easier, and so that the sublimity of the ecclesiastical prayer for Israel may without obscurant fog radiate in its original luster on Good Friday as well."

In a letter sent to Angelo Mariani, the secretary of the Congregation of Rites, dated January 16, 1928, Abbott Schuster briefly rendered his expert opinion.[20] He agreed wholeheartedly with the arguments advanced in the memorandum and added his own "modest opinion" hoping for a rapid revision of the Good Friday prayer "so that which corresponds to the public attitude of other times, which, however, is difficult to reconcile with the spirit of the Church, may be removed from it." The historical and philological rationales advanced by the Friends of Israel had clearly persuaded this liturgical expert. A few days later, on January 20, 1928, Schuster returned to the matter in another letter to Mariani, stating that "the triple suggestion with regard to replacing the word *perfidis,* the *Oremus,* and the kneeling seems to me fully justified by the classical tradition of the Roman liturgy. The aim is to abolish once again a late and superstitious custom."

Mariani immediately ordered an examination of the version of Codex Z of the *Manuale Ambrosianum,* which in the edition published by Marcus Magistretti (1862–1921) in 1904 had served as a model for the planned reform in the memorandum.[21] In fact, it contained the formulation *plebem Iudaicam* (Jewish people) in place of *Iudaicam perfidiam* (Jewish faithlessness). However, even this invitatory of the eleventh century said, "Oremus et pro perfidis Iudeis," which meant that the *Manuale Ambrosianum* could not be used as the model for a reformed Good Friday prayer, even though it contained the objectionable word *perfidis* only once instead of twice, as in the Tridentine version.[22]

The liturgical committee of the Congregation of Rites had the pertinent facts of the history of the liturgy re-examined in a compilation titled "Variazioni."[23] They came to the conclusion that the word *perfidiam* is found in all missals and sacramentals. The kneeling was omitted only in the ninth century, initially in non-Roman liturgies. The Oremus was eventually dropped over the course of the second half of the thirteenth century. However, it is still to be found in Parisian and Venetian missals of the sixteenth and seventeenth centuries, for the last time in an edition published in 1676.

In spite of this somewhat ambiguous finding, the liturgical committee of the Congregation of Rites decided in its session of January 18, 1928, to accept the argumentation in the memorandum and Schuster's opinion, and to revise the Good Friday prayer in accordance with the recommendations put forward by the Amici Israel.[24] This Roman congregation felt it important to remove all liturgical anti-Semitism in order to send a clear signal. At a time when anti-Semitism was becoming more socially accept-able in Europe they would deny even Catholic beer hall "congregants" one of their favorite arguments, namely, that anti-Semitism wasn't all that bad, and was in fact in line with the best traditions of the Church. After all, had they not just prayed on Good Friday for the perfidious Jews—who were as untrustworthy in matters of faith as they were in matters of money?

Before the Tribunal of the Holy Office

Before publishing a decision that had to do with matters of faith, espe-cially a reform to a liturgical text of the importance of the Good Friday prayer, the Congregation of Rites, like all other Roman offices, had to get the consent of the Holy Office. For this purpose, Mariani, as secretary of the Congregation of Rites, on January 25, 1928, sent all the files to the as-sessor of the Congregation for the Doctrine of the Faith, Nicola Canali (1874–1961).[25] All signs pointed to rapid confirmation; the review looked like a routine matter, especially because Cardinal Secretary of State Merry del Val was himself a member of the Amici Israel. The Holy Office, how-ever, had other ideas and proved unwilling to rubberstamp the decision of the Congregation of Rites. In fact, they decided to try before the Grand Inquisition both the reform of the Good Friday prayer and the petitioners themselves! The newly available documents allow us for the first time to trace internal curial discussions and arguments among various congrega-tions and individuals about how the Church viewed and dealt with the Jews and anti-Semitism.

The consultors had the first go at it. One of their experts was asked to write an opinion, which was then discussed among the consultors in as-sembly before the cardinals in the congregation took up the matter. But not just any consultor was entrusted with this task; it was delegated to the papal court theologian, the Dominican Father Marco Sales (1877–1936), an ex officio member of the Suprema who was the eyes and ears of the Holy Father in all matters before the congregation. As was customary, the ex-pert first summarized for the consultors and cardinals the progress of the matter to date.[26] Sales held forth on the Amici initiative and the memorandum, gave an account of the expert opinion and the conclusions of the Congregation of Rites, including the old and the new wording of the prayer, and then made known his own personal opinion. He had to admit that from a dogmatic, ecclesiastical perspective he could not deny the desired reform his *nihil obstat*. "Viewed solely from the perspective of doctrine and faith," he noted, "there can be no objection to the question placed before us." That, however, was actually the task of the Holy Office as the predecessor of the Congregation for the Doctrine of the Faith. In his opinion, Sales took a different tack, that of *convenienza*: "If we ask about the usefulness of the reform, I am of the humble opinion that none exists."

First, to Sales, the Amici Israel was little more than a "cosa privata," a private club—a characterization that seems somewhat strange given its exalted membership. "If we were to revise the time-honored holy liturgy that dates back to ancient times merely at the behest of this or that private association," Sales continued, "there would be no end to it. Because if the 'Friends of Israel' wish to suppress everything that seems harsh to Jewish ears, another association could—just to cite one example—demand that the name of Pontius Pilate be stricken from the profession of faith because it is seen to undermine the authority of the Romans." The same reasoning could be used to demand that the Improperia be eliminated from the Good Friday liturgy. These admonitions to the Jews contain considerably harsher formulations than the word *perfidia*. Furthermore, Sales continued, not without a touch of cynicism, one could demand elimination of the imprecatory psalms from the liturgy "under the false pretense that they engender hatred, and that they contradict the charity preached by our Lord Jesus Christ."

Second, the papal court theologian rejected in the strongest terms the philological interpretation made in the memorandum, in particular the differentiation between *perfidus* and *perfidiosus*. For him, it was clear that "*perfide* generally indicates he who breaches a promise or an agreement that has been concluded," especially if such behavior has become habitual. "And this is precisely what God himself accuses the Jews of in Scripture." As proof of his claim, Sales cited three passages from the Old Testament. He pointed to passages in the fifth book of Moses in which the Jews are expressly called breakers of the covenant (Deuteronomy 31:16, 20, 27); Psalms 78:57, where it is said, "They turned back, deceitful like their ancestors; they proved false like a bow with no tension"; and 2 Kings 17:15, which reads, "They rejected his statutes, the covenant which he had made with their fathers." This negative view of Jews documented in the Old Testament was also found in the New Testament in St. Stephen, "who knew them well": "You stiff-necked people, uncircumcised in heart and ears, you always oppose the Holy Spirit; you are just like your ancestors" (Acts 7:51). On the basis of the biblical evidence, Sales, who had in his publications made a name for himself as an advocate of the classical school of Catholic exegesis, was certain that "only the Jews had a pact with God and a covenant with him, and only the Jews constantly violated this pact, and only they would continue constantly to violate it. It should come as no surprise, then, that they are called *perfidi,* and that we use the expression *perfidia Iudaica* to distinguish them from the pagan." Third, Sales rejected the fine points relating to the history of the liturgy made by the Congregation of Rites with regard to the omission of kneeling and the Oremus, and the inclusion of *perfidis* and *perfidia.* In a sweeping statement, Sales claimed that all three elements of the Holy Week liturgy could be traced to "venerable antiquity" and were therefore not subject to reform of any sort. Finally, no one could accuse Pius V, under whom the missals of 1570 were written, "of anti-Semitism or its promotion," as he had always advocated for the Jews. By formulating his argument this way, Sales insinuated that the Good Friday prayer for the Jews approved by Pius V could not by that very fact be open to an anti-Semitic interpretation—a rather far-fetched and forced claim.

In conclusion, Sales pointed out that the Jews had explicitly accepted their responsibility for Christ's crucifixion in Matthew 27:25: "His blood be upon us and upon our children." Thus there could be "no plausible reason that the revision proposed by the Amici Israel should be accepted." In "deepest submission," as the closing of a consultor's opinion used to read, he concluded, "Nihil esse innovandum"—nothing should be changed. And with that, the proposed reform of the Good Friday prayer for the Jews was rejected by the consultor.

Yet things were to get much worse for the Amici. The fact that the Congregation of Rites had acted on their petition for reform had the effect of shining a spotlight on the group and its theoreticians. Although the Holy Office was concerned only with the dogmatic correctness of the liturgical reform, as the Sales opinion demonstrates, the proceedings took on a dynamic of their own. Naturally, any move by the Suprema against the Amici Israel would have been an extremely delicate matter because of the cardinals and bishops—not to mention the three thousand priests and monks—who counted themselves members.

The dispute in principle between the Holy Office and the Amici Israel was triggered by a printed invitation to the second anniversary of the founding of the group, which was sent to all members. Father Himmelreich was to speak about the reform of the Good Friday prayer at the planned annual meeting, scheduled for February 24, 1928, in the hall of the Cancelleria Apostolica in Rome. Anton van Asseldonk was to have discussed Zionism. As a member, Cardinal Merry del Val, the secretary of the Holy Office, also received an invitation—right in the middle of deliberations over the Good Friday prayer.[27]

Merry del Val was one of the hardliners in the Curia. In his role as cardinal secretary of state under Pius X, from 1903 to 1914, he had been one of the prime movers for the prosecution of the so-called modernists in the Catholic Church. The cardinal suspected all priests and theologians who advocated for reforms within the Church because they believed in a fundamental reconciliation between Catholicism and modernism, dogma and science, Catholic thinking and democracy. Even though Pope Benedict XV had put a halt to his predecessor's obsession with heretics and had rehabilitated some clergy who had been unjustly reprimanded, certain circles within the Roman Curia remained fundamentally skeptical of all modernist tendencies—and of their proponents. Some in Rome resented the politically and economically successful Jews, who had used the rights and freedoms that they had gained in the nineteenth century to push for innovation, whereas the antimodernists and integralists in the Vatican viewed Catholics as the big losers in the modernization process. Merry del Val, who was not reappointed cardinal secretary of state in 1914, and who had been unsuccessful in the papal election of 1922, was a prime example of this mentality. As a representative of an extreme reactionary wing, he had been unable to command a majority in the College of Cardinals. Instead, Achille Ratti emerged as the compromise candidate. But contrary to what some had hoped, Pius XI did not reappoint Merry del Val as secretary of state, instead retaining Pietro Gasparri, his predecessor's secretary of state. This move signaled that in terms of politics and society he intended to seek compromise and negotiated solutions. As a consolation, Merry del Val was made secretary of the Holy Office, the third most important office in the Roman Curia. With that, he was given free rein to act on his antimodernist tendencies in the supreme office of the faith.

The integralist Merry del Val had joined the Amici Israel because he thought it was a religious brotherhood whose sole purpose was to pray for the conversion of the Jews. Getting as many Jews as possible to convert by the power of prayer, thereby saving them from eternal damna-

The head of the Holy Office, Raffaele Merry del Val, took on the petition for reform of the Good Friday intercession—and vehemently rejected any reform of the liturgy.
(Marie Cecilia Buehrle, *Cardinal Merry del Val* [Glasgow, 1957])

tion, was a goal that fit in well with his view of the world. The group's liturgical reform and what he viewed as their pro-Zionist program at the planned annual meeting, however, brought Merry del Val into conflict with the Friends of Israel. He felt that the movers and shakers who had produced the first publicity flyer in 1926 had gone behind his back, and he reacted with condemnation and prohibition—as he usually did. At first the Roman vicariate decreed that the annual meeting could not take place in Rome. This ban was most likely imposed at the behest of Merry del Val.[28]

The Holy Office was not responsible solely for questions of faith and morality. Censorship also fell under its purview, and so Merry del Val immediately initiated an examination of the sixty-seven-page pamphlet *Pax super Israel*. Ordinarily, a work had to be denounced before it could be considered for placement on the Index of Prohibited Books; in other words, the congregation would have had to act in response to outside condemnation. But in this case, the denunciation was internal; the accuser was also the judge. And Merry del Val was in a hurry. Instead of the thorough but usually very time consuming book-banning process, involving at least one printed opinion written by a consultor, which then had to pass through the consultors in assembly before being examined by the cardinals, Merry del Val suggested a significantly quicker process to get to the same goal. Individual sentences from this work that were considered particularly dangerous or that contravened Catholic doctrine would be printed in a solemn papal decree and condemned. He formulated the actual intent of the pamphlet as follows in a brief summary for the information of the congregation: "The entire attitude of this little book is decidedly positive toward the Jews with rather adverse imputations about the Church and its servants. As if the bride of Christ stood accused of negligence, or even worse of unjustified aversion toward the people which is called the Chosen."[29] In other words, according to Merry del Val, the Amici Israel had expressly accused the Church of anti-Judaism or anti-Semitism.

Merry del Val then had a list compiled containing several "erroneous or offensive-sounding statements"; a now unknown member of the congregation added footnotes and comments. In the end, six "dangerous turns" were summarized in the form of propositions and judged from a theological point of view:

1. First, the sentence stating that Christ was the firstborn, and the truth, and the King of Israel, on which the entire argumentation of the text is based, was accorded only limited validity. Because this biblical statement cannot simply be negated, the Holy Office attempted to relativize it with the argument that not all descendants of Israel in the flesh were, as St. Paul stated, also true Israelites in the religious sense.

2. The claim made by the Amici Israel that a common priesthood connects the Jews with the Catholic Church was completely incomprehensible to a member of the Holy Office. Because the Jews "persist in their received obstinacy" there can be no such connection between the synagogue and the Church.

3. The Holy Office rejected out of hand the concept of conversion advanced by the Friends of Israel. Instead of outright conversion and defection by Jews to Catholicism, they spoke of a softer "transition from the Kingdom of the Father to the Kingdom of the Son." The expert found such formulations "simply outrageous." Indignant, he asked how it was possible that the Jews, who had made common cause with those who had nailed Jesus to the cross, thereby killing the son of God, could even have belonged to the Kingdom of the Eternal Father in the first place.

4. The expert denounced the notion advanced by the Amici Israel of a spiritual bond between Jews and Catholics as a "reckless principle" —and even as "an irreverent rebuke of the Church." It was simply impossible for Jews and Catholics to share a life of grace. This argument in particular opened up a nasty gaping abyss.

5. Passages in *Pax super Israel* in which statements about the Jews by the Church Fathers were characterized as unjustifiably harsh in part elicited amazement. The accusation that this erroneous judgment was the result of a lack of understanding of the Jews on the part of the Fathers enraged the consultor. After all, the writings of the Church Fathers and particularly their interpretation of Holy Scrip-

ture were the definitive sources of Catholic epistemology. Questioning their authority touched the foundations of Catholic neoscholastic dogmatics and theology.

6. The Amici had always grounded in the Bible their statements about the relationship between Catholics and Jews. Without stating so explicitly, the member of the Holy Office accused them of nothing less than crypto-Protestantism. In rejecting the text, he drew on a formulation that was extremely problematic for the Catholic theology of the time—the sound Catholic theological doctrine that the original source of revelation is not Holy Scripture but tradition. This claim clearly contradicted the Council of Trent, according to which Scripture and tradition were both considered sources of revelation, although the sequence of the Tridentine decree must be observed, with Scripture preceding tradition.[30]

Cardinal Secretary of State Merry del Val had in midtrial expanded the scope of the Roman Inquisition with regard to the Amici Israel. Not only the Good Friday prayer but also the group's pamphlet would be questioned. As a result, the consultors took up both Sales's opinion and the six propositions at their meeting on February 27, 1928.[31] Taking their cue from the papal court theologian, they rejected the reform of the Good Friday prayer with little discussion. Instead of arguing to ban the book, in the form of either a papal brief or a simple indexing based on the six statements from *Pax super Israel* that were considered dangerous or at least objectionable, as would seem to have been called for given the documents that were presented, the consultors mounted a much more sweeping attack. Given the "dangerous turn" that the Central Committee of the Amici Israel had supposedly taken, they demanded that the association be dissolved. Another section of their decision is also noteworthy: Abbot Schuster was to be brought before the tribunal and admonished in the strongest terms for his repugnant statements. For an expert from one congregation who was performing his duties, and whose opinion had been unanimously lauded by those who commissioned him—the cardinals of the Congregation of Rites—to then be held to account for his opinion by consultors from a completely different congregation (even if by the Suprema) was unprecedented in recent curial history.

On March 7, 1928, the cardinals of the Inquisition began to deal with the issue in the second step of the trial before the Holy Office. Merry del Val himself presented a detailed opinion.[32] It was relatively rare for the head of the Supreme Office of the Faith to work on a cause himself. One can sense in his handwriting and wording just how worked up he was, how tricked and ill-used he felt as the figurehead in a matter that in his view was extremely explosive in terms of Church politics and theology. As far as he was concerned, the activities of the "so-called Friends of Israel" must be stopped once and for all.

Merry del Val's opinion was divided into three parts. He rejected the proposed reform out of hand as "completely unacceptable, even nonsensical." The Good Friday prayers were a particularly ancient and venerable rite of the Catholic Church that could not simply be put up for discussion. The liturgy had been "inspired and sanctified" over the centuries and aptly expressed "the abhorrence for the rebellion and treachery of the chosen, disloyal, and deicidal people." The secretary of the Holy Office viewed the Good Friday liturgy as a summation both of Holy Scripture and of the statements of the Church Fathers about the Jews. What the New Testament had to say about this people could be summarized in the pertinent and oft-cited scene in the passion of St. Matthew: when Pontius Pilate decided to free Jesus, the Jews demanded that Barabbas be freed instead. When Pontius Pilate washed his hands in innocence, the Jewish people cried out, "His blood be upon us and upon our children" (Matthew 27:25). There was a certain internal logic to the cardinal's claim that given the architecture of the entire Good Friday liturgy, which is extremely critical of the Jews, it would not be enough simply to revise the prayer: "To conform with this peculiar request, we would have to eliminate most of the Good Friday liturgy, including the admonitions, the readings from St. Augustine, etc."

True, Holy Scripture and the realization and emphasis of the day of the Lord's death in the liturgy speak not of individual Jewish believers but only of the Jewish people as a whole. For Merry del Val, the people as such were damned. They failed in their historical mission of salvation. Of course individual Jews could always convert to Catholicism, Merry del Val remarked, more than a little cynically. According to Catholic precept, baptism alone constituted membership in the new people of God, independent of sex, origin, or ethnicity. One becomes a Christian through baptism; Jewishness is an accident of birth. The prayers in the Good Friday liturgy, Merry del Val continued, were not about individual Jews. They were always about the "stiff-necked Jewish people burdened with the curse that they as a people with their principles undertook the responsibility for having spilled the blood of the holiest of the holy." Echoes of a *völkisch* interpretation are obvious, and they would become even sharper as the opinion proceeded.

To begin with, Merry del Val dealt in detail with contemporary *ebraismo*. St. Paul's remarks about Israel's disobedience in his letter to the Romans, which culminates in the quotation from Isaiah, "All day long I stretched out my hands to a disobedient and contentious people" (Romans 10:21, quoting from Isaiah 65:2), formed the starting point for his reasoning. A deeply pessimistic analysis of the present situation led to the following conclusion: "That day persists. Hebraism with all its sects inspired by the Talmud continues perfidiously *(perfidamente)* to oppose Christianity; and today, after the war, it attempts more than ever to reestablish the Kingdom of Israel in opposition to Christ and his Church." This formulation makes clear how the cardinal understood the term "Hebraism," that is, where he perceived the primary Jewish opposition to the Church to lie. Zionism, with its vision of a Jewish return to the Promised Land, settlement in the land of Israel, and the creation of a Jewish state, was to him deeply disturbing.

Proceeding from his pessimistic view of the world, Merry del Val asked a rhetorical question concerning the Amici Israel's optimistic analysis of the present, which claimed to see increasing signs that the Jewish people were about to change their ways. "Where is this supposed beginning of contrition on the part of the Jewish people?" Merry del Val asked. And his answer: "I would not wish to see the Amici Israel fall into a trap devised by the self-same Jews who everywhere insinuate themselves into modern society and attempt by all means to dispel the memory of their history, and to exploit the good faith of Christians." In essence, the cardinal accused the Amici Israel of being a fifth column of a Jewish world conspiracy. Employing a classic *topos* of anti-Semitic rhetoric of the day, Merry del Val was saying that just as Jews had secretly infiltrated all modern societies, they were now attempting to do the same to the Catholic Church. As far as he was concerned, the naïve Friends of Israel must be protected from this infiltration. After this digression, Merry del Val returned to the actual subject of the first part of his deliberations and concluded that he was unalterably opposed to any revision or omission of the Good Friday prayer for the Jews or of the rite associated with it. As a result, the Holy Office was forced to respond to the inquiry of the congregation of rites, "Negative et amplius."

What he meant by *amplius,* "and even more," he made abundantly clear in the second part of his opinion, which concerned the Amici Israel itself. Merry del Val considered the group's principles and plans to be fundamentally reprehensible and even damnable. How he categorized this association of priests in the history of ideas is particularly illuminating. For him, "this community may be placed more or less within the context of interconfessionalism and religious indifferentism." Here we see Merry del Val's antimodernism coming to the fore; indeed, these code words had been used just two decades earlier by Pius X in his condemnation of modernism. After this statement of fundamentals, the cardinal went about dismantling the key principles underpinning *Pax super Israel.* In doing so, he tried to make the opinions of individual Amici Israel members look ridiculous by the very manner in which he dealt with them. The following quote from the text of his opinion shows the biting irony with which he sought to discredit the Friends of Israel:

> We are asked to speak not of the conversion of the Jews but rather of a simple transition from a less perfect thing to a more perfect thing. We are asked to recognize that the Jewish religion is a revelatory religion, without being permitted to say that such revelation has no value other than in relation to Christian revelation and faith in Christ, by which it will, so to speak, be absorbed. We are asked to recognize that the Jews have a priesthood and . . . we are asked to permit Judaism and Chris-

tianity to live, so to speak, side by side and in harmony. It is claimed that the apostles did not call the Jewish people "deicidal," whereas St. Peter openly said to the Jewish people in his speech in Solomon's portico, "The author of life you put to death, but God raised him from the dead; of this we are witnesses" (Acts 3:15). We are asked to speak not of the ritual transgressions of Jewish sects, nor of their association with freemasonry, nor of the usoriousness that they have practiced on a large scale against Christians, and so on and so forth.

Here, too, Merry del Val made use of current anti-Semitic *topoi*. It was no surprise, then, that the cardinal secretary of the Holy Office would call for the dissolution of the Amici Israel, or at the very least for it to be restricted to praying for the conversion of the Jews. In addition, he demanded withdrawal of the guiding principles issued by the general committee to the members and a retraction of *Pax super Israel*.

As with the decree proposed by the consultors, withering criticism was again leveled at Abbot Schuster in the final third of the opinion. Merry del Val argued for a "grave admonition" of the Benedictine monk and expert of the Congregation of Rites because he "was prepared to be goaded to the extreme in wishing to eliminate the supposed 'superstition' from a rite of the Holy Church."

As one would expect from these unequivocal recommendations, the cardinals of the Supreme Congregation in their decision largely followed the opinion of the assembly of consultors and of Merry del Val. All reforms of the Good Friday prayer for the Jews were rejected, and a decree to that effect was sent to the Congregation of Rites. The Amici Israel was to be dissolved or at least turned into a simple community of prayer; all copies of the dangerous pamphlet *Pax super Israel* were to be retracted and destroyed; and finally, the main petitioners, that is, Abbot Gariador, Knight of the Cross van Asseldonk, Father Laetus Himmelreich, and the expert and consultor of the Congregation of Rites, Abbot Schuster, were to be summoned before the Holy Office, where they would be gravely admonished.[33]

During the usual audience for the secretary of the Holy Office on the following day—the third and last stage of the proceedings—Pius XI him-

self dealt in detail with the entire matter because without his explicit consent no decision would be binding.[34] In contrast to the usually brief minutes of such discussions, which generally contain little more than the
pope's approval of a decision by the cardinals or at most one or several
minor modifications, the postscript in this case is rather extensive. This
shows how involved Pius XI was in this matter, which is unsurprising
given the explosiveness of the issue and the prominence of so many of
the members of the Amici Israel: "His Holiness paid personal attention to
the entire question, listened attentively to the reading of the cardinal secretary's opinion, and examined the offending little work." After examining the documentation, Pius XI came to the conclusion that this was an
extremely serious matter that touched on questions of faith in an imme-
diate way, and that it must be resolved without delay. He therefore con-
sented to the recommendations made by the cardinals the previous day,
while adding numerous modifications to the original text to make it more
precise.

Pius XI was not content with a mere retraction of the reform petition—
an option that in any case was still contained in the recommendation of
the cardinals of the Holy Office. Rather, such requests were to be expressly condemned by the Church—a passage that the secretary under-
lined in his minutes. The pope rejected any change to the liturgy of the
Catholic Church apodictically. The Congregation of Rites, which had
been open to the reform petition, was to be informed of this decision immediately—"senza ritardo," in the words of the pope. All this demonstrates just how dissatisfied Pius XI was with his liturgical experts in the
Curia; they should have been able to put a stop to this matter from the
outset.

With regard to the Amici Israel, "after due consideration and taking
into account the worrisome, erroneous, and dangerous turn that the committee has taken . . . the Holy Father has concluded that it should be dissolved." Pius XI was particularly irritated by the apparent repurposing of
the prayer brotherhood for the conversion of the Jews into a political
group within the Church; "in a worrisome manner," he declared, it "has
deviated onto false terrain." The pope was, however, clear that this double
decision—rejecting the reform of the Good Friday prayer and banning

the Amici Israel—could not simply be reported as such in the *Acta Apostolicae Sedis.* Rejection of the recommendation to strike "perfidious Jews" from the general prayer would elicit negative reactions from the public and open the Holy See to accusations of anti-Semitism. For this reason, Pius XI was particularly concerned that the dissolution decree of the Holy Office be formulated as carefully as possible. The decree should state that the Catholic Church had always rejected all forms of anti-Semitism, and that the Church's commandment to love had always explicitly included Israel and the Jews. In addition, the text was to make clear "that the Church had always prayed for the conversion of the Jews, but that it could under no circumstances support initiatives that contradict the universal liturgical tradition and the doctrine of the Church, even though they may have arisen from a holy and praiseworthy intention." The president of the Amici Israel, Abbot Gariador, was "to be informed of this act" before publication of this decree of dissolution "out of personal consideration for himself and his colleagues." After publication, both he and Fathers van Asseldonk and Himmelreich were to be summoned before the Holy Office and admonished.

The pope was particularly incensed at Abbot Schuster for his role as consultor of the Congregation of Rites. He, too, was to be admonished by the Holy Office. The Holy Father had a "pained impression" of his expert opinion, and so Schuster would be required to justify himself before the Suprema because he had spoken out before the Congregation of Rites "in such a grave form that was insulting to the Church." Furthermore, Pius XI ordered that Schuster's nine-volume work on the Roman Missal, *Liber Sacramentorum,* be combed through to determine his position on the Good Friday prayer for the Jews. Finally, the pope was "shocked" and "impressed" by Merry del Val's argument that the Jews had played no small role in the foundation of the Amici Israel, and that the entire movement showed signs of "infiltration by the selfsame Jews."

Just how concerned the pope was with this matter may be gauged by the fact that he summoned Merry del Val to another audience the following day, March 9, to discuss with him once more the *grave questione* of the Friends of Israel. Pius XI affirmed his decisions of the previous day and ordered a *decreto motivato* (reasoned decree). In fact, over the next several days the pope intervened personally in the editorial process, often request-ing complete rewrites of this text. The pope and the Holy Office took such pains with the wording so as to avoid even the slightest appearance of anti-Semitism in the dissolution of the Amici Israel and everything connected with it. That this sensitivity was the motivating factor in the editorial process is made clear by the preface to the Italian-language draft that was submitted to the cardinals of the Holy Office for their delibera-tions, on March 14, 1928. It stated baldly, "La motivazione del Decreto è basata sulla necessità di prevenire nei riguardi della S. Sede l'accusa di 'antisemitismo'"—the wording of the decree was motivated by the need to anticipate potential accusations of anti-Semitism.[35] It was therefore no accident that language designed to document the Church's consistent de-fense of the Jews was inserted into the text. Of course, not all the cardi-nals of the Holy Office agreed with this turn of events. Some even argued for deleting the statement "the Church condemns anti-Semitism" because that wording was not sufficiently nuanced. "In the end, the term anti-Semitism in its literal sense was selected, that is, in the sense of a system-atic suppression of the Jewish race. In particular, in order to leave room for a figurative anti-Semitism that is permissible (or even necessary) in the moral sense, it was not stated" that the Church condemned "'every sort of anti-Semitism,' but rather 'anti-Semitism.'"[36] In the opinion of these cardinals, this wording meant that only racial anti-Semitism was con-demned, whereas theological anti-Semitism on the part of the Church would be considered legitimate and even necessary. This differentiation would later play a crucial role in official comments on the decree.

The decree dissolving the Amici Israel was published on March 25, 1928, in the *Acta Apostolicae Sedis*. Interestingly, the text made no mention of why the Holy See was so interested in banning the Friends of Israel. The group's original reform petition was not mentioned, nor was its admoni-tion by the Inquisition and the Pope for this transgression. Neither the faithful nor the bishops would have learned from the official register that the Congregation of Rites, the dicastery responsible for Church liturgy, had joined the Amici Israel in its petition, that is, that a fierce controversy had been raging between the individual offices within the Curia over this matter. This effectively obliterated the actual reasons for the decree, as the pope had demanded in his audience with Merry del Val. The curt statement in the decree that the Amici had, in addition to other transgressions, advanced dangerous opinions that stood in contradiction to the Catholic liturgy was so general that the actual target of the criticism was not discernible. Both the Holy Office and Pius XI were clearly afraid to name names.

It would have been difficult, if not impossible, to explain to the public why the Catholic Church, which had always advocated for the Jewish people and rejected all forms of anti-Semitism, was not prepared to delete language in the Good Friday liturgy that sounded anti-Semitic, in spite of the fact that the Congregation of Rites had declared the reform liturgically correct and the papal court theologian had in his role as expert of the Holy Office pronounced it dogmatically unobjectionable. The Church would have been sovereign in the area of liturgical reform. There was no reason for the pope and the Curia to take third parties into account, as they did with "mixed matters" such as confessional schools, civil marriage, the protection of Catholic associations and organizations, pastoral care in the military, or church taxes—all matters in which the Church was forced to deal with various nation states. The conclusion of the Lateran agreements one year later and the Reichskonkordat of 1933 are further examples. But the need to get along with totalitarian systems in the interest of protecting the Catholic Church and to ensure pastoral care, all too frequently cited in Catholic scholarship to excuse the Church's hesitance to advocate for persecuted Jews, would not have been an issue here.

Nor, significantly, is there any mention of the liturgy in the version of the decree approved by the cardinals of the Holy Office on March 14, 1928. At the audience for Cardinal Secretary Merry del Val the following day, during which he scrutinized the text sentence by sentence with the pope, Pius XI insisted on "a simple allusion to the holy liturgy" at the end.[37] The decree of March 25, 1928, cited *Pax super Israel* as the real reason the Holy See had to deal with the "association called the Friends of Israel."[38] In other words, an issue which had in fact been secondary to the trial before the Inquisition was now being portrayed as the actual cause, and the entire matter was being painted as a book-censorship proceeding. Interestingly, the pamphlet that was supposedly at the center of the proceeding was never placed on the Index, despite having been banned.

Most likely out of deference to the numerous high-ranking members of the association, the dissolution decree recognized "the praiseworthy side of this association, which consists in urging the faithful to pray to God, and to involve themselves in the conversion of the Israelites to the Kingdom of Christ." The text of the decree stressed that it should come as no surprise that an association with such goals should "count a whole array of bishops and cardinals among its members" in addition to many faithful and priests. During the audience on March 15, the question of whether cardinals and bishops should expressly be named as members of the Amici Israel was a point of intense debate between Pius XI and Merry del Val, precisely because it would constitute an affront to those concerned. In the end, the pope decided to leave the cardinals and bishops in the text as "a positive argument" that the Church in principle harbored no prejudices against the Jews.[39]

Next came the apologia with which the Church sought to rebut any potential accusations of anti-Semitism before decreeing the dissolution of the Amici Israel. This passage for the first time repudiated modern anti-Semitism in the magisterium. Here, too, the pope insisted on the term "anti-Semitism," which Merry del Val had apparently wished to delete. Although Pius XI resolutely rejected both the Amici Israel's pamphlet and the memorandum about the reform of the Good Friday prayer, he did embrace the warnings about "modern anti-Semitism" contained in both texts. This is noteworthy because neither the Nazis' seizure of power, which would make racial anti-Semitism a guiding principle of governance, nor even the anti-Semitic direction taken by Italian Fascism at the end of the 1930s could yet have been predicted. The pope's insistence on condemning racial hatred shows how closely Achille Ratti had been following the development of twentieth-century ideologies. Most other political and religious leaders did not at that time recognize the problem, the dimensions of which would become clear only later.

Once the admirable intentions of the Friends of Israel had been dispensed with and the Church inoculated against the accusation of anti-

Semitism, the decree moved on to its actual purpose, the dissolution of the Amici Israel. The reason cited was that the group had in the two years since its founding "assumed a manner of acting and thinking that stands in contradiction to the *sensus ecclesiae,* to the teaching of the Church Fathers, and to the holy liturgy." In addition, all publications that might similarly promote erroneous initiatives were in principle banned. The final version of the decree was ratified by the cardinals on March 21 and approved by the pope the following day.[40]

Abbot Schuster had been summoned to appear before the Holy Office on March 16, even before publication of the decree. The commissioner of the Congregation, the Dominican priest Giovanni Lottini (1860–1951), was given the task of admonishing the Benedictine monk in accordance with the decision of the pope and cardinals. The minutes of Schuster's hearing tell us that Schuster demonstrated abject submission *(ossequientissimo)* and recanted all statements that he had made about the planned reform of the Good Friday prayer. He stated that his sole aim in writing the opinion for the Congregation of Rites had been to facilitate the conversion of Jews.[41] Schuster was even clearer in the letter of submission that was demanded of him and written on the same day:

> With my whole heart I, as a most obedient son of the Holy Mother Church, retract and withdraw from my opinion on the question of the prayer for the Jews in the Good Friday service all that which displeases the most reverend fathers of this congregation and which they deplore. My swift pen betrayed the intention of my thoughts because the adjective "superstitious," which I used, referred not to the rite of the liturgy, which is sacred and venerable, but rather to an attitude widespread in the Middle Ages with regard to the Jews. . . . In each case, *sentio cum Ecclesia,* I censure everything that it rebukes; I draw a line wherever it draws a line; I take its side whenever it is attacked; I attack whenever it attacks.[42]

This letter is one of the most shocking documents in the file. Schuster was a scholar of the liturgy, a devout Benedictine abbot who had spent his entire adult life examining the history of the liturgy of the Catholic Church. He had out of deep scholarly and spiritual conviction come to the conclusion that the reforms advocated by the Amici Israel were more than justified both liturgically and spiritually. The forced retraction of the opinion he had rendered to the Congregation of Rites cast a pall over a life devoted to scholarship.

In their session of March 21, the cardinals accepted Schuster's unconditional retraction with the same satisfaction as did Pius XI. Apparently, given his complete act of submission, the pope's anger at Schuster subsided very quickly as the admonition appears to have had no further consequences. To the contrary, in 1929, Pius XI named Schuster archbishop of Milan and then elevated him to cardinal. In 1996, Pope John Paul II beatified the Benedictine abbot for his piety. Critics of this move pointed to Schuster's close ties to Fascism and a number of written and public statements that could be interpreted as openly anti-Semitic.

The president of the Amici Israel and the signatory to the petition, Abbot Gariador, was summoned to appear before the Holy Office on April 3, 1928.[43] He accepted his admonition without question, as his letter of submission, dated April 11, testifies.[44] Matters turned out rather differently for the secretary and spiritus rector of the group, Anton van Asseldonk, who was summoned to appear before the Holy Office on March 28.[45] He was "very saddened" by the suppression of the association and sent his letter of submission, on April 12, only after consulting with his confessor. In it, he attempted to make the best of the dissolution of the Amici Israel by underscoring the positive aspects of the decree. He thanked the Holy Office for praising the good intentions of the Friends of Israel and expressed his pleasure that the text of the decree had "solemnly—and better than we ever could have—most forcefully condemned anti-Semitism."[46] In addition, he held that this decree expressly legitimized efforts to continue to pray for the Jewish people and to work for their conversion.[47]

The cardinals of the Holy Office, however, were not at all satisfied with his letter of submission. They again summoned him to appear and, on April 14, forbade him in the sharpest terms to comment in any manner on decrees enacted by the office for the doctrine of the faith.[48] Three days later, van Asseldonk was again summoned to the Palazzo del Sant'Ufficio, where he was subjected to the most severe rebukes. Not only was he forbidden to interpret the decree of dissolution, but he was also prohibited from making any public statements about any aspect of the matter.[49] In their session on April 18, the cardinals of the congregation accepted the letters of submission of Abbot Gariador and van Asseldonk with their usual sense of satisfaction. With that the file on the Amici Israel was closed.[50]

A Catholic Way of Anti-Semitism?

The entire matter did, however, have public repercussions. An article published in *Jewish World* on April 16, 1928, voiced strong objections to the dissolution decree.[51] The Holy Office and, it seems, even Pius XI himself were stung by the article, which was shown to the pope during the audience on May 3, 1928. The decision was made to forward the edition of *Jewish World* to the Jesuit Enrico Rosa (1870–1938), publisher of the influential Catholic journal *Civiltà Cattolica*. He would then print a refutation at the behest of the pope.

In the field of Catholic journalism, Father Rosa had been "an interpreter and fearless defender of the directives of the Holy See for thirty years," to quote his obituary.[52] He honored his obligation to the pope in a ten-page article in the May edition of *Civiltà* titled "Il pericolo Giudaico e gli 'Amici d'Israele.'"[53] At a minimum, the pope approved this addendum to the decree of dissolution; it may even be considered his official commentary.

Father Rosa distinguished between two types of anti-Semitism: an "unchristian type of anti-Semitism" and a "healthy evaluation of the danger emanating from the Jews." Racial anti-Semitism, which fed on "party politics or passions . . . or material interests," had been justly condemned outright in the decree of dissolution. However, the Church must "with the same zeal protect against the other extreme, which is not less dangerous and all the more seductive given the appearance of good," that of friendship with the Jews, to which the Friends of Israel had fallen prey. The "danger emanating from the Jews" should never be underestimated. The Jews had become "presumptuous and powerful" since their emancipation at the turn of the nineteenth century. They had come to dominate large portions of the world's economic life. They possessed well-nigh "dictatorial power" in trade, industry, and finance, and they had been able to build up "their hegemony in many sectors of public life." In addition to their social and political dominance in many European countries, which was out of all proportion to their numbers, Rosa accused the Jews as a whole of having manipulated all revolutionary activity from the French Revolution of 1789 through the July Revolution of 1831 and the German Revolution of 1848 up to the 1917 Bolshevik Revolution. In addition, "as the actual leaders of occult sects, they are forging plans for world hegemony." This accusation raised the specter of a global Jewish-freemason-Bolshevik conspiracy. Some of the arguments advanced by Rosa about the "Jewish peril" could well have been lifted from the writings of racial anti-Semites of the time. To this extent, he fundamentally blurred the line that he himself had drawn between the "dangerous" modern biological anti-Semitism now banned by the Church and a "good" Christian anti-Semitism that was necessary for the Church. In any case, the boundaries seem to have been far more fluid than he would have been prepared to admit. In an article titled "Semitismo e antisemitismo" in *L'Avvenire d'Italia,* published on May 30, 1928, Father Rosa again attempted to elucidate the meaning of the decree of dissolution and to defend it against attack.[54] Both of his articles found their way into the official files of the Holy Office.

The differentiation between two types of anti-Semitism that Father Rosa attempted in his commentary on the decree of dissolution of the Amici Israel, with the blessing of Pius XI, would later have important repercussions. It became the explanatory model par excellence for the behavior of the Catholic Church toward the Jews up until the Second Vatican Council. The early modern concept of the dual protectorate, to which Thomas Brechenmacher has drawn attention, disappeared from memory. According to this model, which continues to draw controversy, Church leaders had always protected Catholics from the Jews as a matter of course, but by equal measure they had also protected the Jews from persecution and the murderous attacks of fanatical Catholics. Catholic statements on the "Jewish question" well into the 1950s are replete with attempts to distinguish as Father Rosa had between an "evil," biologically motivated racial anti-Semitism, banned by the Church, and a "good," theologically motivated anti-Semitism.

An article from 1930 by the Jesuit Gustav Gundlach (1892–1963) exemplifies this trend. Published in the first edition of the influential *Lexikon für Theologie und Kirche,* his "Anti-Semitismus" captures the spirit of Father Rosa.[55] Gundlach, however, was no more successful than Rosa in insulating "good" anti-Semitism from "evil"; the boundaries he advanced were just as porous. Gundlach defined anti-Semitism in general as "a modern movement aimed at fighting Jewry politically or economically," which was motivated by either *völkisch*-racist considerations or by statist-political anti-Judaism: "The one fights Jewry simply because of its racial and *völkisch* otherness; the other because of the excessive and damaging influences of the Jewish part of the population within the selfsame citizenry. . . . The former type of anti-Semitism is unchristian because it is in opposition to charity and fights against a people only on account of their otherness as a people and not because of their actions." This type of anti-Semitism automatically turned against Christianity as well "because of its deep connection with the religion of the people first chosen by God." The second type, by contrast, "is permitted as soon as it fights the actual damaging influence of the Jewish part of the population in the areas of economics and party politics; theater, film, and the press; the sciences and art . . . by moral and legal means." Gundlach explicitly rejected all legal exceptions for Jews. He did, however, list an array of positive and permissible means for combating the Jews: a Christian penetration of society; the suppression equally of Semitic and Aryan "vermin" among the people; and finally the strengthening of moral-faith factors within the Jewish people against "the liberal assimilated Jews most open to moral nihilism, who . . . are active in opposition to human society within the camps of world plutocracy and of world Bolshevism, and thereby induce dark streaks within the Jewish soul, which was driven from its native soil." Interestingly, Gundlach hardly adduces any theological arguments. Nor does the article ever mention baptism or even the possibility of conversion to Christianity. Gundlach does not even take note of Christian anti-Judaism with its customary *topoi* of Jews as "Christ murderers," accusations of ritual murder, or the desecration of the Host. Particularly lacking in the section on anti-Semitism permitted by Christianity is any clear demarcation from the rhetoric of racial ideologues, who, after all, were propagating the anti-Semitism banned by the Church.

Comprehensive studies by Olaf Blaschke and Urs Altermatt have only recently examined the question of the connections between a specifically "Catholic anti-Semitism" and modern racial anti-Semitism. Publication of their studies triggered some intense reactions. The preliminary consensus that has crystallized out of the controversy is that Christian or Catholic anti-Semitism—usually called anti-Judaism to make it more palatable—undoubtedly existed. The question of the continuity or discontinuity between Christian anti-Judaism and "modern" racial anti-Semitism remains a matter of controversy. Whereas some interpret "modern anti-Semitism as a direct consequence of the tradition of Christian anti-Judaism, and as an attempt on the part of Christianity to adapt to modern industrialized society," others view these two varieties of anti-Semitism as "largely opposite to each other" because racial anti-Semitism "denies a fundamental aspect of the Christian doctrine of salvation, the potential conversion of the Jews."[56] In contrast to the resistance thesis (which states that because of their faith Catholics fundamentally rejected National Socialism along with its racial theories), the indifference thesis (that the majority of Catholics were neither for nor against Jews), and Blaschke's model of an "endogenous Catholic anti-Semitism" (that Catholics needed the Jews as a "scapegoat" to stabilize the Catholic milieu), an ambivalence thesis appears to be making increasing headway among scholars in the field. Briefly, it states that, "although Catholics distanced themselves from 'racial' anti-Semitism, they did not reject all anti-Semitism, but instead supported the 'better' Christian anti-Semitism."[57] This interpretation is supported by the internal curatorial debates in 1928 around the Amici Israel reconstructed here.

Perhaps this is a good time to ask about the function of anti-Semitism and anti-Judaism within the Roman Curia. Some statements by Merry del Val and Father Rosa seem—at least at first glance—to support the thesis of Blaschke, who views anti-Semitism as a basic structural feature of Catholicism. But on closer inspection, the specific anti-Semitism of the Curia looks more like a facet of the manner in which the Catholic Church, or perhaps better, an influential group within the Church, positioned it-self vis-à-vis modernism. Merry del Val immediately classified the efforts of the Amici Israel under "interconfessionalism" and "indifferentism," part of a conceptual framework that he, as a leading antimodernist under Pius X, had used in combating not only the Christian union movement in Germany but also modern "liberalism." What we are really dealing with here is the intransigent, radical-ultramontane antimodernist Catholicism that took control of the Church in the nineteenth century and was swept away only by Vatican II. This school of thought, however, represented not the Catholic Church as such but only a particular camp within it. The events surrounding the Amici Israel demonstrate the extent to which the power of this school of thought had, by 1928, already begun to crumble within the Roman Curia, requiring harsh disciplinary measures to ensure its continuance. At least in the intermediate term, the future belonged to the conciliators, among them the Amici Israel. Goldhagen's blanket accusation that the Catholics, the Catholic Church, the pope, and the Curia had *all* been anti-Semitic simply cannot be sustained. The Amici Israel and its program demonstrate the opposite. Their position was philo-Semitic or what might be termed *anti–anti-Semitic*. All the tendencies that marked the competing interests of the Church in relation to the Jews emerged in the Vatican during the controversy over the reform of the Good Friday prayer. These included hardline anti-Zionists and anti-Semites, "classic" Christian anti-Judaists, and even philo-Semites. Even in this question, the Curia was not a monolithic bloc but reflected the very different camps and orientations within the Catholic Church as a whole.

The unambiguous condemnation of modern anti-Semitism contained in the decree of dissolution of March 1928 has time and again been cited in defense of the Catholic Church against the accusation that it remained silent during the persecution and murder of the Jews and had been indifferent to their fate. In fact, in contrast to most other major social institutions, the Catholic magisterium had condemned racial anti-Semitism long before the National Socialists came to power. With foresight, the pope had warned of the dangers of modern Jew hatred well before Kristallnacht and the implementation of the Final Solution.

But that is only one side of what has until now been evident purely on the basis of an imminent interpretation of the text of the decree. Precise analysis of the back story of the decree made possible by the archival sources has now permitted detailed understanding of the other side, if you will. This newly available evidence shows that Pius XI not only failed to initiate steps against anti-Semitism—which would have come under his purview—but actually rejected and condemned such action outright. The pope was unwilling to end anti-Semitism in the liturgy by scrubbing "perfidious Jews" from the Good Friday liturgy; moreover, every single person who championed this reform was forced to recant his error before the Holy Office. Pius XI did not even have the courage to inform the public of his action. After all, how could he have justified it? But because he predicted that the Holy See would be accused of anti-Semitism if it came out that he supported retention of "perfidious Jews" in the liturgy despite a clear decision to the contrary by the Congregation of Rites, he had inserted into the decree of dissolution a sort of prophylactic defense in the form of a condemnation of modern anti-Semitism. This text can simply no longer be advanced as a heroic act on the part of the pope in the battle against anti-Semitism. To the contrary, it is a mark of moral impoverishment because it is easy to condemn hatred of Jews in others while not changing one's own anti-Semitic conduct, in this case, the wording of the liturgy. Pius XI wasted his big chance. It took decades and more than six million murdered Jews for the Church to summon the courage to cleanse its relationship with the Jews of anti-Semitism, even in the liturgy.

Let Us Pray for God's Chosen People

Reform of the Good Friday prayer, including elimination of the passages about "perfidious Jews," would have been a clearer sign of opposition to anti-Semitism than the general condemnation contained in the decree of dissolution of the Amici Israel. A worldwide change in the Catholic liturgy would probably have had a greater effect than any antiracist encyclicals of the sort planned by the pope in 1938, or than any other papal pronouncements against anti-Semitism, for that matter.

Still, the Benedictines of Beuron did summon the courage a decade after the dissolution of the Amici Israel to write a new translation of "pro perfidis Judaeis" for a German audience, which was included in the 1938 edition of the Schott Missal. Instead of "perfidious" in the sense of "ignominious," it now read "faithless" Jews.[58] Although this did not remove the problematic terminology from the official Latin prayer text, the negative connotations were somewhat lessened among the faithful, most of whom knew little or no Latin. Archbishop Conrad Gröber of Freiburg (1872–1948), who was frequently referred to as "brown Conrad" for his alleged support of National Socialism, gave this revision his stamp of approval. No permission from Rome was needed.

But this change was to be unique. Other missals and popular editions held to the old wording criticized by the Amici Israel. In Rome, it took another decade for the Congregation of Rites to legitimize the wording "unbelieving Jews," in a response published in 1948 in *Acta Apostolicae Sedis* to an inquiry about the correct translation of the Good Friday prayer. The decree now admitted that the meaning of the word *perfidus* in many translations prepared for use by the faithful was offensive to Jewish ears. Although Rome was unwilling to approve outright the translation "unbelieving," the congregation agreed not to disallow the translation of *perfidis* in this sense.[59]

One change that had been rejected by the Holy Office in 1928 was enacted by Pius XII after more than a quarter of a century. In the context of reform of the Holy Week liturgy, genuflection was inserted into the intercession for the Jews between the invitation to prayer and the oration. And the wording became available in German for the first time, appearing in the January 1956 edition of *Feier der Heiligen Woche* [Celebration of Holy Week].[60] In the reform initiated by Pius XII the individual prayers were also given headings for the first time. The prayer for the Jews was now titled "Pro conversione Judaeorum." This injudiciously chosen formulation placed the people of the Old Covenant at the same level as unbelievers, whose prayer was titled "Pro conversione Infidelium." In fact, the term *conversio* continued to convey associations with the Church's "mission to the Jews"—and this just after the Second World War.

Pope John XXIII (1958–1963) initiated a particularly crucial reform in 1959. He omitted the word *perfidis* from the invitation to prayer during the Good Friday liturgy in St. Peter's. The oration was preceded by silent prayer with genuflection (as Pius XII had conceded four years previously), and in the oration itself he replaced *judaicam perfidiam* with the simple *judaeos*. This change fulfilled the promise of the Amici Israel. Thirty years earlier, Abbot Schuster, Abbot Gariador, and van Asseldonk had been forced to renounce this "false" formulation of the prayer before the Holy Office.

Scholars have been unable to determine precisely why the pope took this step. In his sensitivity toward the Jewish people, Angelo Giuseppe Roncalli seems to have been a latter day "Amicus Israel." His text of the Good Friday prayer for the Jews, which became binding for the Church worldwide in 1960, largely follows the formulation of the prayer submitted by the Amici Israel to the Congregation of Rites in 1928. It is unclear whether he took his cue from Anton van Asseldonk. A letter from van Asseldonk to the pope, dated October 28, 1959, which is listed in the index of individual documents from the files of the Congregation for the Doctrine of the Faith evaluated here, at least seems to point in this direction. Unfortunately, the text of this letter is not available because it has not yet been released for research purposes.

But in spite of these changes, Catholics continued to pray on Good Friday for the conversion of the Jews. The breakthrough in relations between Catholics and Jews occurred with Vatican II and the new missal of 1970, a version marked by great respect for the Jewish people. Article 4 of "The Declaration on the Relation of the Church to Non-Christian Religions 'Nostra aetate'" proclaimed on October 28, 1965, dealt specifically with this topic. Karl Rahner (1904–1984) and Herbert Vorgrimler were surely correct when they stated in their commentary to this declaration that between Jews and Christians, "there is more to cleanse than merely a brutally unresolved past in which Christians committed many sins and bloody and moral persecutions on the Jews, and today blatant lies. The fact is that until this council, inhumane and unchristian anti-Semitism was continuously nourished by many parts of the Catholic liturgy, catechism, and sermons."[61] The text of the decree attested to the common spiritual patrimony of Jews and Christians, rejected the blanket condemnation of Jews as accursed by God, and, "mindful of the patrimony" that the Church shares with the Jews, decried the "hatred, persecution, displays of anti-

Semitism, directed against Jews at any time and by anyone." The Church further rejected "any discrimination against men or harassment of them because of their race, color, condition of life, or religion" because it is foreign to the mind of Christ. "Since the spiritual patrimony common to Christians and Jews is thus so great, this sacred synod seeks to foster and recommend that mutual understanding and respect which is the fruit, above all, of biblical and theological studies as well as of fraternal dialogues." Jews should not, "Nostra aetate" continued, "be presented as rejected or accursed by God."[62]

The respect for Israel evident in "Nostra aetate" is made even clearer in the new formulation of the Good Friday prayer, which is still valid. It states, "Let us pray for the Jewish people, the first to hear the word of God, that they may continue to grow in the love of his name and in faithfulness to his covenant. *Silent prayer. Then the priest sings or says:* Almighty and eternal God, long ago you gave your promise to Abraham and his posterity. Listen to your Church as we pray that the people you first made your own may arrive at the fullness of redemption. We ask this through Christ our Lord. Amen."[63] The prayer for the Jewish people is now in sixth place, between the prayer for the unity of Christians and the prayer for all those who do not believe in Christ. This represents a complete change from the text as it existed before Vatican II. That is, the validity of God's promises to Israel are permanently recognized.

In the Holy Year 2000, John Paul II in his universal prayer prayed for forgiveness for the sins of Catholics "committed by not a few of their number against the people of the Covenant and the blessings." The pope recalled "the sufferings endured by the people of Israel throughout history."[64] Perhaps he was also recalling the prayer contained in the old Tridentine Missal and the failed reform of 1928.

But that is not the end of the story. On July 7, 2007, Pope Benedict XVI in his apostolic letter "Summorum pontificum" made easier the use of the pre–Vatican II Tridentine liturgy contained in the missal of 1962. That which generations of faithful had held sacred "could not suddenly be forbidden or deemed harmful," the pope said in explaining his defense of this "extraordinary expression of the one Roman rite."[65] But the formulations of the Good Friday prayer in the old and new Roman missals, which in the opinion of the pope merely represent two interpretations of the one liturgy, are well-nigh impossible to reconcile. In spite of John XXIII's modifications, the missal of 1962—even though it dispenses with the words *perfidis* and *perfidiam*—continues to speak of the "blindness" of the Jewish people, from whom the "veil" must be lifted. As might be expected, the pope's letter has been roundly criticized, not only by Jewish religious leaders, but by many Catholics as well. They fear that the headway made in Jewish-Christian dialogue since the Second Vatican Council could well be halted. The extraordinary form of the Good Friday intercession now approved clearly contradicts the spirit of "Nostra aetate."

And the criticism has hit home. On February 6, 2008, *L'Osservatore Romano* published a new formulation of the Latin Good Friday prayer for the Tridentine Mass. Benedict XVI, however, did not simply replace the old text with the post–Vatican II Latin version from the missal of Paul VI; rather, he decided on a compromise that simply avoids the most objectionable passages. The English translation of the Latin liturgy reads, "Let us also pray for the Jews. That our Lord and God may enlighten their hearts, that they may acknowledge Jesus Christ as the Savior of all men. (Let us pray. Let us kneel. Let us stand.) Almighty, ever living God, who will that all men would be saved and come to the knowledge of the Truth, graciously grant that all Israel may be saved when the fullness of the nations enters into Your Church. Through Christ Our Lord. Amen."[66] In this formulation, there is no longer an intrinsically Jewish path to salvation. The conversion of all peoples to Christ explicitly includes the people of Israel. The ordinary and the extraordinary forms of the "one" Catholic liturgy now coexist in an irreducible tension, at least as far as the Good Friday prayer is concerned. This cannot have made dialogue about the relationship between the Catholic Church and Judaism any easier.

Three

The Pact with the Devil?

The Reichskonkordat (1930–1933)

In the wake of the failed reform of the Good Friday prayer in 1928, the subject of anti-Semitism seems to have been of little further interest to the Roman Curia. In any case, there is no mention of it in the files of the Holy Office or in the documents of the Office of the Secretary of State, which Pacelli took over from his mentor, Pietro Gasparri, on February 9, 1930. Nor does the subject come up in any of the pertinent reports from the nunciatures in Munich and Berlin. Only in early April 1933 did it again appear on the agenda of the Roman Curia. Up to then, the Curia had focused on three events that would assume critical importance in terms of the relationship of the Catholic Church to National Socialism and the role they played in the context of Hitler's seizure of power. These events were the Center Party's consent to the Enabling Act of March 24, 1933, by which Hitler obtained dictatorial powers; the retraction of the condemnation of National Socialism by the German bishops on March 28; and finally the commencement of negotiations for a Reichskonkordat between the German government and the Holy See in April of the same year.

The controversy raging among researchers is whether there was any connection among these three events, or whether they had nothing to do with one another. In other words, was the promise of a Reichskonkordat the price paid for the Center Party votes to establish a legal dictatorship?

Did the bargain entail the disempowerment of Catholicism as a political force in Germany and the lifting of the bishops' condemnation of the NSDAP, which opened the way for Catholics to participate in the Nazi movement? Such a connection is plausible only if all actions of the Catholic Church—including those of the Center Party, the German episcopate, and the Roman Curia—were engineered by a single agent. That is the only way in which a concordat could have been traded for the Enabling Act and a bishops' declaration. If, by contrast, all three Catholic actors had worked independent of one another, such horse trading would make little sense. For proponents of the "package-deal thesis" [*Junktimsthese*], the Roman Curia was pulling all the strings because—even in the absence of solid evidence—the hierarchical structure of the Catholic Church would allow for nothing else. In other words, Eugenio Pacelli, Pius XI's cardinal secretary of state, was to blame for everything. At his instruction, the bishops and the Center Party made concessions to the National Socialists in return for his beloved Reichskonkordat, for which he had spent twelve long years struggling in vain during his nunciature.

But it may be argued that looking at Pacelli exclusively and concentrating on the period from the end of January to the beginning of April 1933, that is, from Hitler's appointment as Reich chancellor to the start of negotiations around the Reichskonkordat, leads to a problematic narrowing of perspective. Indeed, though Pacelli was the point man in the Roman Curia by virtue of his position, he was part of a personal network, without knowledge of which his actions cannot be completely understood. The pope made all the final decisions, which is why the discussions between Pius XI and Pacelli, about which Pacelli kept meticulous records, take on such importance. What information did the secretary of state convey to Pius XI? What information did he withhold? In which instances did the Pontifex leave decisions to Pacelli? In any case, Pacelli was dependent on the information flowing in from papal nuncios around the world. The Vatican diplomats and ambassadors accredited by the Holy See were also important political interlocutors whom he regularly received for discussions in the Vatican palace. The pertinent nuncial reports and Pacelli's notes about audiences with the diplomats are thus important sources in helping us answer these key questions.

Chronologically, the ascendancy of the National Socialists and the beginning of Pacelli's role as head of Vatican diplomacy essentially coincided. Nazi electoral successes forced the Church to rethink the relationship between the Catholic faith and the National Socialist worldview. Naturally, the German bishops played an important role in this reconsideration, but so did the magisterium. The crucial theological question revolved around whether "good" Catholics should be permitted to get involved with this "evil," ideologically hostile group. Or were Catholicism and National Socialism fundamentally irreconcilable? In addition to questions of theology and worldview, there was also the political question of whether the Catholic Center Party and the Nazis could work together. Here, it would be useful to understand precisely what the Vatican knew about these issues. The Curia was involved in the decisions made by the bishops and the Center between 1930 and the end of 1932. During these years, did Pacelli ever consider exerting direct influence on Germany? Did he ever in fact intervene with the Center or the episcopate? Or did German Church politics simply bypass the cardinal secretary of state? We must answer these questions for the years 1930 to 1932 before we can judge the events that occurred between the end of January and the beginning of April 1933. Only if we know the channels and persons on whom Pacelli relied in his "German game" between 1930 and 1932 can we get a sense of which players merit attention in the months after Hitler's appointment.

The Cardinal Secretary of State's Secret Notes

To reconstruct the Roman view of the questions at issue here, we first need to examine the nuncial reports from Germany. Cesare Orsenigo in Berlin and Alberto Vassallo di Torregrossa in Munich sent Pacelli regular reports about developments in Germany. They wrote at least once per week, sometimes more often. Orsenigo's impressions of political matters were more important than the information coming out of Munich; Orsenigo was simply closer to events in the capital, which enabled him to send firsthand assessments to Rome more quickly. Whereas some of the nuncial reports with their appendixes are rather lengthy, Pacelli's instructions were generally brief, on occasion limited merely to a thank you. These sources have been accessible since February 2003 and have been thoroughly mined by both Italian and German researchers. Two other categories of sources, however, are analyzed here for the first time; they became available only in September 2006. These include Pacelli's personal notes about his almost daily discussions with Pius XI and the audiences that he presided over with ambassadors to the Holy See. Both sources reveal that transactions within the Curia changed immensely.

In contrast to the more or less collegial process by which consensus was worked out in the Curia in the nineteenth century, political decision-making devolved on two persons after World War I, the pope and his cardinal secretary of state. Previously, the Congregation for Extraordinary Ecclesiastical Affairs, which was under the authority of the Office of the Secretary of State, had always been involved in "extraordinary," that is, politically explosive, questions. But by the time Pacelli became cardinal secretary of state in 1930, it played virtually no role at all. The cardinals were only rarely called together to advise the pope about an important question. In fact, the pertinent files from that time contain only a few opinions from consultors, with extensive analyses of problems and potential scenarios. The fierce and contentious discussions of the cardinals at sessions of the congregation, which were customary in the nineteenth century, and of which precise minutes can be found in the series "Sessioni," are, unfortunately, also lacking. In this respect, our high expectations when the archives relating to the pontificate of Pius XI were opened were not met. No session of the cardinals took place in the spring of 1933, when Hitler was appointed Reich chancellor, or when the Center Party agreed to the Empowering Act, or when the persecution of the Jews began and many people urged the pope to intervene with the German government on their behalf. Minutes relating to Kristallnacht in 1938 are simply nonexistent. The same holds true for the negotiations for the Reichskonkordat in the summer of 1933—up to that time, agreements between the various states and the Holy See had been the domain of the Congregation for Extraordinary Ecclesiastical Affairs. Nor do we have documents relating to the "annexation" of Austria in 1938 and the problematic role played in that event by Cardinal Theodor Innitzer (1875–1955) of Vienna, or about the genesis of the 1937 encyclical *Mit brennender Sorge* [With deep anxiety].

As regrettable as the lack of minutes may be for research, we had good reasons to concentrate on only two decision-makers, Ratti and Pacelli, mainly having to do with their understanding of their offices and authority. In addition, Pacelli was convinced that after twelve years in Munich and Berlin he was the expert in all matters German in the Roman Curia. And who in the Curia would have been qualified to say otherwise? It is therefore not surprising that Pacelli largely handled affairs involving Germany by himself, bypassing the congregation.

The dynamics and the drama of unfolding political processes and the fact of instant global communication by telegraph, for example, made flexible and rapid responses indispensable to Pacelli. He neither could nor wanted to wait for weeks or even months for an expert opinion from consultors of the Congregation for Extraordinary Ecclesiastical Affairs, the minutes from their deliberations, and finally a report with recommendations to the pope himself. Of course, Pacelli could have telephoned at any time to summon a cardinal of the congregation to the Office of the Secretary of State for advice. Unfortunately, because of the sparseness of the sources we may never know whether he ever availed himself of this option. Be that as it may, the overall effect was that the Office of the Cardinal Secretary of State, which had always been important, now became paramount to Vatican affairs. Pacelli thus became the key diplomatic agent of the Catholic Church and its leader on the world political stage during the fateful years of the 1930s. One need only think of the Spanish Civil War, the Nazi dictatorship with its annexation of Austria, Stalin's Soviet Union, and the Sudeten crisis, all of which cast dark shadows as the world inched its way toward war. It is clear, however, that the cardinal secretary of state had to coordinate his actions closely with the wishes of the pope, the monarch of both the Church and the Papal State. He may have been the most powerful cardinal in the Sacred College of Cardinals, but he was still only the secretary to the Vicar of Jesus Christ. But who was playing the better hand of cards? Was it the pope because of his office or the cardinal secretary of state who pulled all the diplomatic strings? Could the some-what unworldly scholar Achille Ratti have had much impact on the politi-cally well versed and experienced power politician Eugenio Pacelli? Or was Pius XI really the all-powerful Pontifex maximus whom Pacelli could not hope to outmaneuver?

As mentioned, among the numerous series of files recently made avail-able, two deserve special attention. Both involve Pacelli's handwritten notes. In the first series, he documented the important outcomes of his regular private audiences with Pius XI.[1] In the second, he summarized topics touched on in his discussions with diplomatic representatives to the Holy See.[2] In these, he also noted his own responses to inquiries by the diplomats. Both of these holdings were for Pacelli's exclusive use. No one else in the Curia was ever permitted to look into these private notices. For this reason alone, the series should be accorded a high level of authentic-ity. Because they were not meant for public consumption, the sentences are sometimes incomplete and the handwriting sketchy. Both series bring us closer to the center of the Vatican decision-making process and give us direct insights into how both Pacelli and the pope worked and thought.

As a rule, Pacelli had a private audience with the pope every other day; at certain times they met daily, at other times three or even four days would pass between discussions. The private audiences took place during the summer months as well, which Pius XI usually spent at his summer residence, at Castel Gandolfo, in the Alban Hills. At these times, Pacelli, who stayed at the Vatican during the summer, would be driven to Castel Gandolfo. These discussions were canceled only when Pacelli took his an-nual vacation, usually in Rorschach, Switzerland, on the Lake of Con-stance, as he had since his time as nuncio. Since becoming secretary of state in the summer of 1930, Pacelli had taken to recording the important topics and results of these private audiences with the pope in his minus-cule handwriting on small sheets of paper. He maintained this practice until Pius XI's death in February 1939. In general, he would jot down key words and phrases, filling up two pages front and back per meeting.

Just when Pacelli wrote his notes, which he most likely did to help him remember actions that the pope wished him to take, is unclear, especially

Pacelli's notes of his audience with Pius XI on April 1, 1933. The text reads: "Write to the Berlin nuncio that further Jewish persons have reported to the Holy Father about the danger of anti-Semitic excesses in Germany, of which it is said that they have already occurred in some places. He should see whether and what might be undertaken. [Days may come in which one will have to be able to say that in this matter something was done. Such a thing is part of the good traditions of the Holy See.]"

(Copyright © Archivio Segreto Vaticano, A.E.S., Stati Ecclesiastici, 4 periodo, pos. 430a, fasc. 348, fol. 21r) since some of the entries show different levels of editing, with deletions and insertions, not infrequently with different pens and inks. The process was probably as follows: before the audience, Pacelli wrote up a sort of agenda and noted the main points, with headings, that he wanted to discuss with the pope. Many of the notes contain a reference to the report from the nuncio with the protocol number, which can be understood only by consulting the letter itself. These circumstances make it clear that in addition to the provisional agenda that he brought to the audience, Pacelli also brought the files corresponding to the headings—that is, the nuncial reports, memoranda, or other letters—for reference purposes, to read crucial passages to Pius XI, or to let him examine the documents himself. Pacelli then noted the pope's decisions under the pertinent heading. This means that we have before us Pius XI's opinions on various matters, even if filtered through his secretary of state. Pacelli would then, for example, translate these decisions into an instruction for a particular nuncio. Pius XI did not simply rubberstamp his secretary of state's suggestions. He not infrequently elaborated his own conceptions or rejected Pacelli's recommendations out of hand. The French ambassador to the Vatican, François Charles-Roux (1879–1961), commented on Pius XI's political independence in his memoirs: "There are popes who, once they have given their minister their trust, surrender almost all their political concerns to him. This was true, for example, in the case of Pius X and Cardinal Merry del Val, whom Pius relied on to transact his business. That was not how Pius XI proceeded. By nature he could not have endured such a method. With him, the role of secretary of state meant less freedom, but in exchange, more regularity in collaboration with the Holy Father, but for that he was no less demanding."[3]

For example, Pacelli suggested three times that the pope endorse more strongly Franco's national Catholicism in the Spanish Civil War, and three times the hesitant pope turned him down. A bit resigned, Pacelli noted at the end of the audience on August 11, 1936, "For the third time I presented to the Holy Father the idea, suggested by many, to approach the task of atonement and reparation for the pain that Spain had caused. The Holy Father did not believe that he could accommodate this request."[4] Nonetheless, he had approved the official article "The Holy See and the Religious Situation in Spain," which Pacelli had in fact written, and it appeared that same evening in *L'Osservatore Romano*, the official newspaper of the Vatican. In the article, Pacelli made clear that the Holy See had lodged a vigorous protest with the Madrid government about the "barbaric" persecution of priests and members of orders by "elements armed by the government itself."[5]

Pacelli also wrote notes about his discussions with ambassadors to the Holy See, which are of particular importance. He received representatives of the diplomatic corps several times a week and apparently made a lasting impression on many of them, including Charles-Roux: "A prelate, tall, gaunt, darkish complexion, slightly graying, ascetic facial features, alert gaze, benevolent mien, the red cap sitting upon his small, aristocratic head, the purple satin cape upon his shoulders, a belt of the same color over his black soutane with braids and gleaming buttons, a gold cross hanging by a chain upon his chest. That describes Cardinal Pacelli, who after his audience with the pope seeks out his own chambers to receive guests."[6]

Immediately after each meeting, Pacelli again jotted down the most important points covered in these meetings with diplomats on small sheets of notepaper. And even though much of what he wrote is in telegram style, there are nonetheless numerous well-formulated passages in which Pacelli cites verbatim an ambassador's opinion or inquiry. The notes in which the secretary of state recorded his own responses to certain questions are of particular interest. This is where we learn most about his personal assessment of a given political situation. Pacelli usually received many diplomats each day, sometimes in groups, sometimes in succession. He also granted long individual audiences. Reading these notes enables us to appreciate how his understanding of the information that individual ambassadors to the Holy See imparted about conditions in the various countries developed over the years. Topics of international interest such as the National Socialist seizure of power or the Spanish Civil War were usually discussed by several diplomats, giving Pacelli a rather nuanced picture of the situation. He was frequently queried by members of the diplomatic corps about his assessment of the situation and the potential for intervention by the Vatican on one side or the other.

The Bishops, the Center Party, and the NSDAP before the Seizure of Power

Pacelli was well aware of Hitler and National Socialism. As nuncio in Munich and then Berlin he had often been confronted with the movement. He had reported to then Cardinal Secretary of State Gasparri about events in Munich on November 9, 1923, one day after the failed Hitler putsch. After severe riots, he was pleased to report to Rome on November 12, "Hitler arrested. Order seems to have been restored."[7] On November 14, he emphasized that the entire uprising by Hitler and his followers had been of a markedly "anti-Catholic" character. That was no surprise to him because the radical right-wing mouthpieces of Ludendorff, Hitler, and their cohort, newspapers such as the *Völkische Beobachter* or *Heimatland,* had for some time been "ranting" against the Catholic clergy.[8] These attacks were also aimed at Cardinal Faulhaber, who had spoken out against the persecution of the Jews. In fact, in May 1924, Pacelli wrote to Gasparri in connection with the Hitler trial that in his opinion nationalism, or National Socialism, was "perhaps the most dangerous heresy of our time."[9]

Hitler engaged Pacelli's attention again in the summer of 1929, shortly before the end of his term as nuncio in Berlin. The nuncio to Vienna, Enrico Sibilia (1861–1948), had requested from him information about "a certain Hitler." Pacelli responded to his colleague in Vienna on August 5, 1929, to the effect that

> a notorious political agitator, Adolf Hitler, is known as such. He was born in 1889, in Braunau am Inn, in Upper Austria, did his volunteer military service in the German army, and then joined the National Socialist movement, which, originating in Austria, spread throughout all of southern Germany under his influence, under the name "National Socialist German Workers Party" (NSDAP). In 1923, he organized his followers along military lines into the so-called Storm Detachment and undertook a putsch, together with general Ludendorff, which came to a deservedly bad end. He was sentenced to five years in prison on April 1 but was released early at the end of this year. In February 1925, he founded the National Socialist German Workers Party, which enabled

him to regain his followers, who in his absence and against his will had joined the German Völkisch Freedom Party.

Out of concern for public safety, a number of German states had banned Hitler, a foreigner, from speaking. However, this ban had been lifted in 1927. In conclusion, Pacelli stated, "I need not add that during my stay in Bavaria I myself have never had any sort of personal contact with him."[10]

Ambassadors to the Holy See had since the beginning of 1931 repeatedly discussed with Pacelli the political situation in Germany, which was changing drastically, primarily as a result of the ascent of Hitler and his party. The first to broach this subject, on January 9, 1931, was the German ambassador to the Vatican, Diego von Bergen (1872–1944). He tendered several critical remarks about the foreign press review *Illustrazione Vaticana,* in which "National Socialism in Germany" was described as being in league "with the Communists and anarchists."[11] According to his notes, Pacelli refrained from commenting, as he would two months later when Bavarian Ambassador to the Vatican Otto Ritter zu Groenesteyn (1864–1940) informed him about the "Hitler movement," which he viewed as "very dangerous." The "Hitlerians" had spent "at least thirty million marks" during the last elections. "And although it is unclear where the money came from, some have theorized that it came from the Italian Fascists." Groenesteyn apparently feared that the National Socialists might seize power in North Germany, specifically in Prussia, and he requested support from the Holy See in Bavaria so that it might remain an independent state and not be demoted to the status of a mere Prussian province, "in the interest of the Catholic Church as well, because otherwise there will be no stopping the Hitler movement."[12] A week later, Belgian Ambassador Max van Ypersele de Strihou (1870–1941), who had filled that position since 1926, informed Pacelli of the hostility of the German bishops toward the NSDAP. They had declared the worldview of the National Socialists to be fundamentally incompatible with that of Catholicism.[13] But here, too, Pacelli refrained from comment. Over the next several months, he spoke with Bergen only in general terms about "the difficult situation

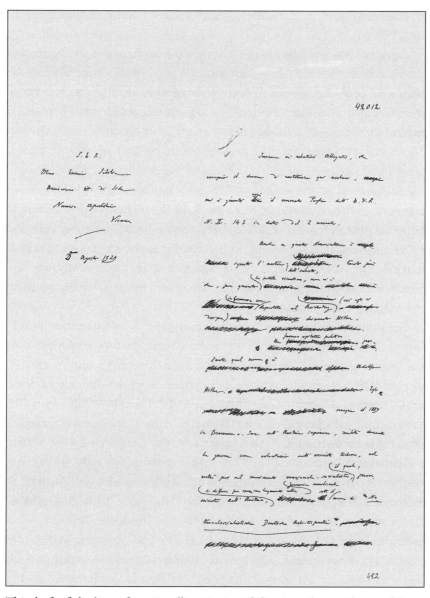

This draft of the letter from Pacelli to Enrico Sibilia gives clear evidence of the care that Pacelli took in formulating his thoughts.

(Copyright © Archivio Segreto Vaticano, ANB vol. 94, fasc. 1, fol. 682r)

in Germany," and in particular about "the continuing economic problems."[14]

Tensions increased during the summer of 1931 between the Curia and the Fascist regime in Italy as a result of controversies surrounding the pope's pet project, Catholic Action. No fewer than six ambassadors, those from Germany, Belgium, France, Bavaria, Austria, and Ireland demanded explanations from Pacelli about statements on this matter made by Pius XI, which were perceived to be particularly sharp. This was one of the few times Pacelli allowed himself a personal response. "For my part, I stressed the seriousness of the situation," he told the diplomats.[15] Here we see something of the role allocation in the Ratti-Pacelli team when it came to potential political conflicts, at least between the lines. The pope tended to be impulsive and effervescent, and sometimes not the least shy about making injurious statements; his secretary of state, the consummate diplomat, was always restrained and balanced, intent on avoiding anything that might feed the flames.

The political and economic crisis in Germany was frequently the subject of discussions between the secretary of state and the diplomats over the following months. The ambassadors from Germany's neighbor states, in particular, repeatedly drew Pacelli's attention to the difficult situation in the Reich and to the "struggle between Hitler and Brüning."[16] The Bavarian chargé d'affaires was especially clear when, in December 1931, he stated that the economic disaster in the Reich would primarily redound to the benefit of the Nazis: "The Hitler party, growing steadily, is the party of the desperate."[17] In early 1932, French Ambassador Louis Gabriel de Fontenay (1864–1946) also brought up the "Hitlerians." Pacelli responded that many feared a Nazi win would open up a "bridge to Bolshevism"— which would make an alliance between France and Germany useful.[18] On April 1, Fontenay speculated about a possible National Socialist election victory in Prussia, but noted that the party should not be permitted to achieve an absolute majority. In this context, the ambassador laid out a scenario for Prussia that, once Hitler was appointed Reich chancellor barely a year later, would be discussed in the Curia in terms of the Reich as a whole. Apparently, the French government saw a chance for the Center Party to exert influence on the NSDAP, because the Nazis would need

the Catholic party to achieve a majority in government. The National Socialists would, as a result, be moderated and kept in check.[19] At least between the lines, the ambassador may have been probing to see whether
the Holy See might be prepared to exert an influence toward this end on
Catholic politics in Germany. Unlike in the spring of 1933, the secretary of
state declined to comment. Nonetheless, one of the crucial points of
Church politics had at the very least been raised.

Over the course of the next several months, the Bavarian ambassador
returned repeatedly to his fears of an imminent seizure of power by the
National Socialists. For example, at the end of April 1932, he expressed
deep concern over the fate of Bavarian Minister President Heinrich Held,
who may have "perhaps exposed himself too much in the battle against
the National Socialists."[20] On May 20, he informed Pacelli that the Bavarian People's Party had split into two camps. One side favored a coalition
with the National Socialists; the other, with Held at the lead, advanced
the prospect of continuing political collaboration with the Social Democrats. Groenesteyn made it clear where his sympathies lay. The National
Socialists were igniting an "orcus of terror" such that one could well
imagine what would happen in Germany if they actually came to power.[21]
One month later, however, even the ambassador from Bavaria could see
no way out other than a center-right coalition, and he expressed his hope
"that the Center Party may find a way to liaison with the nationalist parties."[22] Pacelli rejected Groenesteyn's recommendation of an ecumenical
council against Bolshevism on September 2, 1932, because of the supposed
difficulties that stood in the way of such a synod.[23] However, their common opposition to Bolshevism became manifest as a result.

The audience on October 21, 1932, with the French ambassador to the
Holy See, Charles-Roux, who had just recently been appointed on June
27, is of particular interest. It was one of the rare instances in which Pacelli
actually noted his response to a diplomat's concrete question: "He requested from me information about the situation in Germany, which I
gave him." Pacelli predicted that the National Socialists would lose votes
in the upcoming elections, and that the Communists would gain. The
Center would surely lose several seats that it had won in the previous election as a result of favorable circumstances. In addition, he told Charles-

Roux of the Center Party's rejection of the government of Franz von Papen (1879–1969) and of the impossibility of building a majority coalition consisting solely of the Center and Papen's DNVP.[24]

A week later, the Bavarian ambassador raised the question of the November elections. He reported to the secretary of state about a trip to Munich made by Reich Chancellor von Papen, and about the speeches he gave there, which had been met favorably, even by many Catholics. Catholics were turning away from the Bavarian People's Party, which, "instead of supporting the Papen government, which had rescued Germany from the danger of National Socialism, had instead attacked it most harshly," just as had the rest of the Center Party. That is why these Catholics would no longer vote for the BVP or for the Center in the next election, but rather for the DNVP. Pacelli replied that, according to his information, the reason the Center was forced to deny its support to the government of the ultra-right former Center politician Papen had to do with a feared split in the party and the threatened loss of the labor wing.[25] After the election, both the Bavarian and the German ambassadors to the Holy See returned to the subject. While Groenesteyn regretted the personal attacks made against Papen by Kaas and Held, the leaders of the Center and the Bavarian People's Party, Bergen informed the cardinal secretary of state that a coalition consisting of the Center and the NSDAP would be incapable of achieving a majority.[26] With that, the ambassador now raised the question that seemed to him most crucial, namely, the potential for collaboration between the Center and the parties of the right, that is, the DNVP and the NSDAP. He apparently hoped to gain Pacelli's sympathies for such a solution to the German governmental crisis, especially since—if we give credence to Brüning's memoirs—the latter had two years earlier, in August 1931, recommended to the then Reich chancellor a coalition with the right wing.[27] Again, however, Pacelli kept his own counsel.

Thus the political situation in Germany, the rise of the NSDAP, and the possibility of a brown-black coalition had come up many times in Pacelli's audiences with the ambassadors. Pacelli received important assessments of the German situation from both Bergen and Groenesteyn, as well as from the ambassadors from other European states. But on the basis of the evidence of his own notes about these encounters, he abstained from judgments and played it close to the vest. He was the very picture of a discreet diplomat.

In addition to the information about the political situation in the Reich obtained from his discussions with diplomats in the Apostolic Palace, Pacelli, naturally, relied on the reports from the nuncios in Berlin and Munich, who were directly subordinate to him.[28] For example, on September 18, 1930, Pacelli's successor in Berlin, Cesare Orsenigo, reported on the surprising outcome of the parliamentary elections four days earlier. Orsenigo sensed a fundamental "deep distrust of parliamentarianism" in the astonishing gains made by the NSDAP, from 809,000 to more than 6 million votes. As a result, Orsenigo did not share the assessment of some commentators that Hitler's party was merely a "transient phenomenon." On the contrary, he assumed that it would continue to grow because the party would not be faced with governmental responsibilities and would therefore continue to attract increasing numbers of protest voters. Although "quite a few Catholics" were members of the party, its program was highly suspect from a religious perspective. But as in many other reports from those times, Orsenigo stressed the strict opposition of the NSDAP to Communism and the "surge of Sovietism."[29] This opposition to Bolshevism was nourished not, however, by religious principles but exclusively by the party's nationalism. And although the Center had retained its percentage of the votes, the situation created by the elections left little hope of consistent policies or even of a stable government.[30]

On September 30, 1930, the vicar general of Mainz had declared Catholicism and National Socialism to be incompatible "because the program of the NSDAP contains precepts that are irreconcilable with Catholic doctrine and principles." These included the "overestimation of the Germanic race and the denigration of all foreign races . . . that in many lead to complete hatred of foreign races," tendencies that were denounced as "unchristian and un-Catholic."[31] Orsenigo was skeptical of these expressions of principle, clear though they may have been. Although many Catholics certainly greeted the so-called Mainz Declaration enthusiastically, others among the faithful criticized it for its "exaggerated strictness." The Church—so the vicar general wrote to Pacelli on October 8—had guaranteed the enmity of Hitler's party, even though its attitude toward

Catholicism had not up to that point been completely negative and might still have developed in a more positive direction.[32] It seems that the Office of the Secretary of State was not completely unified around the Mainz Declaration. Whereas Undersecretary of State Giuseppe Pizzardo (1877–1970) argued for having Orsenigo warn Bishop Hugo of Mainz not to act in the future without the prior consent of the Holy See, Pacelli disagreed with this critical position.[33] Instead, he requested that the Berlin nuncio continue to monitor German conditions carefully, and to report back as appropriate.[34] In fact, Orsenigo next reported on the "wise restraint" of the other German bishops on this question. In his opinion, the attitude of the NSDAP toward religion and the Church was and continued to be ambivalent. Although some statements coming from National Socialist leaders justified retaining the Mainz condemnation, others held out hope "for a more reasonable and respectful attitude on the part of the party toward the Catholic Church." The nuncio identified two elements within National Socialism. One consisted of Catholics, "who are enrolled in the party in great numbers," are exclusively interested in political goals, and have positive feelings toward the Church. The other group tended "toward open opposition" to Catholicism and largely "consisted of nonbelievers and Protestants." Orsenigo was of the opinion that the NSDAP would retain its "double-faced attitude toward religion" as an election tactic because this was the only way it could make full use of its potential voter base. He further expressed the hope that once the party had become fully established, its religion-friendly wing would win out—but only if there prevailed "a patient and careful wait-and-see attitude on the part of Catholics."[35]

When, at the end of 1930, Orsenigo in Berlin heard of exploratory talks between Brüning and Hitler about collaboration with the Nazis in a joint government, he reported to Rome with satisfaction that both the Center Party and the German bishops were now "much more careful" in their statements about National Socialism.[36] In January of the following year, Orsenigo had to report that these talks had failed. The Center had been forced to recognize "the impossibility of political collaboration" with the NSDAP, particularly since the latter had done nothing to invalidate the charges contained in the Mainz Declaration. As a result, by the beginning of 1931, the nuncio no longer thought it advisable for the bishops and the Center Party to change their policies or direction. He wrote to Pacelli that "it would be a tactical error to split with the Social Democrats at this point." Without collaboration with the SPD, the Brüning cabinet would be finished and parliamentary agreement on emergency legislation unachievable.[37]

Once the coalition between the NSDAP and the Center, or at least toleration of the Brüning government by the NSDAP, had collapsed, all the German bishops eventually came in line with the hard, uncompromising course prescribed in the Mainz Declaration. As early as November 1930, Cardinal Faulhaber had, at a synod for the archdiocese of Munich and Freising, labeled National Socialism "a heresy" that "cannot be brought into harmony with the Christian worldview."[38] Pastoral instructions from the Bavarian Conference of Bishops to the clergy, on February 10, 1931, identified heresies in the Nazis' cultural policies, particularly their rejection of the Old Testament and the Ten Commandments, as well as their denial of papal primacy, and the party's racism: "Catholic clergy is strictly forbidden to participate in the National Socialist movement in any form. . . . Participation by National Socialists in religious services in closed ranks under uniform and banner is and remains forbidden." Whether individual Nazis could receive the sacraments was left to the judgment of each pastor. They would continue to be treated just like individual liberals or Socialists. Indeed, the bishops noted, "even among the adherents of such heresies, there have been and continue to be those who do not wish to betray their confirmation vows or the Church."[39] Munich Nuncio Alberto Vassallo di Torregrossa immediately informed Pacelli about this step taken by the Bavarian episcopate. He also alluded to the attempts by the *Völkische Beobachter* to play down this condemnation by remarking that the opinions alleged by the episcopate in no way represented the National Socialist worldview. Vassallo's words speak for themselves. In tone and content they make clear the fate that would threaten the Church if the National Socialists ever came to power.[40]

In the spring of 1931, the other German bishops—separated by ecclesiastical province—followed the Bavarian example and condemned National Socialism. The declaration of the bishops of the Upper Rhine, on

March 19, 1931, for example, read, "Bishops as shepherds and preachers of the Catholic faith and morals" must "warn against National Socialism because of and as long as it pursues and spreads views that are irreconcilable with Catholic teaching. It is therefore forbidden for Catholics to accept these views as true and to profess them in word and deed." The racism and the primacy of the Aryan race propounded by the Nazis were declared incompatible with Catholic universalism. "For this reason," the declaration continued, "it is completely impossible for the Catholic Church to permit itself to be led, constrained, or seduced in its doctrine and its actions by the 'morality and moral sense of a single race' such as the Germanic."[41] Orsenigo immediately informed Pacelli of the declarations of the German bishops, and he expressed the hope that these admonitions would save German Catholics from being absorbed into a party "that more and more diverges from Catholic principles."[42]

In October 1931, Orsenigo informed Pacelli of a "total crisis" in the gov-

As nuncio, Cesare Orsenigo had no easy task during the fateful year 1933.

(Monica M. Biffi, *Mons. Cesare Orsenigo. Nunzio apostolico in Germania: 1930–1946*, Archivo Ambrosiano 75 [Milan: NED, 1997])

ernment in Berlin. He was doubtful that a new cabinet could be formed under the leadership of the Center Party that would "not be distorted too much toward the right, that is, in the direction of the National Socialists," and he told Pacelli that the installation of a National Socialist government could not be ruled out. Even if "this experiment" were to fail, which many observers considered likely, given that a government led by the National Socialists would be viewed with extreme skepticism in Europe, it would probably "lead to a rise in Communism."[43] A few weeks later, Orsenigo again wrote about the political and religious situation in Germany in a detailed report. The "most delicate point" was the relationship between Catholicism and Protestantism and between Catholicism and the National Socialists. The "old anti-Catholic hatred" had been reawakened among the Protestants. In fact, certain Protestant circles and newspapers evinced a "complete devotion to National Socialism." Whereas they touted Protestantism as reliable on the national level, they charged German Catholicism with a dependency on Rome that "is inconsistent with the interests of the nation." Orsenigo reported a consistent upward trend in the numbers of "Hitleriani." The desire for national rebirth in Germany was driving young people in particular into the arms of the Nazis, which would probably lead to their becoming the strongest party in Prussia after the upcoming elections. Without an absolute majority, however, the National Socialists would be forced to find a coalition partner. Orsenigo recommended a double strategy: the Catholic Church should hold fast to the religious principles inculcated by the bishops with regard to National Socialist ideology, while at the same time practicing a studied politeness in their practical dealings with the leaders of the NSDAP. Doing so would motivate party members "to cleanse themselves of elements that indulge in anti-Catholic behavior" so that they may be capable of "loyal cooperation." Basically, the Berlin nuncio was again hoping for a coalition between the Center and the NSDAP. After all, though the Center Party had put up a fierce fight against the National Socialists, it was "only out of political, never out of religious, motives." Orsenigo considered this separation of politics and religion to be extremely useful for finding potential ways out of this muddled situation.[44]

Over the following months, Orsenigo sent numerous detailed reports about the difficult political situation in the Reich, about Brüning's fall, the appointment of Franz von Papen as Reich chancellor, and his subsequent failure in office. By late 1932 and early 1933, his reports about the death spiral of the Weimar Republic were reaching a climax. Papen sought out Orsenigo and asked him to mediate for him with the Center Party. Papen apparently hoped to use the Catholic party, which he had left two days after being appointed Reich chancellor in early June 1932, to avoid exclusion from the Center, and to return to power in spite of its "enmity," which he was convinced still prevailed. But the nuncio rejected Papen's request as well as his intention to travel to Rome to lay the matter directly before Pacelli. Orsenigo wrote to Pacelli, "Solely with the intent of sparing Your Eminence such a visit, which would probably elicit problematic comment, I ventured to tell him, 'I do not have the courage to advise Your Excellency to undertake such a trip. I would consider it opportune to refrain.'" Orsenigo told Papen that the cardinal secretary of state preferred not to be approached on purely political matters.[45]

Although, as we have seen, Pacelli was well informed about the political situation in Germany, he rarely discussed the topic with the pope from the time he assumed his position until the appointment of Adolf Hitler as Reich chancellor. Internal Church questions such as the appointment of bishops, Church finances, pastoral care in the military, book censorship, and finding common ground for concordats with other countries are, however, found relatively frequently in the sources. Pacelli apparently viewed Germany as his own terrain, at least politically. This is underscored by the fact that he and the pope frequently discussed the political situation in other countries, particularly in Fascist Italy.

When Pacelli reported to the pope on December 19, 1930, about accusations made by the Italian ambassador to the Holy See, Count Cesare Maria de Vecchi di Val Cismon (1884–1959), against German-language priests in South Tyrol, whom he charged with "pan-Germanism," Ratti apparently lost his composure: "'They are crazy people!' the Holy Father exclaimed." Once the pope had regained his self-control, the cardinal secretary of state continued, "Write to the bishops nonetheless so that they also advise these priests and demand of them that they act judiciously. . . . They are not to make German propaganda but to proclaim the Gospel."[46]

When Count Vecchi, barely a year later, mocked the somewhat undiplomatic tone that Pius XI adopted toward the Fascist state, the pope again became enraged. As bishop of Rome—he dictated to Pacelli—he had an ineluctable pastoral duty, and it was absurd to demand "that he perform his pastoral duties diplomatically. Whenever the honor of God and the salvation of the faithful in his diocese are at stake, he can act only as a bishop. A moral and religious primacy of the Fascist government is none of our business." The Holy Father, the note continued, well understood which matters were to be treated as pastoral and which as diplomatic: "The Holy Father will not fail to express his deserved protests against states whenever necessary at the time and in the manner that he deems suitable."[47]

The pope expressed himself with similar clarity when he asked Pacelli, in connection with the fierce battles between Church and state in Mexico, whether in this instance the use of force in the Church's war of resistance might not be permissible. Pius XI gave the following instructions: suitable formulations must be found to express that the Holy See blesses and strengthens all those who in this struggle defend the rights of God and of religion. In the present circumstances, however, "armed resistance could be neither authorized nor encouraged." According to Pacelli's notes, the Holy Father emphasized that this applied "under the present circumstances. Because a glance at history shows that the popes not only frequently authorized external and internal crusades but actually initiated them." As examples, he listed the wars waged against the Turks and the heretics. In fact, he stated, those wars had also defended civilization. Pius V had fought the Turks at Lepanto; Pius IV (1559–1565) did so against the Protestants by means of the Council of Trent. But "under the present circumstances, His Holiness can neither authorize nor encourage; to put it bluntly, he expressly condemned armed conflict."[48] From these few examples, it is apparent that Pius XI had a clear political point of view, which he had no trouble stating to Pacelli.

But whereas the world political situation regularly came up in the daily audiences between the pope and Pacelli, and the pope gave the cardinal secretary of state clear instructions on which steps to take and how the Holy See should position itself politically, we find no such directives with regard to Germany. Interestingly, it was the pope himself who first raised an issue relating to Germany in one of the audiences, in spite of the fact that his secretary of state generally determined the agenda. On February 3, 1931, Pacelli noted, "At the beginning of the audience, the Holy Father showed me an article from *Figaro,* dated January 31, 1931." The conservative Paris newspaper reported on a speech given by the chairman of the Center Party, Prelate Kaas. The pope alluded to the "erroneous path that the Center had been taking for many years in Germany. I then explained to him the difficulties in which this party found itself, particularly given the present composition of the German parliament, in which the Communists on the one hand and the National Socialists (extreme nationalists) on the other had made such gains. If the Center wished to pursue the politics of international understanding, it would be forced to rely on the Socialists—something the Holy Father finds disturbing. If, on the other hand, it decides to join with the parties of the right, a politics of peace is impossible." Because of the increased growth in the parties of the right in parliament, relations with Poland and France would worsen drastically. "In other words, there is nothing left to do other than to leave the government and go into opposition. This would, however, have the most serious consequences because the parties in the government could hoist their candidates into ministerial offices, thereby wreaking much damage." As Pacelli summarized the situation for Pius XI, "It is therefore impossible to understand what to recommend in this situation. It is *un fatale andare*—as the Holy Father remarked."[49]

The audience on May 2, 1931, was the first time Pacelli spoke about a political issue relating to Germany. He reported on a request by Hermann Göring (1893–1946), the chairman of the NSDAP faction in parliament, for an audience in the Vatican. He had turned to the cardinal secretary of state on April 30, in a handwritten letter, as "one of the responsible leaders of the NSDAP and a particularly close confidant of the head of this party, Adolf Hitler." Göring continued that it was "close to his heart to discuss with Your Eminence the problems of our movement."[50] Although Göring turned directly to Pacelli, the secretary of state apparently considered the matter so potentially explosive that he decided to consult with Pius XI. The matter was also delicate because Mussolini had declined to receive

Nazi functionaries to avoid straining his relationship with the German government. Receiving the German right in the Vatican would have been tantamount to recognizing it without considering the position of the Italian state. The pope rejected the idea of a personal meeting with Göring out of hand and forbade Pacelli to receive him as well. "It is a dangerous matter because it seems to go against a decision of the bishops," the pope told Pacelli. Pius XI decided that only Undersecretary of State Giuseppe Pizzardo should receive Göring. The pope instructed Pacelli to brief Pizzardo and to discuss this *cosa delicata* with him in person after the German bishops had unambiguously established their opposition to National Socialism in their declarations. Pizzardo met Göring the next day, May 3, in the Vatican, and prepared the minutes for his superior. They indicate that Göring had tried to dissipate Catholic objections to the Nazis and their anti-Christian attitudes. "He had come to Rome to rest, but Hitler had asked him to undertake this step with the Vatican." The party, he said, recognized the authority of God and of the pope in moral and religious questions. Pizzardo noted that, as the pope had feared, the talks had in part actually concerned an objection, expressed by Hitler, to the position taken by the German bishops against the NSDAP. The opinions of Alfred Rosenberg (1893–1946) and other propagandists did not, according to Göring, represent the opinion of the party and had long been superseded. Göring was particularly critical of the German bishops' support of the Center Party in view of its supposed left-wing orientation and close association with the Socialists. Göring characterized the SPD as a hotbed of atheism, bent on Germany's destruction.[51] It is unclear whether Pacelli ever told the pope about Pizzardo's discussions with Göring. If he did, he seems never to have committed anything to paper.

The pope returned to the German bishops' condemnation of National Socialism one month later in a completely different context. Given the increasing conflicts between the Curia and Italian Fascism, he indicated in an audience that he could no longer rule out condemning Mussolini's party, "as the German bishops had already done with Hitler's party."[52] At the end of 1931, members of the German high nobility requested that Pius XI lift the Church's condemnation of National Socialism. When Pacelli presented him with a letter to that effect in an audience, the pope realized that he had run out of room to maneuver and commented that all he could do now was refer them to the decision of the bishops.[53]

Surprisingly, the increasingly difficult political situation in Germany never again came up in 1932 in discussions between Pacelli and the pope. The only matters discussed were individual formulations of the planned concordat with Baden.[54] And although the Holy Father instructed his secretary of state on April 17, 1932, to congratulate Reich President Paul von Hindenburg on his reelection in the name of the Holy See, there is not a single word on the fall of Heinrich Brüning or the appointment and resignation of Franz von Papen.[55] By contrast, the pope and his secretary of state spent a good deal of time on a report sent by Orsenigo about the training of priests in Berlin. Pius XI angrily denied the blessing sought by Bishop Christian Schreiber (1872–1933) for a planned preparatory seminary, because it was anticipated that the students would be sent to a Protestant secondary school in Berlin.[56] This episode gives evidence of a partially narrowing Vatican perspective. Germany was plunging headlong into chaos—and the pope was well informed of events there—but he found troubling the notion that Catholic candidates for the priesthood should attend a Protestant secondary school.

It should be noted that Pacelli and his diplomatic corps were not the pope's sole source of information about Germany. This may be seen in his sovereign handling of the only volatile issue relating to Germany that Pacelli presented to him for his decision, namely, Göring's request for an audience. Although Pacelli had been well briefed by Vassallo di Torregrossa and Orsenigo about the bishops' condemnation of National Socialism, his notes give no evidence that he ever passed these reports on to the pope. But Pius XI judged matters correctly even without this information. He realized that behind Göring's request lay Hitler's intention to play the Holy See against the German bishops, to motivate the pope to intervene in favor of the NSDAP. He was not, however, about to become a pawn in a campaign against the German episcopate, and, as we have seen, he went so far as to forbid Pacelli to receive Göring. The sources may not warrant the conclusion that Pius XI harbored a certain distrust of his "German" cardinal secretary of state, but it cannot be ruled out. In any case, Pius XI considered the German bishops' condemnation of National Socialism to be a model for how the Curia might respond to Italian Fascism.

Trading a Reichskonkordat for an Enabling Act?
A Research Controversy

"He asked for my evaluation of the situation in Germany," Pacelli noted on February 1, 1933, immediately after a discussion with French Ambassador Charles-Roux, who had just returned to Rome from consultations with his government in Paris. Two days earlier, on January 30, Reich President Paul von Hindenburg had appointed Hitler Reich chancellor. The National Socialist assumption of power had triggered concern in Germany, as the secretary of state noted. Because of this, the French government was discussing a scenario in which the National Socialists, if they could not in fact be denied, were kept in check by a coalition with the Center Party. The hope in Paris was that the Holy See would be able to exert its influence on political Catholicism toward this end. For his part, however, Pacelli viewed this scenario as utopian, as his response to Charles-Roux makes clear: "I said that in my opinion it was improbable that the Center would enter the government unless it received adequate guarantees. However, as far as religious life is concerned, the National Socialists have in the past taken a less favorable position." As Pacelli saw it, the evidence for this conclusion lay in the voting behavior of the National Socialists when it came to the projects that were so close to his heart, the concordats with Bavaria, Prussia, and Baden. The NSDAP delegates had consistently voted no in the state parliaments, including in Karlsruhe just a few months earlier. The cardinal secretary of state called Hitler a "brilliant agitator." But as he told the ambassador, he doubted that he was suited to the task of governance and statesmanship, especially since "his party consists of people of the most varied orientation." Behind the political crisis in Germany, Pacelli continued, "the question of the restoration of the monarchy had played a certain role." This issue could become more urgent "if a dictatorship were to come instead of a parliamentary government (which the current one seeks to be)." When queried by Charles-Roux, Pacelli added that in his opinion the question of the Polish

Corridor had played no role in Hitler's appointment, even though it naturally "stirs every German's heart." For this reason, Pacelli concluded, he thought it unlikely "that the government would be considering an act of violence or military attack in this regard."[57]

This response is unusually lengthy. One of Pacelli's comments was particularly noteworthy, namely, that he considered collaboration between the Center and the NSDAP to be highly improbable given the lack of guarantees. By contrast, no mention was made of any influence exerted by the Holy See or the cardinal secretary of state on the Center Party. This response leads right into one of the most contentious research controversies in recent Church history relating to the period from January to April 1933. At issue is the behavior of the Catholic Church and its various institutions toward the Nazi government. Interest focuses on three sets of questions.

First, how did the Hitler government convince the German bishops to lift their condemnation of National Socialism, which they had articulated consistently since the 1930s, thereby enabling Catholics to join the "movement"? After all, the German episcopate "corrected" its rejection of National Socialism on March 28, 1933, declaring that the general "bans and admonitions" were no longer necessary.[58]

Second, in order to transform the parliamentary Weimar system into a dictatorship by legal means, Hitler needed the Center Party's consent to the Enabling Act. Without the votes of the Catholic party, he would not have been able to achieve the two-thirds majority needed to amend the constitution in parliament. In fact, on March 23, 1933, the Center agreed to the so-called Law to Remedy the Distress of the People and the Nation. What reasons did the representatives of the Catholic political party have for taking this fateful step? Was it a belief in the necessity of a strong government, or was Hitler's governmental declaration of the same day decisive? Or was the promise of a Reichskonkordat behind their move?

Third, what role did the Holy See play in this turn of events? Was Rome involved in the decisions of the Conference of Bishops and the Center Party, or was the Curia surprised by developments in Germany and unable to exert influence? What role did the Reichskonkordat play? Were democracy and the Center Party being sacrificed so that the *Codex Iuris*

Canonici of 1917 could be implemented in Germany as well? Or did Pacelli have no choice other than to play along with the German government because he would have gotten in the way by rejecting the offer of a concordat?

Basically, all these questions may be traced back to the single question at the center of a vigorous controversy that is associated with the names Klaus Scholder (1930–1985) and Konrad Repgen. Was there a connection between the Center Party's consent to the Enabling Act, the German bishops' retraction of their condemnation of National Socialism, and the start of negotiations between the German government and the Vatican for a Reichskonkordat? Karl-Dietrich Bracher had already proposed the existence of such a package deal in the 1950s, when the German Federal Constitutional Court was examining the validity of the Reichskonkordat. Since then, the Protestant Church historian Klaus Scholder and his school have repeatedly attempted to demonstrate this connection in a series of articles. The Catholic historian Konrad Repgen and the Kommission für Zeitgeschichte [Commission for Contemporary History] of the Catholic Academy in Bavaria have contested this theory with equal vehemence. Because no unambiguous sources have as yet been adduced, the primary and secondary arguments underpinning both positions have tended to be hypothetical. For example, it is still a matter of conjecture whether the idea for a concordat was first proposed by vice-chancellor Papen or by Hitler himself. It is equally unclear when the chairman of the Center Party, Prelate Kaas, first learned about the government's intentions. Was it before the vote on the Enabling Act on March 23, 1933—as claimed by Brüning in his memoirs, and in turn by the Scholder school—which could very well have influenced the voting behavior of the Center Party? Or did Kaas first learn of the German government's intentions on April 8, when he ran into Papen on the train to Rome—as Repgen theorizes?

There are numerous secondary questions that the newly released sources in Rome cannot answer. The Vatican Secret Archives, however, should be able to shed light on the issue that Scholder himself considered crucial, namely, the role of the Roman Curia in the triad consisting of the Enabling Act, the bishops' declaration, and the Reichskonkordat. In his own words, "the question of the participation of the Holy See in the events in March" is of central interest: "With that, we come to a crucial point in the entire controversy. Was the Vatican completely uninvolved in the momentous decisions made by German Catholicism in March, as Repgen claims? And even more, was Rome in some sense a victim of these erroneous or at least infelicitous decisions because they made it impossible to reject Papen's offer of negotiations? Or is the thesis correct . . . that all in all German Catholicism—both ecclesiastical and political—rejected National Socialism with admirable firmness and resolution until Rome considered it necessary to scuttle this front for the greater good of its concordat policy?"[59]

Rome's Marionettes or Independent Actors? The Center Party and the Bishops

Analysis of the three important series of files—the nuncial reports, audiences with diplomats, and discussions with Pius XI—yield a precise picture of the information available to the pope and the Curia, and of the discussions between them during those critical weeks in the spring of 1933.[60] As already discussed, Pacelli considered collaboration between the Center Party and the NSDAP to be improbable on February 1. He had not discussed any potential Vatican intervention of this sort with Ambassador Charles-Roux. Two days later, on February 3, 1933, the cardinal secretary of state received the ambassadors of Bavaria, Italy, and Austria.[61] Hitler's seizure of power never came up in his discussion with the Austrian chargé d'affaires. About his meeting with Groenesteyn, Pacelli noted in general terms that he had reported only "about the difficult situation in Germany."

Toward the end of his audience on February 3, Count Vecchi di Val Cismon, the Italian ambassador to the Holy See, did address the "seizure of power by the Hitlerians in Germany," noting that "he had long predicted it." The National Socialists "have assumed power, and they will never give it up no matter how the elections turn out." As evidence for his view, the ambassador quoted Mussolini: "Only he relinquishes power who wishes to." There was a reason the National Socialists were in constant contact with Mussolini, who even advised them: "They have their militias, and they won't allow their power to be taken away." Hitler was not antimonarchist in principle. Pacelli noted that when asked whether the Versailles Treaty had not in fact limited armaments and the military in Germany, the ambassador stated that the National Socialists would not "give a damn" about these requirements. In addition, since their assumption of power, they intended to "destroy Communism by fire and sword." The Italian diplomat was basically sending Pacelli a double message: Hitler, like Mussolini, intended a dictatorship that did away with democracy. In his view, National Socialism and Fascism, with which the Church had been able to come to an accommodation, even concluding the Lateran Pacts of 1929, were completely comparable. Additionally, Communism was the principal enemy of both National Socialism and Catholicism, of Hitler and Pius XI. But when Pacelli asked him about Hitler's attitude toward the Church and religion, Vecchi di Val Cismon stated that he really didn't know how matters stood at the moment. Nonetheless, he hoped that the National Socialists would not fight the Church, "because this would go against their own interests." This would, however, be conditional on the German bishops' abandoning their condemnation of National Socialism, because otherwise the movement would be forced to move against the Church. At the end of the audience Pacelli noted, "The ambassador has offered to intervene based on our terms."

Interestingly, Nuncio Orsenigo, too, addressed the condemnation of National Socialism in his first report after the Nazis' ascension to power on February 7, 1933.[62] Unfortunately, the guidelines laid down by the episcopate had not completely achieved their desired effect. Large numbers of young Catholics were going over to the Nazis. This part of Orsenigo's report may be read as a desire to modify the position of the bishops. Although the entire episcopate had eventually come into line with the Mainz Declaration, quite a few bishops had at the beginning shown themselves to be "anything other than unsympathetic to the new party." Orsenigo advised Pacelli of Hitler's desire to collaborate with the Center Party, or at least to motivate the party to tolerate his cabinet for a year: "The Center, which distrusted a Hitler-Papen cabinet for reasons of program and tactics," made its collaboration contingent on several factors. For one, the party demanded guarantees that the Weimar constitution would be retained. The Nazis balked at this condition, and Hitler was forced to announce new elections. Orsenigo's comment that "the behavior of the Center seems at the moment to be the only reason for new elections" is particularly interesting. It might appear as if the political conflict between the Center and the National Socialists was based on a fundamental disagreement between National Socialism and Catholicism, which the nuncio denied. But even Orsenigo had to admit that the tensions between the National Socialists and the majority of Catholics were considerable. Hitler's declarations that he would defend Christianity as the basis for all morality appeared doubtful at best.

On February 16, Orsenigo reported on the hotly contested parliamentary election campaigns. Whereas the Center Party "naturally relied more or less on the totality of the clergy and the Catholics," the National Socialists attempted to show that they did not oppose religion per se, only "the political abuse of religion." Orsenigo held that it was "naïve and inconsistent" for Catholics to support the new Nazi government, because the grounds for the bishops' condemnation had not been addressed. Nonetheless, "fighting them openly in the name of religion for obviously electoral purposes could lead to bitterness, or even trigger a genuine 'Kulturkampf.'" Although it was difficult to predict the outcome of the elections, it was possible that a coalition of two of the three parties in opposition to the left, namely, the NSDAP together with the German National People's Party or the Center, might achieve an absolute majority in parliament. The Berlin nuncio felt that in this case an NSDAP-Center coalition was more likely than a coalition with the DNVP: "Everything now depends on not destroying it all beforehand."[63] In spite of all the problems, Orsenigo apparently hoped for a coalition between the Center and the NSDAP. But a few days later he had to admit defeat. "The conflict between the Center and the National Socialists is now so out in the open and so acute," he noted, "that it no longer appears possible to hope for a dignified but cautious position which might later have offered the Center the potential for becoming a factor for compromise and peace."[64]

The German ambassador to the Vatican, Diego von Bergen, reported to Pacelli on February 10 "about the political situation in Germany, without saying anything of specific interest."[65] Just two weeks later, he was apparently given instructions by the new national government to make peace with the Curia. As Pacelli noted, he first reported on the "very friendly response" from Hitler to the letter of sympathy from the Holy See about the catastrophe in Neunkirchen—by which he meant the explosion of a gas tank in the Saarland that claimed many lives. After this upbeat introduction, "he gave me very detailed assurances that the present government would neither undertake anything against the Catholic Church nor compromise its good relations with the Holy See. Hitler is Catholic by birth," and Konstantin Baron von Neurath (1873–1956), who would remain as the last practicing Catholic in the government, "is well known as a person of the highest correctness; Papen is *cattolicissimo;* and so everything is completely secure." Pacelli apparently did not find this line of reasoning particularly satisfactory: "I expressed several reservations about Hugenberg." While admitting that Alfred Hugenberg (1865–1951) had a reputation as a passionate "Kulturkämpfer," the ambassador assured Pacelli that he was so busy with economic matters at the moment that for that reason alone he would be unable to make any moves against the Catholic Church. In an audience on the same day, the French ambassador mentioned a possible visit by Hitler to Rome. Pacelli had to admit that he knew nothing about such a visit, and so he used the opportunity of his discussion with the German ambassador to ask whether there was any truth to the rumor. Bergen responded that though he "had no official information" about the matter, he considered it "about 60 percent likely."[66]

In contrast to Orsenigo's reports immediately before the March elections, Pacelli's notes are filled with news of the uncompromising anti-Communism of Hitler and his party. On February 8, 1933, while presenting his credentials, the newly appointed representative to the Vatican from the Principality of Monaco, Emilio Lorenzo Dard (1871–1947), expressed the fear "that France would be driven into an alliance with Russia because of the increasingly tight axis between Italy and Hitler's Germany, and that Russia would split with Germany because of Hitler's campaign against Communism."[67] When on March 4, 1933, Groenesteyn, the Bavarian ambassador, "recognized the merits of the present government in the fight against Communism" while at the same time sharply criticizing Hitler's polemics against the supposed inaction of the previous cabinet, which had mostly been led by the Center Party, Pacelli noted tersely, "It is true that they were much too indulgent of Communism."[68] It is clear in such statements that Pacelli then believed that Stalin, Russian Bolshevism, and its offshoots in Europe represented the real devil at work. By contrast, no mention was made at the time of demonizing, let alone challenging, Hitler. Although Pacelli remained skeptical of Hitler's attitudes toward the Church and Catholicism, his anti-Communism went a long way toward neutralizing those concerns. The pope obviously shared Hitler's attitude. It is therefore not surprising that the first sentence in Pacelli's notes about the audience with Pius XI on that day read, "Hitler is the first (and only) statesman who has to date spoken publicly against Communism. Until now only the pope had done so."[69] Over the next several days, Pius XI informed one or several ambassadors of his more positive opinion of Hitler. For example, on March 7, 1933, Charles-Roux noted after a discussion with the pope that he had modified his opinion of the leader of the NSDAP especially because he believed that he had found "an ally against Bolshevism."[70] Pius XI made similar statements to the cardinals in a consistory on March 13, as Cardinal Faulhaber recorded.[71]

The option of collaboration between the Center and the NSDAP, advanced by Orsenigo in February, had since early March repeatedly come up in discussions between the cardinal secretary of state and various diplomats to the Holy See. For example, on March 4, Groenesteyn answered the question about a potential black-brown coalition with a cautious "perhaps."[72] The issue became more urgent after the elections. On March 7, Orsenigo reported to Pacelli that only about half of German Catholics had followed the bishops' instructions and voted for the Center or the Bavarian People's Party. The other six or seven million Catholic voters had "largely voted for National Socialism," in spite of the unambiguous ban by the German episcopate. Even though these figures are clearly too high, and recent studies have shown that at most four million of the total thirteen million Catholic voters cast their ballots for the NSDAP, these exaggerations enabled the Berlin nuncio to convey to Rome the particular "fascination" that National Socialist ideas held for German Catholics.[73] A few days later, Orsenigo told Pacelli about information, circulating in Germany, that came originally from the Roman *La Corrispondenza* news agency, detailing a change of opinion in the Vatican with regard to the Hitler movement. Some newspapers saw this as "a prelude to collaboration with the Center"; others claimed that the Catholic party had made its peace with Hitler. Orsenigo pointed out that in his opinion relations between the Center and the NSDAP had not been fundamentally undermined. Collaboration between the two parties was already a reality in some state parliaments, such as in Hessen.[74] With these and similar wordings, Orsenigo was clearly reiterating his hope for collaboration between the two parties at the national level. But Pacelli poured cold water on the notion, informing Orsenigo that *La Corrispondenza* had "no relations with the Vatican," and that their editors had "never so much as set foot in the Office of the Secretary of State."[75] Apparently, Pacelli wanted to avoid any impression of Vatican influence in German domestic politics in his statements to the nuncio in Berlin.

Surely he did not consider Orsenigo an unreliable person. Rather, Pacelli saw no possibility that the Vatican or the pope could influence the Center to work with the NSDAP, whether in the form of a coalition, support for individual legislation, or even toleration of each other in parliament. When the Italian ambassador, at Mussolini's behest, asked during an audience on March 14 whether there was anything to the rumors that the Holy See "had given the Center instructions to support the present government in Germany," the cardinal secretary of state noted, "I answered in the negative." In any case, Count Vecchi di Val Cismon answered Pacelli, stating that "if it comes to a collision, it will be fatal; they will destroy the Center for years to come." At the end of this audience, the Italian ambassador returned to Hitler's planned visit to Rome to see Mussolini, which Charles-Roux and Bergen had alluded to several weeks earlier, and asked Pacelli directly, "Would you like him to visit the Vatican as well?" Pacelli answered, "I personally see no difficulties," and he justified his view by noting that Hitler "is the head of the legal government; therefore it is only natural that he would visit the Holy Father when he comes to Rome." Pacelli could, however, "give no binding information without consulting His Holiness."[76]

Pacelli, in fact, consulted the pope three days later, on March 17, about this issue. As expected, Pius XI stated that he had no problem receiving Chancellor Hitler in private audience.[77] Pacelli informed Count Vecchi di Val Cismon of this decision the same day. The count then asked, "But do you want him to come?" According to his notes, Pacelli answered that in his "personal opinion, it would be an error if Hitler were not to visit the Holy Father on his trip to Rome. But this is subject to his decision alone."[78]

By mid-March, both the pope and his cardinal secretary of state were undoubtedly interested in good relations with the new German government. A personal meeting between Pius XI and Hitler in private audience in the Vatican, in the context of his planned visit to Mussolini in Rome, seemed like an excellent way of ensuring such relations. Not a trace of

Cardinal Secretary of State Pacelli and Il Duce, Benito Mussolini.
(CH Beck Verlag)

criticism of the National Socialist worldview from the Curia or its head is to be found in the notes Pacelli made at the time. Any skepticism that might have been engendered by Hitler's policies toward the Church was quieted by his clarion call to defeat Communism. Several times, Pacelli confronted ambassadors who had been critical of Pius XI's statements that Hitler was the only anti-Communist statesman. For example, he explicitly countered an inquiry from the Belgian ambassador to the Holy See on March 17, 1933. And Pacelli rejected the fear of the French ambassador that Italy, supported by Germany, would become embroiled in a war with France—much as he had previously quieted his fear of an "annexation" of Austria—with the remark, "Italia non vuole la guerra"—Italy does not desire war. According to Pacelli, Italy would put its foot down here as well. In this connection, the secretary of state made clear a fundamental feature of his policies: strict neutrality on the part of the Holy See in international political conflicts to the extent that they do not immediately threaten pastoral care. As far as political questions such as "annexation" were concerned, "the Holy See is not competent *(estranea)*."[79]

Apart from the general stance of the Vatican toward Hitler's government and the impossibility of influencing the Center to collaborate with the National Socialists, the condemnation of National Socialism by the German bishops in the early 1930s had taken on increasing importance ever since the newly elected parliament was seated. Hitler was faced with the task of encouraging the episcopate to retract its verdict, thereby enabling Catholics to work on building the new Reich, while eliminating the only solid oppositional bloc to National Socialism other than the SPD.

On March 22, Orsenigo sent a detailed report to Rome about the opening celebrations of the new parliament in Potsdam. At the religious celebration, about eighty Catholic deputies belonging to the NSDAP had appeared in uniform. "The lowest point of the day was the official explanation that the Reich chancellor gave for his and Minister Goebbels's absence at the Catholic liturgy," Orsenigo wrote. The stated reason was the bishops' condemnation of National Socialism. Orsenigo voiced his hope that goodwill on both sides might resolve this conflict. For one thing, the ban on Catholics working within the NSDAP had long ago ceased to be effective. "Unfortunately, it cannot be denied that with few exceptions

Catholics have turned to the new regime with enthusiasm" and have "forgotten" the instructions of the bishops. In any case, the norms enunciated by the bishops applied only to "the ideological-religious content of the National Socialist movement, but assuredly not to their political positions." Catholics, "fascinated" with Nazi policies, tried to find a way to separate religion from politics. Thus it was very much in the interest of the Church to resolve this conflict as quickly as possible and to encourage the bishops to relativize their condemnation. Barring that, the conflict could become a "very dangerous spark."[80]

Given the information that was filtering in from Berlin, Pacelli must have been particularly interested in how the German bishops themselves assessed the new political situation. In fact, in mid-March he asked Cardinal Faulhaber, who was in Rome at the time, for his opinion of Hitler and the possibility of retracting the bishops' declaration. Faulhaber's memorandum to Pacelli runs to six handwritten pages and consists of three parts.[81]

In the first, relatively short, section, the cardinal highlighted three aspects of Hitler that were "praiseworthy." First, he had the courage "to proclaim *the name of God*" in public speeches and to trust in His "blessings" and in divine "Providence." The archbishop of Munich and Freising stressed this point because the preamble to the Weimar constitution lacked any reference to God. A constitution grounded solely in popular sovereignty and lacking any basis in divine right—thereby lacking references to transcendence—was simply unacceptable. This was why Faulhaber had rejected the Weimar constitution and was skeptical of any active Catholic cooperation with the Weimar government, a position that brought him into serious conflict with the future, postwar German chancellor Konrad Adenauer (1876–1967) at the Munich Catholics Convention in 1922. Second, according to Faulhaber's memorandum, Hitler had made it his life's work "to 'crush' *Marxism* in whatever form, particularly Communism as an economic and state principle." Finally, he intended to overthrow the capitalistic economic order and "create *work and bread*," thereby "de-proletarianizing" the working class.

In four considerably more detailed points in the second half of the memorandum, Faulhaber laid out what was not praiseworthy about Hitler. First, "he preaches *wild hatred* and the *methods of violence* instead of fighting with spiritual weapons." He was particularly critical of the persecution of "Catholic men of high achievement," such as the former Center Party chancellor Marx or Bavarian Minister President Held, "merely because they belong to the Center or to the Bavarian People's Party." Although the Munich cardinal admitted that the coalition between the Center and the SPD had "obscured the clear Catholic line," it had only been "a tactical and not a principled association." Second, Hitler preached "*the cult of race* and with it . . . the rejection of Christianity as a Jewish import . . . and war with other races." With regard to religious attitudes, which Faulhaber explored in his third point, his memorandum evinces clear skepticism. Hitler's "friend" Goebbels (1897–1945), a Catholic, had married a divorced Protestant woman, and the head of the SA, Ernst Röhm (1887–1934), was known to be a "notorious homosexual." About Hitler himself, he wrote, "It must be noted that since he became Reich chancellor he no longer employs frenzied language against Jews and capitalism." Hitler's speeches were "psychologically attuned to the souls of workers and peasants," and Faulhaber, who was known for the pathos of his sermons, had to admit that they were genuine "masterpieces."

The third part of his memorandum dealt with Pacelli's actual question, and he tried to clarify "what had led to conflict with the bishops." "National Socialism wants to be a new 'worldview,' a new religion, and not just a new politics." Even though Hitler had broken with Ludendorff's "paganism and hatred of Christianity," it all came down to whether Germany "would remain Christian or become old-Germanic and pagan." For Faulhaber the nature of National Socialism as a political religion that intended to replace Christianity could be seen in a number of points, which he listed for Pacelli. These included the rejection of the Old Testament and the history of the people of Israel as an integral component of biblical history and of Christianity; paragraph 24 of the NSDAP program, which sought to replace Christian morality with Germanic morality; tolerance for Alfred Rosenberg's diatribes, in which "Christianity is labeled as the greatest misfortune" and Jesus Christ "is maligned as 'the son of the Jewess'"; and finally Hitler's "curse of the triad of Socialism, Church, and freemasonry." Faulhaber was particularly concerned about the retention of the Catholic schools. He feared that they would be transformed into nondenominational schools, so-called Gemeinschaftsschulen: "In many external respects such as the uniform and the Hitler salute, National Socialism is a copy of Fascism. But whereas the Italian people are Catholic, all great movements in Germany involve Protestant instincts. The Catholic clergy has followed the instructions of the bishops with praiseworthy discipline; Protestant circles have in large numbers turned to National Socialism, and many hope that the Reformation of the sixteenth century will now be implemented to the point of separation from Rome. This is why the German bishops warned against National Socialism." It was important, however, to distinguish between the functionaries of the party, who believed in the entire Nazi program, and the "followers," who were mainly interested in the political and economic aspects, particularly in work and bread. The individual German dioceses had in practice handled the matter in different ways. Whereas in Würzburg and Mainz all members of the NSDAP were denied a Church burial, this level of exclusion occurred in Munich or Freiburg only if there were contributing canonical impediments such as bigamy or the desire for cremation.

In principle, Faulhaber was open to a retraction of the bishops' condemnations. He formulated the following conditions to Pacelli: "If the new government demonstrates in fact that the fears of the bishops were unfounded—if in addition the new government continues to remain strong in the battle against advancing Bolshevism and public immorality, the bishops will gladly give up their distrust of the party and, for example, permit churchgoing in closed ranks, which up to now was viewed as a demonstration and therefore forbidden, and permit the swastika flag at Church burials."

The bishops' condemnations of National Socialism appeared to have become more of a problem in Bavaria during March 1933. In any case, the Bavarian chargé d'affaires to the Holy See repeatedly confronted Pacelli with this issue. For example, in his audience of March 27, Groenesteyn brought up the opinions of Albrecht of Bavaria (1905–1996), the heir to the throne, who, like his father, Crown Prince Rupprecht, saw "no way other than to join the Hitler movement in order to save Germany from Communism, which is more widespread here than we had thought." In the end, Hitler's government declaration was very well received, "but naturally there are conflicts of conscience with regard to the declarations of the bishops." For this reason, Crown Prince Rupprecht and his closest circles sought an assurance from the Holy See that Catholic cooperation with the NSDAP was morally permissible. Pacelli's answer was clear: "I answered the minister that the declaration in parliament was, in my opinion, satisfactory, particularly with regard to the Catholic Church; but as far as questions of conscience are concerned, I answered that I cannot anticipate the decision of the bishops."[82]

In other words, Rome was satisfied by Hitler's declaration of March 23, 1933. The assurances of the Reich chancellor to view both "Christian confessions" as "the most important factors in the maintenance of our national identity," to respect the concordats negotiated between the Holy See and the German states, and to permit and ensure "the influence to which the Christian confessions are entitled in school and education," met with complete assent in the Curia. The pope and his cardinal secretary of state probably viewed Hitler's intention "to maintain and further friendly relations with the Holy See" with particular satisfaction.[83] When Pius XI spoke with Pacelli on March 25, he praised the Reich chancellor's "good declaration."[84] However, the ban on working with the National Socialists could be retracted only by those who had repeatedly pronounced it since 1930, the German bishops themselves. Both Pacelli and Pius XI would have agreed with the content of such a step by the bishops.

On March 28, 1933, Albrecht of Bavaria came to the Vatican and was received by Pacelli. He, like Groenesteyn the day before, asked the secretary of state specifically about ecclesiastical "permission for Catholics to join the movement." This permission was all the more important because radical elements were attempting to dominate Hitler, and it would benefit the Church if "the good" were able to exert an influence on the Reich chancellor. "I answered," Pacelli noted, "that the government declaration before parliament had been received with satisfaction as far as the desire for good relations with the Holy See, and the continued validity of the concordats with the states, and the battle against atheistic organizations were concerned, and *L'Osservatore Romano* had printed this." The cardinal secretary of state thus concluded that the assumption of governmental responsibility and Hitler's declaration before parliament "seemed to confirm a change in the old attitude, as it had been expressed in Rosenberg's writings in particular." Naturally, however, the Holy See could not anticipate the decision of the German bishops—a position for which Albrecht expressed understanding. In addition, Albrecht made clear that Crown Prince Rupprecht and the House of Wittelsbach had initially shown no liking for Hitler. In the present situation, however, the führer was "the last means for opposing the invasion of Communism, which had grown to much greater proportions than one ever could have imagined." This argument would have fallen on fertile ground with Pacelli, even though the actual danger of a Communist takeover in Bavaria was most likely small—probably little more than a right-wing phantasmagoria. Albrecht was even prepared to sacrifice Bavaria's extensive independence from Berlin and the federal structure of the Reich on the altar of a joint anti-Communist entente: "The loss of Bavaria's autonomy is a small evil in comparison to Communism, which is the greatest danger."[85]

Pacelli also discussed this topic with the pope that day. The actual occasion was Orsenigo's report of March 24, 1933, but his discussion with Albrecht was undoubtedly on his mind as well. The nuncio started with a detailed report about Hitler's government declaration, which had been "warmly received by the Catholics as well." In particular, he called attention to the context in which Hitler's statements were made, which he characterized as "a programmatic speech before the vote on extraordinary powers, which could only be granted with the consent of the Center." He further wrote, "I assume that the negotiations conducted recently by Prelate Kaas, to secure the Center's votes for the government, which absolutely must have them in order to achieve the two-thirds majority needed for the adoption of extraordinary powers, influenced the government, particularly with regard to the concordats." There is, however, no evidence in this report that the nuncio attempted to influence negotiations between the Center and the government. The use of the term "concordats" in the plural clearly relates to the three concordats with the states of Bavaria, Prussia, and Baden, which Hitler had approved in spite of the planned coordination of the German states. Orsenigo did not allude to a Reichskonkordat, which would have played a role in these negotiations.

Interestingly, neither the Enabling Act nor the role of the Center came up in Pacelli's discussion of this nuncial report with the pope. The only matter they did talk about was the final section of Orsenigo's letter, in which he reported on a discussion with Göring. The minister had made clear "that the government was very desirous that the question of the episcopate's condemnation of the National Socialist movement be resolved, and that one would gladly avail oneself of the assistance of the apostolic nuncio. Although that would certainly have positive effects on the prestige of the Holy See, it could increase the sensitivity of the episcopate. If I were actually to be called on, I would try to avoid both Scylla and Charybdis."[86]

Pius XI did not, however, grant his nuncio's wish. In order to avoid the difficulties discussed by Orsenigo, the pope commissioned his cardinal secretary of state to instruct the nuncio to report immediately the intentions of the German bishops in this matter. However, he firmly rejected any direct intervention by the Holy See or its onsite representative. "Intervention by the pope is neither necessary nor advisable," Pacelli noted at the audience. The nuncio should, though, speak with the bishops confidentially, as the matter was urgent and necessary owing to Hitler's assurances. The old curial political principle that new situations require new decisions had to be honored, "but the bishops' path may not be blocked."[87]

Pius XI was taking the exact same position that Pacelli had twice taken with the Bavarian ambassador and Albrecht of Bavaria. This makes clear that the initiative to lift the bishops' admonitions against National Socialism must have come from the German bishops themselves and not from the Curia. Rome had not been informed in advance, and Pacelli had not ordered this step. Nor could the prospect that such a gain in prestige would improve the cards of the Holy See in the upcoming discussions with Hitler's government have motivated either the pope or his secretary of state to play an active role in this delicate matter. On the contrary, in spite of Faulhaber's memorandum to the Curia, which they had in hand, more precise information was needed about the intentions of the German bishops. The pope would in principle have approved of a retraction of the condemnation of National Socialism, and, in any case, he sounded out the episcopate in this regard at most indirectly and confidentially.

However, the instruction to Orsenigo to discuss a retraction confidentially with the bishops could no longer have had any effect. In his report of March 26, which Pacelli did not yet have on March 28, Orsenigo reported on an initiative—which "will certainly please Your Most Reverend Eminence"—of the chairman of the Fulda Conference of Bishops, Cardinal Bertram, regarding a revision to the position of the episcopate. The primary reason was Hitler's "reassuring speech"; however, the nuncio perceived that the "real and deciding reason" was the "growing predilection" for the new regime in Catholic circles as well, leading the bishops to fear a "dam break," as Thomas Brechenmacher aptly put it. But Orsenigo vehemently criticized the one-sided approach of the bishops. Instead of contacting the government and setting clear conditions, the episcopate had preferred to formulate a declaration "full of hope." "Because there were no negotiations, it was impossible to consider concessions as a quid pro quo." In any case, the government had on all occasions expressed the "burning desire that the condemnation of National Socialism pronounced by the bishops be lifted. Whether this desire reflects a love of peace alone, or is aimed at paving the way for a mass influx of Catholics into the ranks of Hitlerism," could hardly be discerned at that time, as the nuncio noted critically.[88] Three days later, on March 29, after the declaration of the bishops had been published, Orsenigo wrote to Rome, "My efforts were superfluous."[89]

It turns out that on the day Pacelli discussed this topic with Pius XI, March 28, Cardinal Bertram had published a "proclamation by the German bishops about their stance toward National Socialism" in which he retracted the declaration of irreconcilability between Catholicism and National Socialism. The proclamation stated that the German bishops had over the past several years "on cogent grounds taken a rejecting stance toward the National Socialist movement through bans and admonitions, which would remain in effect for as long as and to the extent that these conditions continue." After Hitler's government declaration, the bishops believed that they could "entertain trust" that the "general bans and admonitions" against National Socialism "no longer need be viewed as necessary" without, however, "lifting the earlier condemnation of certain religious and moral errors."[90]

On March 31, 1933, the pope and the cardinal secretary of state discussed this *dichiarazione* (declaration) in detail. It was the first of seven agenda items at this audience. A decision was made to publish the complete text in *L'Osservatore Romano.* "The Holy Father has . . . declared himself to be in agreement with the declaration of the episcopate and considers it good," Pacelli noted, before continuing, "It is good that we do not absent ourselves."[91]

When on the same day, during an audience, the Bavarian ambassador Groenesteyn raised the question of the German bishops' declaration, he expressed the opinion that he had found it a little "confining and confusing and would have preferred a 'freer' version," whereupon the cardinal secretary of state expressed cautious, one might say diplomatic, criticism of the starry-eyed approach taken by the German episcopate: "I told him that in my opinion and as far as I can judge, it would have been better if the bishops had demanded clear statements from the government about certain points" before they retracted their condemnation of National Socialism. If such guarantees had been made, according to the secretary of state, the declaration could have been published much earlier.[92] In other words, the condemnation of National Socialism, which was so important to its leaders, and which permitted Catholics to join the NSDAP without breaking with the Church, was lifted—and nothing given in return. Pacelli, the chief Vatican diplomat, would have driven a much harder bargain. While the declaration was correct in principle, it should have been used as a political bargaining chip in exchange for real concessions. Here, Pacelli was in almost full agreement with his successor in Berlin, which was not always the case. But the bishops had clearly missed their chance. Now the Church would have to make the best of it. Not least for this reason the secretary of state concluded about his audience with the pope that day that now the nuncios in Munich and Berlin could again take up direct dealings with the representatives of the government, which would enable them to harvest the "fruits of this abnormal situation."[93] He may also have had in mind the first phase of Hitler's seizure of power, made possible by the Enabling Act and the retraction of the bishops' declaration.

It is unclear whether Pacelli was repeating an assertion by the pope or whether this represented his own evaluation. Both men would, however, be sorely disappointed in their expectation of a normalized relationship with the National Socialists. The real challenges for the Curia, the pope, and his cardinal secretary of state were yet to come. Their supposed shield against the devil, Stalin and Communism, would all too soon be revealed as Beelzebub.

The Reichskonkordat, or the Pistol at the Cardinal Secretary of State's Head

Unfortunately, the files from the Vatican Secret Archives that have been made accessible since 2003 and 2006 tell us virtually nothing about the Reichskonkordat. A thorough analysis of the sources, however, indicates that Ludwig Volk (1926–1984) had been able to use all the pertinent curial documents, though without their final signature, in his two ground-breaking publications on the subject, the comprehensive edition of the *Kirchliche Akten über die Reichskonkordatsverhandlungen* [Church files on the Reichskonkordat negotiations] of 1969, and his monograph *Das Reichskonkordat,* published in 1972. Volk's interpretations based on the sources, and particularly those of Konrad Repgen, retain their validity with regard to the crucial question of Rome's role in the three critical events in March and April 1933: the Curia had not been directly involved in the Center Party's consent to the Enabling Act, in the declaration by the bishops, or in the idea of a Reichskonkordat. There is no evidence that the initiative for any of these steps came from Rome. The "German" aspects of the Scholder-Repgen controversy are not, however, touched by this "Roman" insight. Whether the German government's offer to the Curia of a concordat came from Hitler or from Vice-Chancellor Papen is probably of secondary importance. Nor does the question of who in Germany learned about the Reichskonkordat plans from whom and when have any bearing on the core question of the controversy—did Pacelli pull the strings in the background? Moreover, Scholder's objection that Volk relied on too late a date for his analysis of the files because for him "the definitive authorization by Papen for concordat negotiations could have occurred only after March 28" is of no importance in the matter.[94] Furthermore, the Vatican documents since Pacelli's assumption of office, in the spring of 1930, up to the end of March 1933, prove that Rome had not made this connection before March 28 either.

Nor were Adolf Cardinal Bertram, the chairman of the German Conference of Bishops, and with him the German episcopate, simply marionettes manipulated by a coldly calculating Eugenio Pacelli. The same goes for Prelate Ludwig Kaas and the Center Party faction in the German parliament. Both the bishops in their magisterial appraisal of National Socialism as a political party and as a religious worldview, and the Center Party representatives in casting their votes for the Enabling Act, acted completely independently. Instructions from Rome did not influence their moves. Pacelli made some entries in his private diary to the effect that he had turned down several requests by ambassadors and concerned Catholics for the Holy See to exert influence on the Center and the German bishops. In the end, he agreed with the actions of the bishops and the Center because he believed that they enabled the Church in Germany to avoid being sidelined. But Pacelli felt that Hitler had received the support of Catholics with the blessings of the bishops. His admonition to the German bishops, sent via the Munich nunciature on March 29, 1933, makes this very clear. New guidelines regarding the position taken by Catholics vis-à-vis National Socialism would have to be developed by the bishops "only with the requisite caution and restraint."[95] Unfortunately, this admonition came too late.

If Pacelli had had his way, if he had pulled all the strings, Hitler would have paid a heavy price for the Center's consent to the Enabling Act and the bishops' retraction of their condemnation. The cardinal secretary of state would have dictated hard conditions for the concessions that Hitler was so eager to get from the Church. Instead of hoping for a mere promise, he would have demanded clear, legally binding agreements. A Reichskonkordat would have provided the ideal conditions for such agreements, if it had been part of a quid pro quo involving the Enabling Act and the bishops' declaration of March 28—if Rome had known of such a deal, and if Pacelli had wielded influence over the bishops and the Center Party. Pacelli the diplomat would have insisted on the following sequence if he had been intent on a package solution. First, ratification of a Reichskonkordat with assurances for Catholic pastoral care, confessional schools, and Catholic associations and organizations; second, in return, consent to the Enabling Act by the Center Party, and retraction of the irreconcilability declaration by the bishops.

But up to April 8, 1933, Vatican sources never mentioned a concordat between the Holy See and Germany. It did not emerge as a concept until that date, in a report from Orsenigo to Pacelli. With an eye toward Papen's trip to Rome, Orsenigo had spoken in generalities about an agreement on April 2, mentioning that the vice-chancellor was seeking an audience with Pacelli in order to discuss with him "several points regarding the negotiations between the Holy See and Germany." Orsenigo was thinking about the controversial issues of pastoral care in the military, the possible abolition of forced civil marriage, and the confessional schools.[96] On April 8, he was talking about "potential negotiations about a concordat with the Reich" in relation to Papen's trip to Rome.[97]

And in fact, Papen's offer quickly set in motion negotiations for a concordat between the Holy See and the German government, the details of which cannot be gone into here. The Vatican files, and particularly the audiences with Pius XI, show that the pope was regularly informed of the status of the negotiations by his secretary of state. Pius XI was intensely involved in individual formulations during the various iterations of the text of the concordat.[98] Two points that were crucial to both partners soon crystallized, which in the end led to a sort of quid pro quo. For the Catholic Church, apart from protecting the Catholic confessional schools, which was actually the subject of Article 23 of the Reichskonkordat, what was most important was to ensure the continued existence of Catholic associations and organizations, which were the backbone of German Catholic life. Only if these institutions were exempted from the government's policy of forced coordination with Nazi principles could German Catholicism survive a totalitarian state as an independent and halfway intact institution. What was most important to Hitler and the National Socialists, by contrast, was to rid themselves of all inconvenient political competition, which the Catholic parties (the Center and the BVP) continued to be after the elections of March 1933. Catholicism as a political force needed to be eliminated. The model for this would be the Italian concordat, the Lateran Pacts, which the Holy See had concluded with the Fascist state in 1929. Because the Center Party was so dependent on the so-called Center prelates, and their leadership in parliament at the national and state levels had largely been recruited from the ranks of the clergy since the end of the 1920s, Hitler was keen to negotiate a depoliticization clause that forbade clerics to be involved in any political parties. This initial position could have provided the opportunity to work out a "fair" compromise between the state and the Church. If the Curia were prepared to agree to the depoliticization clause and sacrifice the Center Party, thereby clearing the way for Hitler's one-party state, the Reich chancellor would have guaranteed the continued existence of Catholic organizations in Germany, excluding this slice of German society from National Socialist *Gleichschaltung*. Both sides—the Roman Curia and the German government—referenced the Italian model, which had been working acceptably until 1933. In Italy, the Church's renunciation of a Catholic party had eliminated Mussolini's political competition, and this enabled Pius XI to develop Catholic Action as a religious organization.

Obviously, high-ranking members of the Curia expected a similar outcome with National Socialism. Among them was Pietro Gasparri, Pacelli's predecessor as cardinal secretary of state, who had been the architect of the Lateran Pacts. On June 30, 1933, when the Vatican was deliberating about how to press forward with the Reichskonkordat, Gasparri set down in writing how he believed the Curia should proceed so long as Hitler did not declare war "on the Holy See or the Catholic hierarchy in Germany":

(1) The Holy See and the Catholic hierarchy in Germany are to stop condemning the Hitler party;

(2) If Hitler intends to dissolve the Catholic Center Party *as a political party,* this should be acceded to without much ado;

(3) German Catholics should be free to belong to the Hitler party just as Italy's Catholics are free to join the Fascist Party;

(4) Germany's Catholics should, by the same token, be free not to join the Hitler party; all within legal limits, of course, just as is the case with Italy's Catholics with regard to the Fascist Party.

I am of the opinion that the Hitler party corresponds to the national feeling in Germany. Because of this, a political-religious battle in Germany around Hitlerism is to be avoided at all costs, particularly while His Eminence Pacelli is secretary of state.[99]

The subtext of this statement is that a new Kulturkampf in Germany was to be avoided at all cost. Here Pacelli was in complete agreement with his predecessor. What Pacelli was not willing to do was to capitulate on all fronts, as Gasparri was counseling, as a way of denying the National Socialists any pretext for attacking the Church. Rather, he saw the dissolution of the Center Party as a political bargaining chip for the clause in the Reichskonkordat protecting Catholic associations. However, the Catholic party thwarted his plans. The Center Party was unable to withstand the powerful pressure exerted on it by the National Socialists, and it dissolved itself on July 5, 1933—before the Reichskonkordat was ready to be signed. This removed Pacelli's trump card. Rumors that the Vatican was behind this move have absolutely no basis in fact and fail the test of logic. The cardinal secretary of state was very clear, in a letter to his former aide in the Munich nunciature, Lorenzo Schioppa (1871–1935), who was now internuncio in the Netherlands: the Center Party and the Bavarian People's Party had "dissolved on their own initiative completely independent of a decision by the Holy See." Pacelli had always assumed that both parties would "at least wait until the Reichskonkordat was ratified before dissolving." He only read about their action in the newspaper.[100]

As a result, Pacelli was forced to come to an agreement quickly in order to save what was left of the article protecting Catholic associations now that the depoliticization clause was worthless. The critical weakness of Article 31 resulted from the haste into which the Vatican felt itself forced. In the end, this article "protects those Catholic organizations and associations that serve exclusively religious, cultural, and charitable purposes, and are as such subject to Church authorities . . . in their organization and their activity." Catholic associations which, in addition, "also serve social or professional purposes," would also enjoy protection under Article 31, "to the extent they guarantee that their activities occur outside all political parties." The grave problem with this agreement was that the Curia was unable to press for a list as an integral part of the concordat of Catholic organizations and associations to which protection would be extended. The formulation, "The determination of which organizations and associations fall under the provisions of this article are subject to agreements to be negotiated between the Reich government and the German episcopate," would soon enough reveal its pitfalls. In fact, such a list was never compiled. It would always be a matter of interpretation where the religious sphere ended and the political began. Article 32, which contained the actual incentive for the National Socialists to conclude a concordat with the Holy See, and which was modeled after the Italian version, established that the Holy See would issue decrees "that rule out membership in political parties and activity in such parties for clergy and members of orders." But once the Center Party dissolved itself, the political effect of this decree was more or less moot.[101]

The Reichskonkordat was initialed on July 8 and signed on July 20. It gave Hitler's government its first agreement under international law and represented a not inconsiderable foreign policy success. If the Holy See, as the moral power in the world, could conclude agreements with the National Socialists, then what stood in the way of secular states doing the same? However, Pacelli repeatedly made clear that the conclusion of the Reichskonkordat in no way implied recognition by the Curia of National Socialist ideology as such. Rather, it should be seen in light of the tradition of the Holy See of negotiating with all partners—including totalitarian systems—to protect the Church and its mission of pastoral care. The cardinal secretary of state may well have been recalling his own efforts over many years to come to an agreement with Stalin's Russia while he was nuncio in Berlin. Pacelli had offered the Soviet Union diplomatic recognition no fewer than three times—if the regime were prepared to concede a minimum of religious freedom and guarantees of pastoral care. And three times the Soviet leadership rejected these diplomatic feelers. Here, too, an agreement would have implied no endorsement of Bolshevik ideology. Pius XI's statement that he would negotiate with the devil in person to save a single soul in need is significant in this regard.

In the context of the signing of the Reichskonkordat, Pacelli made clear in several letters—including a confidential letter to Schioppa—that the

The signing of the Reichskonkordat. From left: Prelate Ludwig Kaas, Vice-Chancellor Franz von Papen, Archbishop Giuseppe Pizzardo, Cardinal Secretary of State Eugenio Pacelli, Prelate Alfredo Ottaviani, Assistant Secretary of State Rudolf Buttmann of the Reich Ministry of the Interior, Monsignore Giovanni Battista Montini (the future Pope Paul VI), and Counselor of Embassy Eugen Klee, the chargé d'affaires at the Vatican.

(The Granger Collection, New York)

initiative had come from the German government, not from Rome. But he also wrote that, given "the new political situation that has developed in Germany, without the Holy See having played even the slightest part in it, there was no other way to secure the rights and claims of the Catholic Church in a state that is as important as Germany with twenty million faithful than by means of a concordat." The German episcopate had unanimously signaled to him that a Reichskonkordat was the "last hope for avoiding a 'Kulturkampf,' much worse than in Bismarck's times."[102] The cardinal secretary of state also stressed to English chargé d'affaires Ivone Kirkpatrick (1897–1964) the importance of spiritual welfare in concluding the concordat. The "spiritual welfare" had been "the first and, indeed, the only consideration." Kirkpatrick reported to his government that Pacelli had made absolutely "no effort to conceal his disgust at the proceedings of Herr Hitler's Government"; rather, "Cardinal Pacelli equally deplored the action of the German Government at home, their persecution of the Jews, their proceedings against political opponents, the reign of terror to which the whole nation was subjected." Pacelli vigorously opposed the view that "Herr Hitler would settle down" and "revert to more normal methods of government" after the end of the revolutionary seizure of power. As Kirkpatrick noted, he saw no grounds "for such easy optimism."[103] In his memoir, which was published in 1959, the British diplomat retrospectively underscored Pacelli's critical assessment of Hitler. Pacelli, whom he describes as "particularly interested in and well informed about Germany," responded in the negative when asked whether the responsibilities of governing would have a moderating effect on Hitler: "We shall see that with every year power will make him more extreme and difficult to deal with."[104] In his report to London in 1933, Kirkpatrick addressed the crucial point: "These reflections on the iniquity of Germany led the Cardinal to explain apologetically how it was that he had signed a concordat with such people. A pistol, he said, had been pointed at his head and he had had no alternative." He emphasized that "he had to choose between an agreement on their lines and the virtual elimination of the Catholic Church in the Reich." Moreover, "he was given no more than a week to make up his mind."[105]

Even if some of the "German" details in connection with the Reichskonkordat remain unsettled, and even though it is arguable who derived the greatest benefit from the Reichskonkordat, both long-term and short-term, there is no doubt that this agreement further opened the floodgates for the involvement of German Catholics in the National Socialist state. At the same time, the Reichskonkordat contributed to preventing German Catholicism from being coordinated by National Socialism. It served as a sort of forward defensive wall, which the National Socialists continually attempted to chip away over the next twelve years of their regime. They never completely succeeded. The Catholic Church in Germany was the only large-scale social institution that Hitler never managed to co-opt. In contrast to the Protestant Church, Catholicism never developed a phenomenon like the "German Christians," who made National Socialist principles such as the Aryan paragraphs and their application keystones of their church and its services. Nor did there develop a split between Catholics who were loyal to and those who were critical of the regime, as occurred in German Protestantism.

The Reichskonkordat was a pact with the devil—no one had any illusions about that fact in Rome—but it guaranteed pastoral care and the continued existence of the Catholic Church during the Third Reich. The Curia itself did not make this deal by having the Center Party consent to the Enabling Act or by lifting the condemnation of National Socialism. The German Church bears sole responsibility for these steps. But is there not another price—as has often been asserted—that the Vatican has had to pay for the years since 1933 in terms of its "silence" in the face of the persecution of the Jews? The new sources enable fresh insights into the time between 1933 and early 1939. What was known in Rome, and when, about the persecution of the Jews by the Nazis? How did the Curia think about the matter internally? Why did the Vatican never abrogate the pact with the devil in order to defend the human rights of all those who were persecuted, even—and particularly—the Jews? The transition to business as usual, to "normality," in dealing with National Socialism, which Pacelli had dreamed of in early April 1933, never took place. As we know, the opposite occurred. An unremitting state of emergency was declared, a unique machinery of persecution and destruction was set in motion. The Vatican was faced with one of the greatest challenges in its history.

Four

Molto Delicato?

The Roman Curia and the Persecution of the Jews
(1933–1939)

On April 1, 1933, while the SA *(Sturmabteilung)* was supervising the boy-cott of Jewish stores in the German Reich, Pope Pius XI and his cardinal secretary of state, Eugenio Pacelli, were meeting as usual to discuss the most important topics relating to Church policies.[1] At the top of their agenda that day was the anti-Semitism of the new rulers in Germany. A number of high-level Jewish dignitaries had informed the pope of "anti-Semitic excesses in Germany." Pius XI instructed his cardinal secretary of state to have Berlin Nuncio Cesare Orsenigo sound out whether the Holy See could do something about the situation, and if so, what. After the audience, Pacelli added in square brackets, "The day may come when we will have to be able to say that something was done about this matter"—a crucial sentence given that Eugenio Pacelli would become Pope Pius XII in 1939. Because he never made any public and explicit statements about the Holocaust during World War II, critics such as John Cornwell have referred to him as "Hitler's pope."

Ever since the first performance of Rolf Hochhuth's play *The Deputy,* on February 20, 1963, in Berlin, the controversy about the role of the Church and the pope in the Shoah has become ever more heated. Critics claim that by failing to denounce publicly the systematic murder of more than six million Jews, even though he knew about the gas chambers at

Auschwitz and other extermination camps, Pius XII failed in his moral obligation as supreme protector of human rights. Defenders of the pope question the consequences that such a public denunciation would have had. Pointing to the protest of the Dutch bishops in 1942, which led not to a drop in the deportations of Jews but rather to an increase, costing Edith Stein among many others their lives, Pius XII's defenders claim that his "silence" or the fact that he was never explicit in his statements was the correct approach. "For him, the alternatives were not simply between 'speaking out or remaining silent,'" Konrad Repgen noted. "The question, rather, was how clear *must* be the word that is demanded of the office, and how concrete *may* it be once the consequences are weighed."[2] The pope delivered a Christmas appeal in 1942 in which he expressly proclaimed the fundamental inalienable rights of all people. He also remembered the hundreds of thousands of people who, "through no fault of their own, in part merely because of their nationality or race," were subjected to a "fast or slow death." These statements, he believed, were the outer limits of what he could say without risking the Curia's diplomatic standing and the ability to continue working to save the Jews.[3]

But the so-called final solution of the Jewish question was not the first context in which the pope and the Curia were accused of silence. Nor was this criticism first raised after the fact. Rather, as early as the spring of 1933, immediately after Hitler's seizure of power, numerous Jews and non-Jews turned directly to Pius XI, asking him to condemn publicly the persecution of the Jewish people. This meant that the Curia had been more than well informed through a variety of channels of what was going on in the Reich. Only a few days after the audience mentioned above, on April 4, 1933, Pacelli at the pope's behest instructed Orsenigo to look into the possibilities for intervening against the "anti-Semitic excesses." The cardinal secretary of state's reasons for engaging the Roman Curia in this question are particularly interesting: "It is in the tradition of the Holy See to fulfill its universal mission of peace and love for all human beings, regardless of their social status or the religion to which they belong."[4] With this statement, Pacelli had acknowledged in principle the responsibility of the Catholic Church as advocate for and protector of human rights.

Orsenigo's response, dated April 8, was disillusioning, however. He reported on the Law for the Restoration of the Professional Civil Service *(Gesetz zur Wiederherstellung des Berufsbeamtentums),* which had been decreed the day before. This law contained the so-called Aryan paragraphs that enabled the regime to remove individuals of Jewish extraction from the civil service, even those whose ancestors had converted to Christianity. The nuncio concluded, "Yesterday, the anti-Semitic fight took on an official governmental character. Any intervention by the representative of the Holy See would be tantamount to a protest against a legal act of the German state." It would have been unthinkable for a diplomatic representative of the Holy See to involve himself in the domestic affairs of a state to which he was accredited. Moreover, Orsenigo continued, because the Holy See had not in years past lodged official protests against "anti-German propaganda," it could not now do anything about the persecution of the Jews, because this would give the impression that the Church was "more sensitive toward the Hebrew cause than toward the German."[5] As a result, he suggested that the Vatican stay out of the "Jewish question" and leave the matter to the German bishops.

Two days later, in fact, Cardinal Schulte of Cologne, Archbishop Kaspar Klein (1865–1941) of Paderborn, and Bishop Berning of Osnabrück issued a declaration, which Orsenigo immediately sent to Rome. It stated, among other things, "Filled with the most ardent love for their Fatherland, whose national preeminence they have always promoted with all their strength, the bishops observe with the deepest sense of concern and worry how these days of national ascendancy have simultaneously become undeserved days of the most severe and bitter suffering for many loyal citizens, among them also conscientious officials."[6] Orsenigo believed, as he wrote to Pacelli, that the use of the phrase "loyal citizens" could "also be read as an allusion to the Jews." Although numerous exceptions were being made to the Aryan paragraphs, "unfortunately, the anti-Semitic principle has been accepted and sanctioned by the entire government," and "unfortunately this fact will adhere as a black mark of infamy to the opening pages of the history penned by German National Socialism, which is not otherwise without merit."[7] In spite of Orsenigo's evident admiration for the National Socialist seizure of power in Germany, he nonetheless condemned the persecution of the Jews in unambiguous terms. He was not, however, prepared to intervene on their behalf. He and Cardinal Secretary of State Pacelli once again left the talking to the bishops; but they, too, in their tortuous phrasings advocated only for converted Jews. Noting that Mussolini had extracted a promise from Hitler not to indulge in an "anti-Semitic campaign," the nuncio believed that given the high level of influence that, according to the Curia, "Il Duce" had on Hitler, the matter would take care of itself.[8]

On April 10, Cardinal Faulhaber turned to Pacelli and explained to him why the bishops, like the Vatican, were not intervening on behalf of the Jews, and why they remained silent in the face of measures taken by the National Socialists: "We bishops are currently grappling with the question of why the Catholic Church is not intervening on behalf of the Jews, as has so often happened in the history of the Church. It is currently not possible because the battle against the Jews would at the same time become a battle against the Catholics, and because the Jews are able to help themselves, as the rapid termination of the boycott shows." In addition, the Jews had not stood by the Catholics during the Kulturkampf. The Munich cardinal made a cogent case that the Church should advocate primarily for Jews who had converted to Catholicism: "It is particularly unjust and painful that in this campaign against the Jews, there are those who have been baptized for ten and twenty years and are good Catholics, some of whom even had Catholic parents, who nonetheless count as Jews in a legal sense and will lose their positions as doctors or as lawyers."[9] This statement left precious little of the universal mission of salvation of the Catholic Church as protector and advocate of all people and defender of human rights.

Edith Stein's Letter to Pius XI

This did not mark an end to the issue of the persecution of the Jews in Germany for Pacelli or the Roman Curia. Rather, during the spring and summer of 1933, Pius XI received numerous requests, authored by Jews and non-Jews, pleading with him to speak out. Since the opening of the archives in February 2003, one piece of correspondence in particular has gained worldwide attention, the letter sent by Edith Stein (1891–1942). Although the existence of this letter had long been known, it could now for the first time be read and the fate of this petition tracked. It should be noted that the significance of this letter has on occasion been overestimated, especially in the press, because journalists have tended to assume that the letter of a saint—Edith Stein was canonized by John Paul II on October 11, 1998—would have been given top priority by Pius XI and been tantamount to a sort of instruction.

This view, however, ignores the historical realities. In the spring of 1933, Edith Stein was not a person of importance. She had at the time been teaching for barely a year as a lecturer at the German Institute for Scientific Pedagogy in Münster, in Westphalia, and was largely unknown. Al-

Edith Stein wrote to Pius XI "as a child of the Jewish people."
(CH Beck Verlag)

though she had already led an active life up to then, she was a complete unknown in Rome. Born into a Jewish family in Breslau on October 12, 1891, she converted to Catholicism on January 1, 1922. This step was preceded by years of alienation from the Jewish beliefs of her childhood, which, according to Hanna-Barbara Gerl-Falkovitz, may be characterized as an "atheistic" phase in her life. After studies at the universities of Göttingen, Breslau, and Freiburg, and a brilliant doctoral dissertation written in 1916 under the philosopher Edmund Husserl (1859–1938), whose assistant she became, Stein had a conversion experience during the summer of 1921 while reading the autobiography of St. Teresa of Avila, which led her to join the Catholic Church. As a woman Stein could not have pursued a university career, so she decided to teach history and German from 1923 to 1931 at a Dominican girls school in Speyer. During those years, she frequently considered entering a cloister. However, Raphael Walzer (1888–1966), the arch-abbot of the Beuron Benedictine congregation, with whom she was friends, convinced her to lecture at the institute in Münster.

Because Edith Stein feared that a letter from an unimportant lecturer and converted Jew from Münster would get lost in the machinery of the Roman Curia and never reach its addressee, the pope, she availed herself of a "letter carrier" to whom they would have to give the courtesy of an answer, namely, the arch-abbot from Beuron. Stein's letter is undated, but it was probably written in early April 1933. On April 7, she had traveled to Beuron to meet with Walzer and to discuss the matter with him as her confessor. She typed the text at the abbey. Walzer's cover letter to Pacelli was dated April 12, 1933.[10] The petitioner, wrote Walzer, had pleaded with him to convey the enclosed letter to the Holy Father. Edith Stein, he continued, was well known to him and in German Catholic circles generally as a woman of deep faith who led an exemplary life. She was, in addition, renowned in the field of Catholic scholarship. The arch-abbot urged Pacelli to support Stein's request, which Walzer had made his own. If intelligent and contemplative men did not intervene, he noted in this cover letter, Germany and the Catholic Church would be in grave danger: "My only hope in this world is the Holy Apostolic See!"

"Holy Father!" Edith Stein's letter begins, "As a child of the Jewish people who, by the grace of God, for the past eleven years has been a child of the Catholic Church, I dare to speak to the Father of Christianity about that which oppresses millions of Germans."[11] There follows a forceful description of the persecution of the Jews and its consequences. Stein apparently based her observations on events in Münster:

> For weeks we have seen deeds perpetrated in Germany which mock any sense of justice and humanity, not to mention love of neighbor. For years the leaders of National Socialism have been preaching hatred of the Jews. Now that they have seized the power of government and armed their followers, among them proven criminal elements, this seed of hatred has germinated. The government has only recently admitted that excesses have occurred. To what extent, we cannot tell, because public opinion is being gagged. However, judging by what I have learned from personal relations, it is in no way a matter of singular exceptional cases. Under pressure from reactions abroad, the government has turned to "milder" methods. It has issued the watchword "no Jew shall have even one hair on his head harmed." But through boycott measures—by robbing people of their livelihood, civic honor, and fatherland—it drives many to desperation; within the last week, through private reports I was informed of five cases of suicide as a consequence of these hostilities. I am convinced that this is a general condition which will claim many more victims. One may regret that these unhappy people do not have greater inner strength to bear their misfortune. But the responsibility must fall, after all, on those who brought them to this point, and it also falls on those who keep silent in the face of such happenings.

With that, Stein articulated her key insight: whoever looks away, whoever remains silent in the face of injustice, though perhaps not a perpetrator, nonetheless shares blame. Her demand is thus unmistakable: "Everything that happened and continues to happen on a daily basis originates with a government that calls itself 'Christian.' For weeks not only Jews but also thousands of faithful Catholics in Germany, and, I believe, all over the world, have been waiting and hoping for the Church of Christ to raise its voice to put a stop to this abuse of Christ's name." For Stein it was obvious for theological reasons alone that the pope and the Church

Heiliger Vater !

      Als ein Kind des jüdischen Volkes, das durch Gottes Gnade seit elf Jahren ein Kind der katholischen Kirche ist, wage ich es, vor dem Vater der Christenheit auszusprechen, was Millionen von Deutschen bedrückt.

      Seit Wochen sehen wir in Deutschland Taten geschehen, die jeder Gerechtigkeit und Menschlichkeit - von Nächstenliebe gar nicht zu reden - Hohn sprechen. Jahre hindurch haben die national-sozialistischen Führer den Judenhass gepredigt. Nachdem sie jetzt die Regierungsgewalt in ihre Hände gebracht und ihre Anhängerschaft - darunter nachweislich verbrecherische Elemente - bewaffnet hatten, ist diese Saat des Hasses aufgegangen. Dass Ausschreitungen vorgekommen sind, wurde noch vor kurzem von der Regierung zugegeben. In welchem Umfang, davon können wir uns kein Bild machen, weil die öffentliche Meinung geknebelt ist. Aber nach dem zu urteilen, was mir durch persönliche Beziehungen bekannt geworden ist, handelt es sich keineswegs um vereinzelte Ausnahmefälle. Unter dem Druck der Auslandsstimmen ist die Regierung zu „milderen" Methoden übergegangen. Sie hat die Parole ausgegeben, es solle „keinem Juden ein Haar gekrümmt werden". Aber sie treibt durch ihre Boykotterklärung - dadurch, dass sie den Menschen wirtschaftliche Existenz, bürgerliche Ehre und ihr Vaterland nimmt - viele zur Verzweiflung: es sind mir in der letzten Woche durch private Nachrichten 5 Fälle von Selbstmord infolge dieser Anfeindungen bekannt geworden. Ich bin überzeugt, dass es sich um eine allgemeine Erscheinung handelt, die noch viele Opfer fordern wird. Man mag bedauern, dass die Unglücklichen nicht mehr inneren Halt haben, um ihr Schicksal zu tragen. Aber die Verantwortung fällt doch zum grossen Teil auf die, die sie so weit brachten. Und sie fällt auch auf die, die dazu schweigen.

16

Alles, was geschehen ist und noch täglich geschieht,
geht von einer Regierung aus, die sich „christlich" nennt. Seit
Wochen warten und hoffen nicht nur die Juden, sondern Tausende
treuer Katholiken in Deutschland – und ich denke, in der ganzen
Welt – darauf, dass die Kirche Christi ihre Stimme erhebe, um diesem Missbrauch des Namens Christi Einhalt zu tun. Ist nicht diese
Vergötzung der Rasse und der Staatsgewalt, die täglich durch Rund-
funk den Massen eingehämmert wird, eine offene Häresie? Ist nicht
der Vernichtungskampf gegen das jüdische Blut eine Schmähung der
allerheiligsten Menschheit unseres Erlösers, der allerseligsten
Jungfrau und der Apostel? Steht nicht dies alles im äussersten
Gegensatz zum Verhalten unseres Herrn und Heilands, der noch am
Kreuz für seine Verfolger betete? Und ist es nicht ein schwarzer
Flecken in der Chronik dieses Heiligen Jahres, das ein Jahr des
Friedens und der Versöhnung werden sollte?

Wir alle, die wir treue Kinder der Kirche sind und die
Verhältnisse in Deutschland mit offenen Augen betrachten, fürchten
das Schlimmste für das Ansehen der Kirche, wenn das Schweigen noch
länger anhält. Wir sind auch der Überzeugung, dass dieses Schweigen
nicht imstande sein wird, auf die Dauer den Frieden mit der gegen-
wärtigen deutschen Regierung zu erkaufen. Der Kampf gegen den
Katholizismus wird vorläufig noch in der Stille und in weniger
brutalen Formen geführt wie gegen das Judentum, aber nicht weniger
systematisch. Es wird nicht mehr lange dauern, dann wird in
Deutschland kein Katholik mehr ein Amt haben, wenn er sich nicht
dem neuen Kurs bedingungslos verschreibt.

Zu Füssen Eurer Heiligkeit, um den Apostolischen Segen

bittend

Dr. Editha Stein
Dozentin am Deutschen Institut
für wissenschaftliche Pädagogik

Münster i.W.
Collegium Marianum

17

Edith Stein urged the pope to break his silence about the persecution of the
Jews and to live up to his responsibility. The famous letter was found in 2003
when the Vatican Secret Archives were opened.

must intervene. "Is not this idolization of race and governmental power which is being pounded into the public consciousness by the radio open heresy?" she asked Pius XI, and continued,

> Isn't the effort to destroy Jewish blood an abuse of the holiest humanity of our Savior, of the most blessed Virgin and the apostles? Is not all this diametrically opposed to the conduct of our Lord and Savior, who, even on the cross, still prayed for his persecutors? And isn't this a black mark on the record of this Holy Year which was intended to be a year of peace and reconciliation? We all, who are faithful children of the Church and who see the conditions in Germany with open eyes, fear the worst for the prestige of the Church, if the silence continues any longer. We are convinced that this silence will not be able in the long run to purchase peace with the present German government. For the time being, the fight against Catholicism will be conducted quietly and less brutally than against Jewry, but no less systematically. It won't take long before no Catholic will be able to hold office in Germany unless he dedicates himself unconditionally to the new course of action.
> At the feet of your Holiness, requesting your apostolic blessing,
> Dr. Editha Stein

And in fact her petition was presented to the pope. In private audience, on April 20, 1933, Pacelli spoke about the issue with Pius XI. The name Edith Stein, however, does not appear in this context. The heading above the last of his six agenda items reads, "The arch-abbot of Beuron sends letters against the National Socialists." Here he is referring to Edith Stein's letter alone. There is no evidence in the archives of any other letters that Walzer might have sent. Apparently, the pope did not come to any decisions about this question; at least, Pacelli did not note down under this heading any instructions from the pope.[12] Because researchers had been looking exclusively for the name Edith Stein, they never considered searching for her "letter carrier," so they never found the entry under Walzer.

As always, when Pius XI did not articulate any specific instructions— which meant that Pacelli would not have noted anything down—the task of responding to a submission would have been assigned to him as a routine matter. And the secretary of state's response, which Pacelli wrote

Hochwürdigster Herr Erzabt,

Mit besonderem Dank bestätige ich Euer Gnaden den Eingang
des gütigen Schreibens vom 12.d.M.und der ihm angefügten Bei-
lage.Ich stelle anheim,die Einsenderin in geeigneter Weise wis-
sen zu lassen,dass ihre Zuschrift pflichtmässig Sr.Heiligkeit
vorgelegt worden ist.Mit Ihnen bete ich zu Gott,dass er in diesen schwierigen Zeiten Seine hl.Kirche in Seinen besonderen
Schutz nehme und allen Kindern der Kirche die Gnade des Stark-
muts und grossherziger Gesinnung verleihe,welche die Voraus-
setzungen des endlichen Sieges sind.

Mit dem Ausdruck besonderer Wertschätzung und mit meinen in-
nigen Wünschen für die ganze Erzabtei

Euer Gnaden

ganz ergebener

Sr.Gnaden

Hochwürdigstem Herrn Erzabt Raphael Walzer O.S.B.

Erzabtei B e u r o n

18

Pacelli informed Abbot Raphael Walzer of Beuron that Edith Stein's appeal to
intervene against the persecution of the Jews had "dutifully" been presented to
the pope.

(Copyright © Archivio Segreto Vaticano, A.E.S., Germania, 4 periodo, pos. 643, fasc. 158, fol. 18r)

on the same day, was accordingly brief. Naturally, it was addressed not to the actual petitioner, a supposedly unimportant lecturer in Münster, but rather to the arch-abbot, who, of course, was much further up in the Church hierarchy. Pacelli left it to Walzer "to inform the sender in an appropriate manner that her letter had been dutifully presented to His Holiness." One searches in vain for a response to Edith Stein's plea. Pacelli expended not a single word on the persecution of the Jews in Germany. He also remained silent on the actual subject of her letter, continuing the silence of the pope and the Church. All the pious words that concentrated solely on the well-being of the Catholic Church, while not wasting a single syllable on the fate of persecuted Jews, must have sounded like mockery to Stein: "I pray to God with them that He provide special protection in these difficult times to his Holy Church, and bestow on all children of the Church the grace of courage and magnanimity, which are the necessary preconditions for final victory."[13]

Edith Stein was not able to break through the pope's silence. She herself was one of the first victims of the Law for the Restoration of the Professional Civil Service. Jewish by birth, she lost her lectureship in Münster. In 1933, she joined the Carmelite order in Cologne, thereby realizing her life's dream. But after Kristallnacht in November 1938, she was forced to go into exile in the Netherlands. Her request for acceptance by the Carmelite sisters in Switzerland was delayed by the authorities until emigration, which would have saved her, was no longer possible. When the Dutch bishops broke their silence about the persecution of the Jews on July 26, 1942, and jointly protested the deportations in a pastoral letter, the Nazis reacted immediately by expanding their campaign of murder to include baptized Jews. Two of the most prominent victims of the bishops' public protests were Edith Stein and her sister Rosa (1883–1942). Both were arrested on August 2, 1942, and were taken to Auschwitz, where they were murdered in the gas chamber, presumably on August 9.

Rabbis and Lufthansa Pilots: Petitions for the Pope to Protest

The fascicle bearing the significant title "La questione degli Ebrei in Germania" [The question of the Jews in Germany] in position 643 in the German holdings of the Congregation for Extraordinary Ecclesiastical Affairs contains, in addition to Stein's letter, numerous other submissions to the pope requesting that he intervene on behalf of persecuted Jews. The letter written by the future Carmelite is extraordinary in that it is the only one that was accorded a response. The other petitioners did not so much as receive a confirmation of receipt, let alone a reply from the cardinal secretary of state.

In addition to the pro-Jewish petitions, the pope also received anti-Semitic letters whose authors either sought support for the racial policies of the National Socialists or accused the Vatican itself of being infiltrated by Jews. Just to cite one example, Maximilian Roller of the Aid Center for German Victims of Jewish Deceivers (Hilfsstelle für deutsche Opfer jüdischer Betrüger) in Vienna wrote to Pacelli on September 11, 1933.[14] The Vatican, otherwise "so very well informed whenever some young goose somewhere in the furthest reaches of the world takes a roll in the hay," simply did not want to see that an explosion was threatening the Catholic Church in Germany: "The time when the German people could be stultified with the help of the Church and the Jewish press—on this even the Vatican should be clear—is, thank God, gone for good." Herr Roller was essentially accusing the Catholic Church of making common cause with the Jews. The story of the Amici Israel was supposedly "proof of the fact that the Vatican is permeated and overgrown with Jewish blood, Jewish spirit, Jewish principles, Jewish practices, and Jewish crooks up to the topmost pinnacles."

The fascicle also contains a memorandum with the title "The Jewish Question in Germany," which pleads for understanding for the new government's policies regarding the Jews and may possibly have come from the general direction of the German Embassy to the Holy See.[15] Foreign criticism of Hitler's approach was here attributed to an "inadequate understanding of the position and influence of the Jewish people in Germany." In particular, the memorandum stressed the cultural and moral dangers that supposedly loomed as a result of the massive migration of "Eastern Jews" into Germany in previous years. The "Jewish question" was not a religious problem, according to the memorandum, but rather a problem of race. Hebraic blood and German blood were simply incompatible. The German race must protect itself from foreignization by Jewish blood. The Jews exerted a dominant influence in the economy, banking, the sciences, medicine, and jurisprudence. Even in politics, they had, supposedly, insinuated themselves improperly; in fact, "the revolutionary governments after the Revolution of 1918 were largely formed by Hebrews." Since its founding, the German Communist Party (Kommunistische Partei Deutschlands, or KPD) had been dominated by Jews: "The Jew Marx was the ideologue of their doctrine." The Jew Lasalle had founded the SPD; the Jews Karl Liebknecht and Rosa Luxemburg had formed the German Communist Party; and the Jew Karl Eisner had instituted the "reign of terror" of the Bavarian Council Government (Räterepublik). Finally, the Jews were responsible "for the moral and religious corruption in Germany" because they controlled the arts, literature, theater, film, and the newspapers. They had started the movement to legalize abortion. The Ullstein publishing house was owned by Jews. The memorandum closed with the remark that the policies implemented by the German Reich government with regard to the Jews were reconcilable with Church tradition because "the Catholic Church had at many times recognized the dangers that arise from an increase in Jewish influence."

The materials gathered here are typical of a miscellaneous collection. Everything that was received by the Secretariat of State since April 1, 1933, the day of the boycott of Jewish stores, up to the end of the year was compiled into five fascicles on the general subject of "Jews in Germany." Despite some anti-Semitic writings, pro-Jewish petitions predominate. The Vatican had to come to a decision about how to deal with this matter within a few days after the flood of submissions began. A letter from Arthur Zacharias Schwarz (1880–1939), a rabbi in Vienna, was the occasion for the general decision by the secretary of state not to respond to such inquiries on principle. Schwarz, who came from a family of rabbis, had obtained his doctorate at the University of Vienna in 1905, and in 1907 he received his rabbinical degree at the Israelite Theological Institute. He soon became known as an expert in Hebrew script. One of his study trips took him to the renowned Ambrosiana Library in Milan, where Achille Ratti, the future Pope Pius XI, had been a librarian since 1888 and prefect since 1907. The two men seem to have developed a lively scholarly relationship. Apparently, Ratti, who was a paleographer of note, encouraged Schwarz in his bibliographic studies, which resulted in several catalogs of Hebrew scripts in Austrian archives and libraries during the 1920s and 1930s. In 1925, the rabbi concluded the preface of a book with an acknowledgment to the pope: "I did not receive encouragement for my bibliographic studies from the circles to which I belong by origin, profession, or belief. My suitability for describing Hebrew scripts was first adjudged abroad, at a time when I as yet possessed no knowledge. I have always been deeply grateful for this judgment."[16] The person who first adjudged him to be suitable should be clear. Since 1914, Schwarz had been the rabbi in the ninth and later in the eighth district in Vienna. His daughter Tamar eventually married Teddy Kollek (1911–2007), who later became mayor of Jerusalem. After the annexation of Austria, Schwarz was arrested and tortured by the Gestapo. Emotionally and physically broken, he emigrated to Palestine in January 1939, dying shortly after his arrival in Jerusalem, on February 16.

On April 9, 1933, Schwarz wrote to Cardinal Secretary of State Pacelli, enclosing a letter addressed to Pius XI, with the request that he "be so good as to convey it to His Holiness." Apparently, Schwarz foresaw difficulties and, much like Edith Stein, feared that his letter would get lost in the Vatican bureaucracy. Because of this, he justified his request by referencing his long-term close acquaintance with the pope, and in this regard pointed out "that His Holiness has dignified me with his graciousness on numerous occasions." He then referenced a letter written by Ratti himself dated April 3, 1920, and three telegrams and letters that Cardinal Secretary of State Pietro Gasparri had sent him at the behest of Pius XI.[17]

In his letter to the pope, Schwarz also began by invoking his old scholarly relationship before coming to his actual point of concern:

> Your Holiness, mindful of the high graciousness that Your Holiness has in past years deigned to express for my scholarly work, I have requested the favor that this letter reach the hands of Your Holiness. I request permission to make a statement and to express a concern. I have always viewed the grace of Your Holiness as a talismanic jewel, which I have hidden from profane eyes. Your picture lies in my desk,

and I look at it in all the good hours of my life with a gratitude exceeded only by that toward my parents. I feel free of the demon of politics; with the exception of my position as a rabbi in one of the large Jewish synagogues in Vienna, I live only for my studies, and thanks to the word that Your Holiness provided me in June 1907, in Milan, my true heart tells me that in terms of scholarship I am your creation, and that I will ever be so. No other person in the world knows of this letter.[18]

And so, having expressed his reverence for the supreme leader of the Catholic Church, and having declared that Pius XI had been his intellectual mentor, Rabbi Schwarz believed that he had prepared the ground sufficiently and could now lay out his concerns to the pope: "The concern that motivates me, however, is this: high dignitaries of the Church have also protested the persecution of the Jews in Germany. Your Holiness can hardly know the effect that a word coming from Your Supreme Person would have on pious Jews who, like me, reject all radicalism. If it were possible for Your Holiness to express that the injustice committed against the *Jews* remains an *injustice,* such a word would lift up the courage and morale of millions of my Jewish brethren. It would have a particularly calming effect in places where, as here in Austria, these concerns have not disappeared in spite of the efforts of the government." And the rabbi closed, "I feel certain of the forbearance of Your Holiness if I dare to express these thoughts with the duty and with the right that God has placed in my trembling soul. I ask Your Holiness to accept with grace both my childlike feelings and my deepest reverence."

Unfortunately, Pius XI was never granted the opportunity to accept Schwarz's filial sentiments. In contrast to Edith Stein's letter, Eugenio Pacelli never gave him the rabbi's petition. At least, there is no evidence in Pacelli's notes on his discussions with the pope that he ever did so. The notes from the days in question concern internal Church matters and discussions about initial drafts of the Reichskonkordat. Schwarz apparently never received a response, either. In any case, no draft of such a response has been found in the files.

The cardinal secretary of state seems to have shared the position of his undersecretary of state, Giuseppe Pizzardo, who in a handwritten note dated April 26, 1933, stated on Schwarz's request that "the Holy Father may intervene in the persecution of the Jews in Germany." "It seems a very delicate [*molto delicato*] matter to me to reply. Would it not be better for the German bishops to undertake such a step first?" To which he added, "Perhaps later, indirectly, via the nunciature??"[19] Accordingly, New York Rabbi William Margolis (1909–ca. 1950) received no response either to the telegram that he sent to Pius XI on April 22, 1933. He wrote, "In name of all Sacred in Christianity I implore you to lift your voice in unreserved condemnation of the Hilterite persecution period. Your censure will go far to influence German government . . . to effect reversal of policy."[20]

On April 18, Bavarian Dean of the Cathedral Anton Scharnagl (1877– 1955), whom Pacelli knew from his time in Munich, addressed the situation in which the Jews had been placed. In a report he informed the cardinal secretary of state of the political and religious situation in Bavaria during the months after Hitler's seizure of power, and the policy of coordination of the German states. "The Jews are being attacked with particular sharpness and particular harshness," said Scharnagl—after which he immediately proceeded to relativize their situation. Over the course of the boycott in Bavaria, "no outrages have been committed against Jewish stores or their proprietors." Nor had there been "either plunderings or destruction of commercial spaces or mistreatment of their proprietors." After barely twenty-four hours, the entire fuss was over. Scharnagl's primary concern was the progressive blurring of the discrepancies between the Catholic and the National Socialist worldview among wide swaths of the Catholic population. The March 28 declaration by the bishops had given many the impression that "the German bishops now no longer had any objection at all to National Socialism." Scharnagl was particularly aggrieved that National Socialist measures were also "directed against persons who had for decades and perhaps even longer been Christian." Naturally, the Church was responsible for converts, that is, Jews who had converted to Catholicism.[21]

And in fact, though no action was taken to intervene on behalf of Jews in general, Rome was always ready to do something for converted Jews.

Eure Heiligkeit,

eingedenk der hohen Gnade, die Eure Heiligkeit mir in vergangenen Jahren für meine wissenschaftlichen Arbeiten zu erweisen geruhten, habe ich um die Gunst gebeten, daß dieser Brief in die Hände Eurer Heiligkeit gelange.

Ich bitte, eine Erklärung abgeben und eine Sorge aussprechen zu dürfen.

Die Huld Eurer Heiligkeit habe ich stets als ein glückbringendes Kleinod angesehen, das ich vor profanen Augen verborgen habe. In meinem Schreibtisch liegt Ihr Bild und in allen guten Stunden meines Lebens betrachte ich es mit einer Dankbarkeit, die nur hinter der für meine Eltern zurückbleibt. Von dem Dämon der Politik weiß ich mich frei: abgesehen von meinem Amt als Rabbiner in einem der großen jüdischen Gotteshäuser in Wien lebe ich nur für meine Studien und kraft des Wortes, das mir Eure Heiligkeit im Juni 1907 in Mailand mitgegeben haben, sagt mein treues Herz, daß ich wissenschaftlich Ihr Geschöpf bin und immer sein werde. Von diesem Briefe weiß kein Mensch auf der Welt.

Die Sorge aber, die mich bewegt, ist diese:

Gegen die Judenverfolgung in Deutschland ist auch von hohen Würdenträgern der Kirche protestiert worden. Eure Heiligkeit werden jedoch kaum die Wirkung kennen, die ein von Ihrer Allerhöchsten Persönlichkeit selbst ausgehendes Wort auf die gläubigen Juden haben würde, die gleich mir jeden Radikalismus ablehnen. Wenn es Eurer Heiligkeit möglich wäre, auszusprechen, daß auch das gegen die Juden geübte Unrecht ein Unrecht bleibt, so würde ein solches Wort den Mut und die Moral von Millionen meiner jüdischen Brüder erhöhen. Es würde besonders dort Beruhigung bewirken, wo, wie hier in Oesterreich, die Sorgen trotz der Bemühungen der Regierung nicht geschwunden sind.

Ich fühle mich der Nachsicht Eurer Heiligkeit sicher, wenn ich mit der Pflicht und mit dem Recht, das mir Gott in meine erschütterte Seele legt, diesen Gedanken hier auszusprechen wage.

Ich bitte Eure Heiligkeit, meine gleichsam kindlichen Gefühle und meine tiefste Ehrfurcht in Gnaden entgegenzunehmen.

Wien, 9. April 1933.

Dr. Arthur Zacharias Schwarz,

Rabbiner in Wien IX.

30

Rabbi Arthur Zacharias Schwarz of Vienna implored Pius XI to issue a public protest against the persecution of the Jews.

After all, they were Catholics, and the pope owed them the same pastoral care as any other Catholics. Unfortunately, these actions were almost invariably unsuccessful. One telling example is the case of Maria Pfannenstiel (1880–1973) from Speyer. Her son Max (1902–1976), who after the war was supposed to become a professor of geology in Freiburg, lost his position as a result of the Aryan paragraphs because her father was of Jewish extraction. Her daughter, a third-generation Catholic, could not marry her intended because he would then have lost his position in the civil service. "A law will now be decreed in Germany that in principle forbids marriages between Aryans and non-Aryans; whom then should our Catholic children marry?" she asked, concerned.[22] This letter touched on marital law and sacramental theology, the very core of the theology of the Cath-

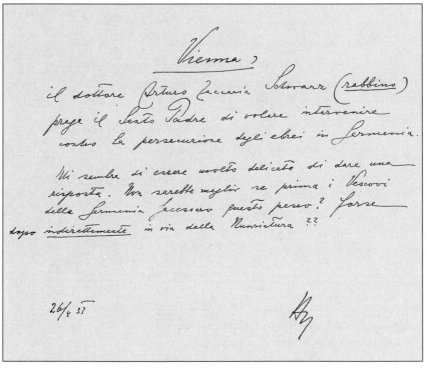

An intervention by the pope is rejected as "molto delicato" in a note handwritten by Undersecretary of State Giuseppe Pizzardo.

(Copyright © Archivio Segreto Vaticano, A.E.S., Germania, 4 periodo, pos. 643, fasc. 158, fol. 32r)

olic Church. However, the efforts of the nuncio to obtain a dispensation in this marital matter did not have the desired result, as Undersecretary of State Pizzardo informed the petitioner. This episode makes clear how little scope the Curia had to achieve anything, even in individual instances. The question of how beneficial in practice a public declaration by the pope would have been must at least be raised.

On April 28, 1933, Orsenigo reported to Pacelli about the visit of a Jewish man to the nunciature in Berlin.[23] To the man's question whether something might be done "to ease the persecution of the Jews," the nuncio reassured him that "everything possible has already been done," and that, in accordance with the Catholic principle of universal charity, the Church intended to continue doing so in the future. This in spite of the fact that barely two weeks earlier Orsenigo had written a letter to Rome stating that the Church could do nothing further about anti-Semitism given that the Aryan paragraphs had now made it official government policy. When his Jewish visitor asked whether Jewish students who had been removed from public schools might be taken in by Catholic schools, Orsenigo denied the request, referring to the principle of confessional education. No one, he added, could detect "an anti-Semitic weakness in this denial" on the part of the Catholic Church. Nonetheless, Orsenigo indicated to his visitor that it might be possible for the German Catholic Charities (Caritas) to cooperate with the Order of Malta to place Jewish hospitals that were being forced to close under Catholic auspices. This could only be done, however, with state approval. "The gentleman left contented," was how the nuncio summarized the meeting. This hardly seems credible, especially since the nuncio added, "Here the distancing of the Semitic element from society expands apace along a broad front," in spite of ample appeals for moderation to the government from persons of high social standing, too. In his answer, the cardinal secretary of state expended not a single word on the inconsistencies in Orsenigo's report. Rather, Pacelli thanked Orsenigo for his involvement, letting him know that he was very satisfied with the outcome of this conversation.[24]

Orsenigo informed Pacelli on May 8, 1933, about how Hitler, in his own words, viewed the "Jewish question."[25] Under Bishop Berning of Osnabrück, representatives of the Fulda Conference of Bishops had had a discussion with Hitler on April 26 that was also attended by Papen, Göring, and Prussian Minister of Cultural Affairs Bernhard Rust (1883–1945). At the meeting, Hitler affirmed that there could be no private or public life in Germany without a Christian religious foundation, which is why he publicly advocated a Christian education for Germany's youth: "We need faithful soldiers because they make the best soldiers." His studies of history had taught Hitler, however, that over the past several centuries Christianity had no longer been able to muster the strength to fight liberalism, Socialism, and Bolshevism with spiritual weapons alone. "With regard to the Jewish question," Orsenigo wrote, "he assured us that he viewed the Jews as vermin and, recalling the position of the Catholic Church up to the end of the fifteenth century, regretted that liberalism had not seen this danger." Hitler concluded that members of this race constituted a "danger to the state and to the Church," and that he was therefore "performing a great service to the Church" by acting accordingly. He distanced himself from Rosenberg's *Myth of the Twentieth Century*, which he called a private work. It was his top priority to avoid any conflict with the churches. Orsenigo's report of May 8, 1933, gave Rome a precise understanding of Hitler's anti-Semitism. Once it was received, they knew exactly where things stood: Hitler intended to exterminate the Jewish "vermin."

Lufthansa pilot Victor Haefner (1896–1967) wrote to Cardinal Secretary of State Pacelli from exile in Paris on June 29, 1933. Like Rabbi Schwarz, Haefner tried to ensure that his letter would be read by mentioning his personal acquaintance with Pacelli: "May I remind you of the flight from Berlin to Freiburg im Breisgau, when I flew you, esteemed Nuncio, to Freiburg. At the time, I was a pilot with Lufthansa-Berlin."[26] Haefner had led an interesting life by the time he wrote this letter. During World War I he belonged to the Royal Bavarian Air Corps and was stationed in Palestine, where he fought against the English. The Bavarian pilots seem to have had a good relationship with the Jewish settlers in the area. After the German defeat, Haefner returned to Bavaria, having in the meantime been promoted to wing commander, and was repatriated to Sonthofen. By his own account, he worked as a civilian pilot for Lufthansa or one of its predecessor companies until 1925. On June 18, 1925, Haefner was sentenced to five years in prison and ten years' loss of civil rights for "disclosure of military secrets." According to the press, he had given sensitive military information to "Western powers."[27] He served his sentence at Spandau Prison in Berlin. Released early, on December 24, 1930, he received a letter from the general state prosecutor in the Superior Court of Justice in Berlin to the effect that the rest of his prison sentence had been commuted, and "the duration of his loss of civil rights limited to the time up to December 31, 1935."[28] This would not be his last brush with the authorities, however. In November 1931, Haefner, a Catholic member of the SPD, was arrested at the airport in Constance, as he was about to fly anti-Fascist leaflets from Germany to Italy.

In his letter to his former passenger, Victor Haefner mainly wrote about Franz von Papen, who in his capacity as negotiator for the German Reich was discussing the Reichskonkordat with Pacelli in Rome. Haefner requested that Pacelli read his letter aloud to "Herr von Papen, whose hands are covered with the blood of his coreligionists." Haefner expressed the hope that Pacelli would hear him out as a Catholic and a German. He vehemently criticized the Catholics in Hitler's government, who permitted "coreligionists to be locked up, beaten, and abused." He then addressed the regime's treatment of the Jews: "I was in protective custody in Spandau Prison in Berlin. There I met a sixty-five-year-old counselor-at-law, who spent six days in the so-called SA barracks. This man, a Jew, looked [in such bad condition] that I had to turn away. I experienced the war at the front, but I had never seen such a massacre! Animalistic—sadistic!" Haefner concluded, "It is the greatest cultural shame that we German Catholics have had to witness over the past century." He begged Pacelli to "give von Papen a good dressing-down" and to express only contempt for him because he had become nothing more than one of Hitler's henchmen. The destruction of the Catholics would follow the destruction of the Jews if it were not stopped: "The excommunication of these creatures should be the first response of our Church."

Haefner, who had evaded the Nazis by fleeing to Paris, was, as a penniless refugee, apparently supported by French Jews. In his letter, he stressed the humanity of the Jews worldwide, who not only helped their own persecuted coreligionists from Germany but also "us Catholics." He then expressed the hope that Hitler would be defeated: "We finished off Prince Bismarck, and so we will also finish off the Nazis." In a postscript, Haefner wrote, "May I please receive confirmation of my words!" As a committed anti-Fascist and anti-Nazi, he was forced in 1939 to flee France to England. On January 28, 1942, the National Socialist regime stripped him of his citizenship as someone "harmful to the Reich." He never received a response from Rome.

On October 24, 1933, Louis Michel, an American Jew of German descent, wrote to Pius XI as the "Defender of all mankind's Fraternity and Humanity" and "Gracious Catholic Humanist," asking him to speak "words of deliverance that will help to free the unhappy Jews of Germany from any further persecution and desolation."[29] Michel expressed the conviction "that only you, the most powerful spiritual church leader in the world, can be the mightiest force sent by God Almighty himself to break the painful chains and the dreadful agonies of the unjustly declassed and sorely humiliated Jews." After pointing out the close relationship between Catholicism and Judaism, Michel talked about "the heartless present Jew-baiter Adolf Hitler," who counterposed his self-styled God, Wotan, to the true God, Jehovah. Germany "today is nothing but a huge, one-sided enslaved Hitler lunatic asylum." The Jews were permanently threatened with hunger, fear, and death; many saw suicide as their only way out, "to escape the cruel fiendishness of the high-executioner Hitler and his lying, murderous gangs of dishonest and homicidal murderers." In his methods of persecution, the National Socialist führer was "more barbaric than even Nero was, more bloodthirsty than Caligula, more sinister than Alba and Torquemada." Interestingly, Michel characterized National Socialist ideology as a political religion without, however, using that phrase. This American Jew was convinced that the God-sent representative of Jesus Christ was the only person who could restrain this evil.

At the time, this conviction was particularly common among Jews in the English-speaking world. And so, the brief report that appeared in the September 1, 1933, issue of the *Jewish Chronicle*, titled "The Pope Denounces Anti-Semitism," should not be too surprising.[30] Supposedly, after Pius XI had received reports about the persecution of Jews in Germany, he "publicly expressed his disapproval." "He stated that these persecutions are a poor testimony to the civilisation of a great people." Furthermore, the pope recalled that not only were Jesus Christ and Mary, the Mother of God, members "of the Hebrew race," but the apostles and many saints were as well. The Bible, too, was of Hebrew origin. According to the article, "The Aryan races, he declared, had no claim to superiority over the Semites." After doubts were raised about the authenticity of this declaration, which had been published by numerous news agencies, the editor of the *Jewish Chronicle* wrote to the cardinal secretary of state on September 8 and asked him to clarify "whether it is true or not."[31] He never received a reply; the Vatican never responded one way or the other to this report.

There is some evidence that this impulsive pope came to understand the true nature of Hitler's regime over the course of 1933. For example, in audience on December 18, 1933, he advised Pacelli to deal sharply with the National Socialist negotiators about the concrete provisions of the articles in the Reichskonkordat that protected Catholic associations. If there was no movement on this front, "the Holy Father would find a solemn opportunity at Christmas to speak out in public." Instead of "being complimentary, as would be appropriate upon the conclusion of the concordat, one would have to be sad." Pacelli noted, "There is no reason to trust in the reliability of the rulers in Germany. The Holy Father believes that Monsignor Orsenigo errs on this point."[32] French Ambassador to the Vatican Charles-Roux once wrote that Pius XI was rarely able to resist "the charm of the unforeseen," and took the opportunity, "whenever he deemed it appropriate, to pronounce a useful truth," regardless of the circumstances.[33] And so it is possible that he actually made such a statement privately, which was then leaked to the public through channels unknown. A letter that Pacelli wrote to Pizzardo on September 21 confirms this suspicion: "I was not displeased by the indiscretion of United Press with regard to the Jews, because it is good for the world to learn that the Holy See has embraced the cause."[34]

Pius XI's Path toward Public Opposition

Over the following years, the legal disfranchisement of the Jews in Germany increasingly crept into all aspects of life. Kristallnacht, in November

1938, added a campaign of violence against Jewish institutions throughout Germany. Synagogues were destroyed and set alight, Jewish stores were plundered, Jewish citizens beaten up, dragged off, or murdered. What was the response from Rome? Could the pope and the Curia really continue their silence in the face of this escalation in anti-Semitic violence?

According to the pertinent series of files from the Secretariat of State and the Congregation for Extraordinary Ecclesiastical Affairs, the subject of the persecution of the Jews played a marginal role in the years after 1933. Nor did the ambassadors to the Holy See do much to raise the issue. Only French Ambassador Charles-Roux broached the subject occasionally with Pacelli, who seems never to have responded to him. For example, on November 17, 1933, Charles-Roux raised the "continuation of anti-Jewish policies" by the Hitler regime, which had the goal of "excluding the Hebrews from all public offices of any consequence."[35] On January 5, 1934, he expressed concerns about "the question of race,"[36] and on August 2, 1935, about the "new German paganism" and the "persecution of Catholics and Hebrews."[37] The issue was virtually never addressed in the regular discussions between the cardinal secretary of state and the pope. One exception concerned a request by the Zionist leader Chaim Weizmann (1874–1952) for an audience with Pius XI, which Pacelli presented to the pope on March 2, 1934. Pius XI decided that it was not advisable to receive Weizmann: "Zionism is a problematic matter. . . . We cannot be on the side of the Arabs because they are the violent conquerors of the Holy Land. But we cannot stand on the side of the Zionists. There is no alternative but to keep out of it."[38]

Nuncio Orsenigo continued to send precise reports to Pacelli about the anti-Jewish measures undertaken by the German government. These included the so-called Nuremberg laws *(Nürnberger Gesetze)* decreed on September 15, 1935: the Reich Citizenship Law *(Reichsbürgergesetz)* and the Laws for the Protection of German Blood and German Honor *(Die Gesetze zum Schutz des deutschen Blutes und der deutschen Ehre)*, which progressively disenfranchised the Jewish population and severely restricted Jews' freedom of action. Orsenigo also reported in detail on the Nazis' Nuremberg Rally, making it clear that the Nazis were cleverly using anti-Bolshevism to intensify their persecution of the Jews. "The Jews are being blamed for it [Bolshevism] exclusively"—so wrote the nuncio—and "it is no wonder that anti-Semitic hounding has resumed with even greater ferocity after the rally." "I do not know whether all of Russian Bolshevism is the exclusive work of the Jews," he commented, "but here they have found a way to make this claim credible, and as a consequence to proceed against the Jews. If, as it appears, the National Socialist government should be of long duration, the Jews will be condemned to disappear from this nation." Despite Orsenigo's clear argumentation, neither the German bishops nor the Vatican took an official position against the Nuremberg race laws. Nor did they ever even lodge a protest.

Nor did the report submitted by Aldo Laghi (1883–1942), the Vatican chargé d'affairs to Switzerland, about the First Jewish World Congress, which took place in Geneva from August 8 to 14, 1936, elicit any reaction.[39] Laghi wrote that the legal suppression of the Jews by the National Socialists "destroys any concept of law that is recognized in the civilized world. Not only does the persecution aim to rob German Jews of all their rights and to ruin them economically; it also attempts to export the poison of anti-Semitism throughout the world."

On September 12, 1938, the master general of the Dominicans, Father Martin Gillet (1875–1951), directed a passionate appeal to Pacelli.[40] In London, the atheists had declared war on God, and in Nuremberg, Hitler was in the process of declaring war on the world. "Why is no voice raised in response to these two declarations of war with a declaration of peace?" Gillet asked. He went on to say that the pope was the only person whose voice would be heard by both the faithful and the non-faithful. He alone possessed the authority to speak out against "nationalism, racism, and anti-Semitism" in the name of civilization. He urged Pacelli, "who sees Saint Peter daily," to press the pope on this issue. Gillet added, however, that the cardinal secretary of state would naturally have a larger overview of "these delicate materials" than he himself, and so he would leave the matter completely up to Pacelli. As a handwritten note on the letter shows, Pacelli apparently read it to the pope. We do not know how he responded.

The lack of response to Orsenigo's report on Kristallnacht, from November 9, 1938, is a great disappointment.[41] The nuncio had tendered a detailed description of that day's "anti-Semitic vandalism." He also made it clear that Goebbels's claim that the riots throughout Germany had been a spontaneous enraged reaction to the murder of Ernst vom Rath (1909–1938), the secretary of the German legation in Paris, was not credible. Rather, these disturbances had been "ordered from much higher up." In addition, the ambassadors of Great Britain and the Netherlands had "acted to defend the property of the Jews." Unfortunately, there happens to be a gap in Pacelli's reports about his audiences with Pius XI for, of all things, the time between September 13 and December 3, 1938. Between September 27 and October 29, the secretary of the Congregation for Extraordinary Ecclesiastical Affairs, Domenico Tardini (1888–1961), represented the cardinal secretary of state before the pope because Pacelli was on vacation in Switzerland. There were most likely no discussions between October 30 and December 3. Thus it is unclear whether Orsenigo's report on Kristallnacht ever reached the pope. The Curia, however, never responded publicly to this very public National Socialist campaign of anti-Semitic "vandalism."

Who, in the final analysis, was responsible for the silence of the Curia? Was it the pope himself? Or was it his chief diplomat, Cardinal Secretary of State Eugenio Pacelli? This question cannot (yet) be satisfactorily answered on the basis of the newly available sources in the Vatican Secret Archives. It is, however, clear that Pius XI had resolved, at the latest during the final year of his pontificate, to intervene more decisively against National Socialism, its racial ideology, and the persecution of the Jews. This "strategy of confrontation," as José Sánchez has called it, picked up momentum as the Fascist regime in Italy increasingly mimicked Nazi racism and anti-Semitic provisions began to creep into Italian law.

For example, on September 5, 1938, a decree "For the Defense of Race in Fascist Schools" barred all Jewish students, teachers, and lecturers from Italian state schools and universities. Pius XI lost his composure at an audience for Belgian pilgrims the next day: "In tears, he read passages from St. Paul which locate our spiritual origins from Abraham. . . . Abraham is our patriarch; he is our primogenitor . . . in Christ and through Christ."[42] According to the pope, anti-Semitism is simply irreconcilable with Catholic faith; it is "a repulsive movement with which we Christians can have nothing in common." Christians are not permitted to take part in anti-Semitism: "Spiritually, we are Semites."

Domenico Tardini made notes on October 23 about an audience that Pius XI had with his liaison to Mussolini, the Jesuit Pietro Tacchi-Venturi (1861–1956), to the effect that the Fascist regime would remain adamant on the race question.[43] Tardini explained to the pope that the Ministry of Culture had banned all Italian newspapers from reprinting the attacks in *L'Osservatore Romano* against Italian and German racism. The pope supposedly had cried out, "But that is outrageous! I am ashamed . . . I am ashamed to be an Italian. And I want you, Father, to tell that to Mussolini! I am ashamed, not as pope but as an Italian! The Italian people have degenerated into a flock of foolish sheep. I will speak, I will have no fear. The concordat presses on me, but much, much more than that my conscience presses on me."

And Pius XI did more than just speak; he tried in concrete ways to assist persecuted Jews in Germany, Austria, and Italy. Thus, for example, in November and December 1938, he instructed Pacelli to have the Vatican's diplomatic representatives in the Americas and Australia sound out those governments about the possibility of accepting Jewish immigrants. The responses were consistently negative. For example, on December 19, 1938, the apostolic delegate for Canada and Newfoundland, Ildebrando Antoniutti (1898–1974), reported to Pacelli about "the greatest difficulties" because the government was not prepared to loosen its strict immigration laws for persecuted Jews.[44]

The pope was particularly aggrieved about Jewish students forced to discontinue their studies. During Christmas 1938, the librarian and archivist of the Catholic Church, Cardinal Giovanni Mercati (1866–1957), had come out in support of Jewish scientists and students. At his suggestion, the pope wrote to the cardinals in Boston, Philadelphia, and Chicago, as well as to Cardinal Jean-Marie-Rodrigue Villeneuve (1883–1947) in Montreal, asking them to support all those who had been forced to give up their studies because "they do not belong to the Aryan race."[45] Such help was urgent for humanitarian and Christian reasons, not least because Jesus Christ, the Savior, had shed his blood on the cross for his own people, the Jews, as well.

The new marriage laws, in particular, which forbade mixed marriages between Aryan and non-Aryan Italians, deeply angered the pope because, unlike in Germany, with its forced civil marriages, an outcome of the Kulturkampf, in Italy the concordat of 1929 recognized Church marriages in civil law. If it had accepted this new law, which countermanded the sacrament of marriage, the Catholic Church would have made itself complicit in the actions of the Fascist state. Article 34 of the Italian concordat stated, "The Italian state, in its desire to restore the institution of marriage, which is the foundation of the family, that dignity which corresponds to the Catholic traditions of its people, recognizes the force in civil law of the sacrament of marriage, which is controlled by canon law."[46] By contrast, the Fascist law of November 17, 1938, declared in Article 1, "Marriage between an Italian citizen of the Aryan race and a person belonging to another race is forbidden. Marriages entered into in violation thereof are null and void."[47] This provision clearly contradicted the concordat because it declared valid Catholic marriages to be null and void after the fact if one of the partners was a non-Aryan Italian. Pius XI had intended to use the tenth anniversary of the conclusion of the Lateran agreements on February 11, 1939, to give the bishops a general accounting of the relationship between the Church and the Fascist state. A *posizione* compiled by Tardini in January 1941 shows that the critically ill pope dedicated the final days and hours of his life to writing this text, which, for Tardini, was "of the greatest importance."[48] In a speech that was more spiritual than political, Pius XI wanted, among other things, to discuss how the state-run press was twisting history, "to the point of its stubborn denial of any persecution in Germany, a denial accompanied by the false and scurrilous accusation of making politics much like Nero's persecution was accompanied by the accusation of arson in Rome."

The manuscript of the speech concludes with a glorification of the mortal remains of the apostles Peter and Paul, on whom the authority of the Roman pope is based:

We can and must say: *exultabunt ossa glorificata,* and we say it heartfully, in the tones of prayer: exult glorified bones of those great ones amongst the friends and apostles of Christ, who have honored and sanctified this Italy with their presence, with their work, with their glorious martyrdom, with the purple of their most noble blood; exult on this memorable day, anniversary of God's being given back to Italy, and Italy given back to God, splendid portent of a blessed future.

And in presence of this portent, you, too, sacred and glorious bones, like those of Joseph of old, prophesy . . . Prophesy the perseverance of this Italy in the faith preached by you and sealed with your blood: sacred bones, prophesy a wholehearted and steadfast perseverance against all the blows and all the snares, that, from far and near, threaten it and clash with it; prophesy, sacred bones, peace, prosperity, honor, above all the honor of a people conscious of its dignity and human and Christian responsibility; prophesy, venerable and beloved bones, prophesy the coming or return to the true faith to all peoples, to all nations, to all races, all linked and all kin in the common bond of the great human family; prophesy, apostolic bones, order, serenity, peace, peace, peace to all this world, that, though seemingly gripped by a homicidal and suicidal craze of weapons, wants peace and with us beseeches it of the God of peace and hopes to have it. So be it![49]

Pius XI in 1933.
(SV-Bilderdienst / Scherrl)

Pius XI died on February 10, the day before he was scheduled to give this speech. On February 15, in his role as *camerlengo,* Pacelli ordered all printed copies of the speech and the plates in the Vatican printing office to be destroyed. Pius XI's handwritten draft and appurtenant materials were taken to the archive. Even after his election as pope, Pacelli never mentioned his predecessor's planned speech. The Italian bishops were informed of the contents of the Pope's speech twenty years later, in February 1959, by Pope John XXIII. It was one of Pacelli's responsibilities during the papal transition to ensure that none of the intellectual and spiritual remains of the recently deceased pope became public. However, after his election he would have been free to publish his predecessor's draft, thereby proclaiming his continuity with the spirit of Pius XI. But Pacelli decided otherwise, just as he did with the other large project planned by Pius XI during the last months of his life, the encyclical against racism.

On June 22, 1938, the pope had asked the Jesuit John La Farge (1880–1963) to draft such an encyclical against racism. He was supported in his work by fellow Jesuits Gustav Gundlach (1892–1963) and Gustave Desbuquois (1869–1959). Interestingly, the pope did not make use of the Holy Office, which would ordinarily have been responsible for matters of doctrine. Nor, apparently, did he inform his secretary of state of his intentions. In fact, Pius XI bypassed the entire Roman Curia, its various organs and members. This alone should make us pause and ask why the pope would have proceeded in this manner. Is it possible that he no longer trusted those around him when it came to this issue?

Gundlach drafted a German version, which in its concluding sections directly addressed racial anti-Semitism, but in a way that differed markedly from Desbuquois's French version. It is not exactly clear whether these drafts ever reached "Fisher senior" (as Gundlach later called Pius XI) or "Fisher junior" (Pius XII). To nail that down, we would have to evaluate the sources in the Jesuit Generalate, in Rome, and the documents from the pontificate of Pius XII in the Vatican Secret Archives, which will not be made available for many years. In any case, Father Gundlach was himself not sure in the spring of 1939. He once wrote that the documents had actually been given to Pius XI, but then later he had his doubts. In all likelihood, however, the pope's increasingly worsening state of health made it extremely difficult for Pius XI to engage with this project. If Gundlach is to be believed, Pius XII, the successor to Pius XI (the "white Pope"), essentially "buried" the entire matter "more or less in passing" in a discussion with Jesuit General Wlodimir Ledóchowski (1866–1942)—the "black Pope."[50] Be that as it may, neither Pius XI nor his successor published this papal encyclical, so perhaps it should go down in history as the "disappeared encyclical."

Gundlach's draft states the following about racial anti-Semitism: "By its nature, the so-called Jewish question is a question neither of race nor of nation nor of ethnicity nor of statehood; rather, it is a question of religion, and since Christ, a question of Christianity." He continues, "The Church today views with indignation and with pain the treatment of the Jews based on provisions that contradict natural law and can therefore never earn the honorable title of law. Completely fundamental claims of justice and love are violated without reticence or inhibition." And finally: "Therefore, as so often before in history, we again undertake to protect the people of Israel from unjust oppression, and again confirm the condemnation with which the Holy Office, on March 25, 1928"—that is, in the decree dissolving the Amici Israel—"condemned all jealousy and all disunity among the peoples and 'very particularly that hatred which today is generally called by the name anti-Semitism.'"[51]

Even though the newly released sources do not permit us to answer definitively the question of responsibility for the silence of the pope and the Curia in the face of the persecution of the Jews, there does seem to be evidence that, at least during the final years of his pontificate, Pius XI wanted to do more in this regard than his cardinal secretary of state, Eugenio Pacelli, was prepared to countenance. In his 1960 article "Pius XII. und die Juden" [Pius XII and the Jews], the Jesuit Robert Leiber (1885–1963), one of Pius XII's closest advisers, came to the conclusion "that Pius XI was in general not easy to dissuade from taking public positions on burning questions; Pius XII was not easy to move toward that end."[52] Not without reason did Bishop Alois Hudal (1885–1963), the director of the German National Church Santa Maria dell'Anima, in Rome, write in his memoirs that the "resolute bearing" of Pius XI, whom he characterized as a "strong, pugnacious personality," preferred "an open break with National Socialism and Fascism to a lingering poisoning." He had "in the interest of peaceful development" frequently been prevented from acting as such "by the intervention of the secretary of state and the Papal Congregation for Extraordinary Affairs." "The more the state of health of the pope left something to be desired," the more the intentions of Pius XI had been "blocked and weakened."[53]

In this context, an article from *Volksstimme,* the official organ of the Social Democratic Party in the Saar region, dated July 13, 1933, is of particular interest. Given that it had been archived under "Jewish question" in Germany, the cardinal secretary of state would probably have known about it. According to the article, "Two diametrically opposed camps and opinions battled over the German question in the Vatican. The irreconcilables, who wanted an open fight with Hitler, drew in particular on Catholic France, Poland, Austria, and Catholic world opinion. The Jesuits were in this camp. The compromise camp was led by Pacelli, the secretary of state and strongest of the political princes of the Church. Pacelli won."[54]

This intervention by Pacelli, preventing a public statement by Pius XI on the "Jewish question," implied no agreement with nor even toleration of anti-Semitism and the resultant persecutions. To the contrary, Pacelli was clear in his rejection of racial anti-Semitism, and he believed that the Church had a general responsibility to support human rights. Rather, his espousal of public silence had more to do with his understanding of the office of the pope as *padre comune* of all faithful Catholics. In accordance with this belief and as a consequence of his experiences in Germany, he pleaded for strict neutrality of the Holy Father in all political controversies, which for him included the issue of the Jews. His priority was not to imperil the pastoral mission of the pope and the Church. This pattern, which had characterized Pacelli's time as nuncio and as cardinal secretary of state under Pius XI, would again manifest during his own pontificate in his response to the famous sermons by Bishop Clemens August Count von Galen of Münster during the summer of 1941. At the same time, a reconstruction of Galen's difficult path into the public arena will give us fundamental insights into the habitus and mentality of an entire generation of leading clergy under National Socialism.

The Bishops Can Speak, the Pope Must Remain Silent: Pius XII and Bishop Galen

Clemens August Count von Galen, the bishop of Münster, was a "perfectly ordinary fellow, with quite a limited intellectual endowment, who therefore had not until very recently seen where things were going, and therefore was always inclined to come to terms."[55] This less than flattering assessment came from none other than Bishop von Preysing of Berlin and dates from the summer of 1941, when Galen gave his three famous sermons in Münster. A completely average person, a child of his time and place, only moderately talented, Galen was not a man who came easily by the moral courage to call the Nazi policy of euthanasia precisely what it was—the murder of innocent human beings. His public protest could easily have ended in death. In other words: he was a man from whom such a step was not to be expected. In fact, Preysing went even further when he cited Galen's tendency to "come to terms." In plain language, he sought compromises that would enable the Church to survive in the National Socialist state. But, Preysing continued, "the more impressive, then, that the Holy Spirit has now illuminated and filled him. How much more significant is such a sign than it would be in the case of a highly intelligent man."

Two key concepts may be helpful in understanding Galen's character: obedience and conscience. Galen was no rebel and no independent or flexible thinker. On the contrary, whenever he attracted attention it was because in a changing world he held fast to principles that he had accepted long ago. He was true to his principles, stable, predictable, modest, and God-fearing in the sense that he never doubted revealed truths. Those who were less well disposed to him would have considered him obstinate, ignorant, arrogant, and intellectually lazy. From the beginning, there was no doubt that Galen would listen to his parents and fulfill the duties and ideals of his aristocratic ancestors, follow the instructions and teachings of the Catholic Church, and be a loyal subject to state authority. At the same time, he was constantly assessing his conscience, as he had learned at home and in his Jesuit education. Actually, there would probably have been no contradiction between conscience and obedience because, in the final analysis, he was firmly convinced that all authority came from God. Nonetheless, Galen constantly posed the question: Is what external authorities—parents, nobility, state, and Church—demand of me congruent with what the inner voice of God says to me? Whenever he could not answer this question in the affirmative—usually after a long period of internal struggle—and decided in favor of conscience over obedience, he experienced moments of intense personal growth.

Galen was ordained a priest on May 28, 1904, after studying theology under the Jesuit faculty at Innsbruck. He was a pastor in Berlin, which he thought of as the "modern Babylon," from 1906 to 1929.[56] In all that time he never warmed up to life in the big city or to the culture of the Roaring Twenties, and he constantly yearned for the pastoral idyll of Catholic Oldenburg. Galen got to know Pacelli during his years in Berlin. The nuncio did not have a particularly high opinion of Galen and criticized his lackluster sermons. His future in the Church did not seem particularly promising until March 1929, when Bishop Johannes Poggenburg (1862–1933) recalled him to Münster to take over as pastor and dean of St. Lambert's Church. The bishop hoped that Count Galen, whose political sympathies he judged to be aligned with the right wing of the Center Party, would be useful in reining in the Westphalian aristocracy, which was tending toward the Nazis. At this point, Galen believed that he had arrived at the end of his career, and that he might best use his final assignment on earth to make end-of-life preparations.

But things were to turn out very differently. As early as 1930, Bishop Poggenburg had raised Galen as a potential candidate for bishop for the newly formed diocese of Aachen. Rome appears to have viewed the stubborn man from Oldenburg as a somewhat awkward candidate. After the death of the Münster bishop on January 5, 1933, Cardinal Secretary of State Pacelli did not place him on the list of three from which the cathedral chapter would elect the new bishop. The capitulars themselves, however, had put him in third place on their own list. Four Prussian bishops had in fact declared Galen to be suitable for the position, but what probably clinched his omission from the list was Nuncio Orsenigo's negative assessment: while Galen "is certainly a very pious and devoted man, obedient to the Holy See . . . some judge him to be little suited for this post, both because of his all too arrogant manner and because he is in his ideas rather obstinate."[57]

On March 9, 1933, the cathedral chapter received a list containing the names of Auxiliary Bishop Antonius Mönch (1870–1935) of Trier; Adolf Donders (1877–1944), dean of the Münster Cathedral; and Heinrich Heufers (1880–1945), cathedral capitular in Berlin. In tendering this list, Rome had interpreted the provision of the concordat with Prussia—that the list would be compiled taking into account the suggestions of the local churches—in such a way that none of the candidates recommended by the Münster cathedral chapter was on the list. On March 21, Heufers was duly elected bishop; but after a long delay he declared, in May, that he would not be able to fill the position for health reasons. Adolf Donders also turned down the seat of St. Ludger. That left Antonius Mönch. Because one could not very well conduct an election on the basis of a single name, Pius XI decided to add Clemens August von Galen to the list. "There is no reason this candidate should not be nominated," the pope remarked in an audience with Pacelli on July 8, 1933.[58] And on July 18, 1933, Galen was elected bishop of Münster.

From the beginning, Galen had been just as critical of the National Socialists as he had earlier been of the Weimar Republic. He described his general understanding of the state in a memorandum dated February 28, 1933: "Freedom and obedience to authority are both the will of God; both are necessary fundamental attitudes for the life of societies on earth. . . . The Weimar state overemphasized individual freedom, while ignoring or denying the authority ordained by God. . . . however, it failed in its promise of happiness. . . . From this disappointment, the new nationalism advocates for the equally false opposite extreme: blind surrender to the authority of an 'authoritarian government,' loyal allegiance to the 'national führer' that will usher in a more beautiful future."[59] Galen was on the front line in the fight against Alfred Rosenberg, author of *The Myth of the Twentieth Century* and chief ideologist of National Socialism. He took over the task of refuting Rosenberg from a Catholic perspective in the *Anti-Myth*, a supplement to the *Kirchliches Amtsblatt der Diözese Münster* [Diocesan gazette of the diocese of Münster], after Cardinal Schulte of Cologne got cold feet and decided not to publish. When Rosenberg appeared in Münster at the district party rally on July 6 and 7, 1935, Galen just one day later turned the traditional Grand Procession, with almost twenty thousand participants, into a powerful protest against so-called neopaganism.

Galen opposed the hesitance of the Conference of Bishops, particularly that of its chairman, Cardinal Bertram. He viewed as useless the policy of secret petitioning and wanted to end the bishops' official silence in favor of powerful public demonstrations by the episcopate. When it became clear that his position would not win out in the Conference of Bishops, he sent a memorandum to the cardinal secretary of state, in early March 1936.[60] The sole focus of this memorandum was the question of how the Church could harness public opinion. Galen pointed out that the government consistently held back in its encroachments whenever the Vatican or the bishops protested in public and the protests were covered by the media. He sharply criticized the bishops for their public silence: "The tactic of negotiating behind closed doors and of not publishing petitions to the authorities was correct as long as there was hope that the authorities were motivated by a desire for peace and considerations of justice. There are no further grounds for such hope." What was needed now was "another tactic, going before the public" because the government would want to avoid any appearance "of being recognized as publicly attacking the Church." He continued, "Looking at the tactical situation in this light, one must ask whether it is not necessary to follow the old tactics of battle, namely, pursuing the retreating enemy, exploiting the enemy's known weaknesses. In our case, this means stepping out in public at every opportunity, denouncing each violation of the vital rights of the Church or of the concordat, protesting openly each new interference in the rights and freedom of the Church. Such a change in tactics cannot involve only a single bishop. . . . Rather, if a single bishop were to proceed, it would feed rumors of disunity in the German episcopate, which would be exploited by our enemies in this sense."

Although Galen had hitherto primarily opposed National Socialism for ecclesiastical reasons without questioning the legitimacy of the regime itself, this would change in 1936. In his sermon at the Xanten pilgrimage on September 6, he for the first time formulated something akin to righ-

teous resistance to an unjust regime motivated by human rights and freedom of conscience.[61] Drawing on the Acts of the Apostles (5:29)—"We
must obey God rather than men"—Galen celebrated the martyrs of
Xanten of late antiquity, to whom humankind owed a debt of gratitude,
not only because "of their Christian faith, but also for reasons of human
dignity, which they defended with their blood and life! Because at the very
moment in which human authority conflicts in its commands with the
clearly recognized will of God, witnessed in one's own conscience, it
ceases to be the 'servant of God,' destroys its own dignity, loses its right to
command . . . attempts wantonly to strangle the God-given freedom of
the human personality, God's likeness in man."

Nonetheless, it was a far distance from a sermon about the historical
martyrdom of the saints of Xanten to a willingness to become a blood
witness to human rights. Galen became even more dissatisfied with Bertram's direction after a major controversy erupted in the German Conference of Bishops in 1940 over the chairman's well wishes to Hitler on his
birthday, an action to which the bishops had not agreed. On May 26, 1941,
Galen wrote to Bishop Hermann Wilhelm Berning of Osnabrück that the
time for obligatory public protest, which might entail "the sacrifice of
one's own freedom and life," was at hand.[62] Up until then, he had soothed
his conscience with the thought that if Bertram and other bishops who
were superior to him "in age, experience, and virtue" remained silent and
were content to participate in "paper and ineffective protests unknown to
the public," it would be "presumptuous and an affront to the other most
reverend gentlemen, perhaps even foolish and misguided, if I pressed forward with a 'flight into the public arena,' possibly provoking even more
brutal measures against the Church. But I cannot much longer quiet my
conscience with such arguments *ex auctoritate.*"

It is interesting that Galen here wrote only about defending the freedom and rights of the Church, for example, opposing the closing of monasteries, and did not yet have his eyes trained on "euthanasia," the destruction of life "unworthy of living." His perspective changed drastically in
the three sermons he gave during the summer of 1941. In these sermons
he linked the protest against the plundering of the monasteries and the
protest against the murder of innocent lives. When the Conference of

Bishops again failed to come out in active support, Galen went public. The tipping point for these sermons, which could hardly have been more clear and unambiguous, may very well have been a conversation Galen had on June 7 or 8, 1941, with the Dominican priest Odilo Braun (1899–1981), a member of the Ausschuss für Ordensangelegenheiten, a committee for affairs relating to religious orders. Braun showed him lists of monasteries that had been seized in other dioceses and urged him to act:[63]

> *Galen:* Not a single monastery has been occupied here.
> *Braun:* Your Excellency, we are required to put out the fire, even if it is our neighbor's house that is burning. We cannot wait until our own roof is ablaze.
> *Galen:* What should we do, a pastoral letter?
> *Braun:* It doesn't have to be a pastoral letter. If a bishop calls a spade a spade in his sermon, we will have gained a great deal.
> *Galen:* Then we will be slapped with a ban on speech.
> *Braun:* I would not adhere to that as a bishop.
> *Galen:* Then we will be imprisoned.
> *Braun:* I think we will have taken a step forward if a bishop is imprisoned.

Galen ended the conversation, saying, "Trust in God and the Holy Spirit and the wisdom of the bishops."

Four weeks later, Galen risked a ban and arrest by directly condemning the regime and its henchmen, the Gestapo: "Every German citizen is completely unprotected and defenseless in the face of the physical superiority of the Gestapo." At this point, Galen was no longer merely defending the rights and claims of the Church; he was now unambiguously advocating for human rights and human dignity. His sermon on August 3, 1941, has not lost its power to move:

> And so we must await the news that these wretched defenseless patients will sooner or later lose their lives. Why? Not because they have committed crimes worthy of death, not because they have attacked guardians or nurses as to cause the latter to defend themselves with violence which would be both legitimate and even in certain cases necessary, like killing an armed enemy soldier in a righteous war.

No, these are not the reasons why these unfortunate patients are to be put to death. It is simply because, according to some doctor, or because of the decision of some committee, they have no longer a right to live because they are "unproductive citizens." The opinion is that since they can no longer make money, they are obsolete machines, comparable with some old cow that can no longer give milk or some horse that has gone lame. What is the lot of unproductive machines and cattle? They are destroyed. I have no intention of stretching this comparison further. The case here is not one of machines or cattle, which exist to serve men and furnish them with plenty. They may be legitimately done away with when they can no longer fulfill their function. Here we are dealing with human beings, with our neighbours, brothers and sisters, the poor and invalids . . . unproductive—perhaps! But have they, therefore, lost the right to live? Have you or I the right to exist only because we are "productive"? If the principle is established that unproductive human beings may be killed, then God help all those invalids who, in order to produce wealth, have given their all and sacrificed their strength of body. If all unproductive people may thus be violently eliminated, then woe betide our brave soldiers who return home wounded, maimed, or sick.

Once admit the right to kill unproductive persons . . . then none of us can be sure of his life. We shall be at the mercy of any committee that can put a man on the list of unproductives. There will be no police protection, no court to avenge the murder and inflict punishment upon the murderer. Who can have confidence in any doctor? He has but to certify his patients as unproductive and he receives the command to kill. If this dreadful doctrine is permitted and practiced it is impossible to conjure up the degradation to which it will lead. Suspicion and distrust will be sown within the family itself. A curse on men and on the German people if we break the holy commandment: "Thou shalt not kill," which was given us by God on Mount Sinai with thunder and lightning, and which God our Maker imprinted on the human conscience from the beginning of time! Woe to us German people if we not only license this heinous offence but allow it to be committed with impunity![64]

Galen's sermons had an electrifying effect precisely because he was no longer simply defending the Church but human rights. For the Allies, these sermons were an impressive indication of the potential for a better

Germany beyond National Socialism. Galen's public protests led to a temporary halt in the killing program. The Nazis were hit and had to take public opinion into account. In the Reich chancellery, some around Martin Bormann (1900–1945), its head, considered hanging Galen to intimidate the other bishops—preferably from the church tower of St. Lambert's. Hitler wanted him to stand trial before the People's Court. In the end, Goebbels's position won out. It was decided to postpone dealing with Galen until the final victory. There was no point in creating Catholic martyrs in the middle of a war, which would only drive the Catholic population to the barricades against the Nazi regime.

Be that as it may, Galen's sermons against euthanasia must be weighed against his silence about the persecution of the Jews. He remained quiet about the Nuremberg laws, Kristallnacht, and the Holocaust. We can only speculate as to the reasons for his silence. It may be that the sources that might enlighten us were destroyed when the Münster Cathedral, the bishop's house, and the archive were destroyed by Allied bombing on October 10, 1943. There is no doubt, however, that Galen came from an "us and them" milieu in which an undertow of religious and social anti-Judaism was more or less part of everyday life. Galen was not untouched by these tendencies. For example, on his trip to Lithuania in 1918, he characterized the city of Vilna as "dirty and full of Jews." Other than that, however, we have hardly any anti-Semitic statements from him. He vehemently criticized the racist premises underpinning National Socialist anti-Semitism and the Nazis' denigration of the Old Testament. In the end, he was convinced of the unity of humankind and of the fact that each individual was created in God's likeness. Galen had close relations with the Münster rabbi Fritz Leopold Steinthal (1889–1969) and immediately asked about his well-being after Kristallnacht.

But persecuted Jews were looking for help from the bishop, particularly after the sermons of the summer of 1941. An anonymous petitioner wrote to Galen, "Reverend, as you know, on September 19 . . . a Jewish sign has been decreed for us, and no one will be permitted on the street without this sign. We are subjected to the mob; everyone may spit on us without our being able to defend ourselves! . . . You are probably also aware that Jews have been hauled away from Stettin, and that this is presently under way in Baden and in Breslau. . . . Will anyone come to our aid? . . . Only the insane idea, the crazy hope that somewhere a helper will appear drives me to write this letter. May God bless you!"[65]

If a public protest by a German bishop caused the National Socialists at least partially to limit their murderous policy, it is frequently asked, should that not have been a clear sign to Pius XII? Should that not have encouraged him to give up his indirect pronouncements and condemn the Holocaust publicly, calling it by its name—systematic genocide?

Galen's sermons must have made an extremely long-lasting impression on Pius XII. They are also the reason the pope made him a cardinal in the spring of 1946. Pius XII apparently read these sermons so often that he could recite them by heart. The pope's housekeeper, Sister Maria Pascalina Lehnert (1894–1983), reported on an audience that the pope had with the new cardinal. "With sparkling eyes," Galen had told her, "how

Triumph in Rome: Galen after being elevated to cardinal in 1946.

(Institute for the History of the Bishopric of Münster, Gottfried Melcher Collection)

Pius XII recited various passages from his sermons, as if he had learned them by heart, thanking him repeatedly for everything he had done."[66]

In a letter to Bishop Preysing, his liaison in the German episcopate, dated September 30, 1941, the pope wrote, "The three sermons given by Bishop von Galen also provide us consolation and gratification such as we have long not experienced as we proceed along the way of the Cross on which we accompany the Catholics of Germany."[67] The moment of "courageous emergence," the Pope declared, had been well chosen. Galen's respect and the "moral earnestness and strength of his protest" had certainly contributed to success. The bishop had "in a very open but noble manner placed his finger on the wounds and injuries . . . that each righteous thinking German experiences as painful and bitter." The pope understood full well that the National Socialists' suspension of their policy would probably only be temporary, and that words alone could not redress the injustice. However, he saw Galen's sermons as evidence of "how much can still be achieved by open and resolute action within the Reich." The pope continued with a sentence that sheds light on his own policy of silence in the face of National Socialist injustice: "We emphasize that [point] because the Church in Germany is all the more dependent on your public action, as the general political situation in its difficult and frequently contradictory particularities imposes the duty of restraint on the supreme head of the entire Church in his public proclamations." Pius XII assured Preysing that public protests by the German bishops had always enjoyed his full support and would continue to be supported in the future. He was aware that his responses to the National Socialist regime, which consisted of secret diplomatic exchanges of memoranda with the German government and papal petitions, had not had the desired effect. This shows that Pius XII would have liked to speak as openly as Galen. From Pius's perspective, Galen could speak publicly because, as a German bishop and head of the diocese of Münster, he was responsible only for his flock, whereas the pope's hands were tied, precisely because of his role as supreme shepherd of all Catholics throughout the world. The pope was obliged to remain politically neutral. That was why he could not hurl a thunderbolt at the National Socialists. As Pacelli realized, at least in 1941, he would have to leave to the bishops the open conflict with the devil.

Five

Dogma or Diplomacy?

The Catholic Worldview and Nazi Ideology (1933–1939)

In the fall of 1933, the National Socialist press enthusiastically celebrated the Reichskonkordat as a recognition by the pope and the Curia of the new regime and the worldview that it represented. After all, if the Vatican held the Third Reich in such high esteem that it was willing to conclude agreements with it that were binding under international law, could any other state or government reasonably doubt the legitimacy and reliability of the Hitler government and the Nazi Party? What was good enough for the pope, with his indisputable moral authority, should be good enough for secular authorities, too. Cardinal Secretary of State Pacelli, for his part, immediately set the record straight: the Reichskonkordat, like every other concordat, had been entered into for the sole purpose of regulating so-called *res mixtae,* matters of a mixed character of equal concern to the state and to the Church. Under no circumstances did the conclusion of such an agreement with the German government imply recognition of the form or the ideological foundations and principles of that government. He responded similarly during an audience on July 15, 1933, when asked by French Ambassador to the Holy See Charles-Roux whether the conclusion of the Reichskonkordat might be seen as "approval of the doctrines of Hitlerism." "I responded that a concordat does not imply such approval," Pacelli noted.[1] Naturally, the cardinal secretary of state could do nothing to prevent the manner in which the Reichskonkordat was put into practice by the National Socialists.

The disagreements that have arisen about the significance of the Reichskonkordat raise a number of fundamental questions about how the Roman Curia dealt with the various twentieth-century totalitarianisms in general and the Nazi regime in particular. Was it really possible to conclude an agreement that was binding under international law with a state whose legitimacy one believed to be fundamentally questionable? Was it not reasonable to assume that the conclusion of a concordat implied recognition of the ideological foundations of the other party to the agreement? Or was it possible for the Curia to distinguish between legal state authority, to which all Catholics owed allegiance according to St. Paul's Epistle to the Romans, and the anti-Christian ersatz religion that underpinned the Nazi regime, which all Catholics were expected to oppose? In the final analysis, these questions involve the basic relationship between dogma and diplomacy, between doctrine and flexible political practice within the Roman Curia. Was it permissible to abstract from eternal articles of faith when the political interests of the Vatican were at stake, or even to interpret them as freely as one deemed necessary? Or should the Curia have resolutely opposed as inimical a totalitarian worldview whose purpose was to replace Christianity, and avoided all forms of traffic with such a devil?

In fact, these questions were the subject of heated discussion within the Vatican itself. Two offices in particular were involved in the debate: the political section of the Curia, the Secretariat of State and the Congregation for Extraordinary Ecclesiastical Affairs, which is subsumed under it, on the one hand, and the Holy Office—the Supreme Sacred Congregation, responsible for all matters relating to faith and dogma—on the other.

No lesser a figure than Eugenio Pacelli, the cardinal secretary of state himself, wrote in his notes about a private audience with Pius XI on February 10, 1934, that a certain tension existed between the Office of the Secretariat of State and the Holy Office, not least because of their different areas of responsibility; as a result, they could not be expected to agree on all matters: "The Holy Office is not the Secretariat of State; by its na-

Ein feierlicher Augenblick von der Grundsteinlegung zum Haus der deutschen Kunst.

Der päpstliche Nuntius Vasallo di Torregrossa spricht eben zum Führer:

„Ich habe Sie lange nicht verstanden. Ich habe mich aber lange darum bemüht. Heute versteh' ich Sie."

Auch jeder deutsche Katholik versteht heute Adolf Hitler und stimmt am 12. November mit:

##

A meeting between Munich Nuncio Alberto Vassallo di Torregrossa and Hitler at the laying of the cornerstone for the "House of German Art," in Munich, on October 15, 1933, conveyed to Catholic voters in particular that they, too, could reconsider their rejection of National Socialism. The Nazi election poster reads in part: "Papal Nuncio Vasallo di Torregrossa speaking with the fuehrer: 'For a long time I didn't understand you. But I have long made the effort. Today I understand you.' And today each German Catholic understands Adolf Hitler and will vote 'Yes' on November 12!"

(Bundesarchiv, Berlin, Plac. 003-003-001)

ture it functions as a magisterium," whereas the Secretariat of State represents the political interests of the Holy See.[2] These statements, which were made in the context of placing Alfred Rosenberg's *Myth of the Twentieth Century* on the Index of Forbidden Books, suggest certain differences of opinion between Pacelli, the political head of the Curia, and the Supreme Sacred Congregation with regard to dealing with National Socialism and its representatives. It may be that the condemnation of one of Nazism's chief ideologists happened to come at a particularly inopportune time for Pacelli. The cardinal secretary of state was in the process of renegotiating the articles of the Reichskonkordat involving the protection of associations, the purpose of which was to prevent as many Catholic associations, important social outposts for the safeguarding of pastoral care, as possible from being subsumed by and coordinated with the Nazi program, or even dissolved. The fact that Rosenberg's book was banned certainly did not make it easier for Pacelli to achieve the result that was ideal for the Church from a political point of view when negotiating with the Nazis. Or could it be that we were seeing evidence of one of his basic character traits? Given Pacelli's personal proclivities, did he perhaps favor diplomacy over dogma in the service of papal politics to the point that he was willing to turn a blind eye when it came to unchallengeable pure doctrine? A heretofore unknown memorandum from the fall of 1933, which is contained in the files of the Secretariat of State, affords an interesting insight into the inter-Vatican assessments of National Socialism in terms of "dottrina e politica," pure doctrine and practical politics.

Catholic Totalitarianism versus Ideological Totalitarianisms

An expert opinion bearing the title "The Holy See and National Socialism: Doctrine and Politics" was written in the Secretariat of State, probably in September 1933, in the context of attempts by the Nazis to portray the Reichskonkordat as recognition by the Church of the regime's legitimacy.[3] The anonymous author of this memorandum was most likely a member of the Congregation for Extraordinary Ecclesiastical Affairs. He probably studied theology at the Gregoriana University or at a comparable seminary. In any case, his opinion gives evidence of a broad neoscholastic education, particularly in his frequent references to Thomas Aquinas and his *Summa Theologica.*

"The greater the Church's accommodations at the political level" in the Reichskonkordat, the expert wrote, "the more important it is to emphasize the immutability of Catholic doctrine." The author recommended a solemn public declaration by the highest authority of the Church, if possible by the pope himself, that would "draw a precise line of demarcation between faith and politics" in order to prevent the concordat—and therefore the Catholic Church itself—from being used by the National Socialists for their own purposes. The author of the memorandum basically believed that it was in principle impossible to distinguish between National Socialism as an acceptable—however nationalistic—party with whose political representatives agreements could be concluded, and an anti-Christian ideology that had to be vehemently opposed by the Church. Such ruminations about a supposedly "good" nationalist German Socialism and an "evil" ideological National Socialism were not uncommon in Germany or in the Roman Curia at the time. For example, at an audience with Pacelli, the German ambassador to the Holy See, Diego von Bergen, distinguished between the "neopaganism" of some Nazis, which the Church could legitimately condemn, and "political National Socialism," which should be off limits.[4] But for the author of the memorandum, the NSDAP was not only a party but also a political religion. Both the cross of Jesus Christ and the swastika, the symbol of salvation through the Hitler movement, made universal and comprehensive claims on the entire person and on all of society; in this sense, both were "totalitarian" and therefore fundamentally irreconcilable. They represented two mutually exclusive worldviews.

The expert's suspicion that the Nazis intended to replace Christianity with their own religion was not pulled out of thin air. The Church was well informed of the Nazis' attempts, particularly in their work with youths, to replace Jesus Christ with Adolf Hitler and to pass him off as a messiah. One of the songs popular among the Hitler Youth, which Bishop Joannes Baptista Sproll cited in a sermon in Rottenburg Cathedral as proof of the Nazis' anti-Christian propaganda, is contained in the same fascicle in which the expert opinion was found:

We are the merry Hitler Youth;
we have no need of Christian virtue,
because our führer Adolf Hitler
is our redeemer and our intermediary.

No priest, no imp can prevent us
from feeling like Hitler's children.
We follow Horst Wessel, not Jesus Christ;
away with the incense and holy water!

Singing, we follow Hitler's banners;
only by doing so are we worthy of our ancestors.
I am neither Christian nor Catholic;
I'm with the SA through thick and thin.

Let them take the Church;
the swastika makes me happy on earth.
I will follow it at every turn.
Baldur von Schirach, take me along![5]

The expert elaborated on the irreconcilability of Catholicism and National Socialism at the level of doctrine before drawing conclusions for the politics of the Holy See. Although the Catholic Church in its universal mission recognized that people are rooted in a particular country and in their love of their homeland in a "benevolent nationalism," "National Socialism immediately becomes idolatry and false doctrine because it considers only the well-being of its own people and forgets that of all other peoples." Among the metaphysical principles according to universal Catholic doctrine is that of diversity in unity, which finds its visual expression in baptism, through which human beings of the most varied races and languages are gathered together into a single people of God. There are no more Jews, Greeks, or Romans; rather, "all those who are baptized are God's chosen people." Those who, like the National Socialists, "believe that only their people are noble and consider all others to be barbarians," are in complete opposition to Christian doctrine and put forth a pre-Christian pagan theory. "The official doctrine of the current German regime," with its emphasis on a biological theory that attributes all moral qualities to race, stands in violation of the principles of Christian universalism.

The irreconcilability of National Socialist doctrine and the doctrine of the Church may be most clearly seen in the racial theories of the former. "The theoreticians of the German regime deny the so-called spirit," which, without roots in their own race, "wanders aimlessly through the world." "They contrast the spirit with the so-called collective soul of the race," which is completely dependent on "physical qualities" and in particular corresponds to "qualities of the blood." This doctrine "of the collective soul and the blood," completely false from a Catholic perspective, was all the more dangerous because it had with Hitler's seizure of power become the official basis for German civil law. Even the Protestant Church in Germany had come to accept racial theories in its doctrine. The expert opinion was here referring to the National Socialist German Christian Party, which had in 1933 won a majority in the church elections, and which later went so far as to use the Nuremberg race laws with their Aryan paragraphs against Protestant pastors. The pope, by contrast, had only recently "ordained as bishops members of the colored races," conferring on them the highest office of the Church, to demonstrate that "the Church knows no racial prejudice." At the same time, continued the expert, "one of the greatest persecutions of Jews that history has ever seen" was being carried out in the Holy Year 1933.

Clearly, the author of the memorandum hoped for a public statement from the Holy Father against the persecution of Jews in Germany to underscore Catholic doctrine, which unambiguously condemned all forms of racism and anti-Semitism. This hope would not be realized in the year of Hitler's seizure of power. Nonetheless, the author of the memorandum was clear that pure doctrine must come ahead of diplomatic compromise and political opportunism.

The discussion of the totalitarianism of National Socialism by the official newspaper of the Vatican, *L'Osservatore Romano,* which barely a year later publicly referred to it as "totalitarismo hitleriano," is of particular interest.[6] The expert contrasted it with the totalitarianism of the Catholic Church. Although he recognized that the National Socialist regime in Germany was in the forefront of fighting the false doctrines of individualism, Socialism, and liberalism, the totalitarian theory of race, which "derives all human values from the Nordic peoples," stands in crude contrast to European civilization, which is based on a synthesis of ancient and

Christian thought. It is impossible for National Socialism and Catholicism to exist side-by-side, let alone form a synthesis, because both make a totalistic claim on the whole person: "The term *totality* cannot be exploited to achieve political or worldly goals. The Church itself strives for totalism when it demands the whole person and all of humanity for God." Here, the author drew radical consequences from the classical catechistic question, "For what purpose are we on earth?" and its answer, "To serve God and to go to heaven!" At issue was no more and no less than being and nonbeing:"The Church works for the personal salvation of each individual. Christianity is convinced of the infinite value of each individual human soul because Christ suffered on the cross for each individual soul." Because of this sacrifice, the Church must make a totalistic claim on each individual, and each individual must decide fully in favor of God, who as the sole reality is deserving of the attribute "total." Christians may have no gods other than the one and only because "the only goal worthy of human beings is the one and only God."

"How far is this doctrine of totality removed from that of the swastika?" the expert exclaimed. For him, the most important aspect of the "totalitarian concept of the Hitler doctrine" concerned the state: "The totality of the human being must serve the state; it must be the symbol of everything. But in this manner, the attributes of the *societas perfecta,* which only the Church of Christ represents, are usurped by the state." This is why Catholic sociologists correctly spoke of a modern deification of the state as a new form of idolatry. The expert saw in this false collectivism a close connection between the "Hitlerian theory of coordination and Marxist Communism." Christianity, by contrast, did not recognize collective souls; it was concerned with the salvation of the individual. The ultimate goal of Christians, their home, was heaven and not the totalistic state—the "highest goal of all human strivings," as Hegel had put it. The political ideal of the Catholic Church was not Machiavelli's *Prince* but St. Augustine's *City of God.*

Here, the expert was implicitly referencing Pius XI. In a handwritten letter dated April 26, 1931, and published in the *Acta Apostolicae Sedis,* which was addressed to Cardinal Schuster, the archbishop of Milan, the pope explicitly rejected the state's claim to total control over the "entirety of its citizens," their "personal, family, spiritual, and supernatural life." This "objective totalitarianism" could not be ceded to a totalitarian state such as Fascist Italy. Such a claim by the state was "absurd" and well-nigh "monstrous." Here, the Catholic Church alone was responsible as a result of the competence conferred on it by Jesus Christ.[7]

In his memorandum to the German government, dated May 14, 1934, Pacelli referenced not only the pope's letter but also the pertinent volume in the Secretariat of State, which also contains the anonymous opinion about the Church's totalitarianism. A "totality of the regime and the state, which also desires to include supernatural life, is absurd and represents a true monstrosity." This is why the "absolutization of the racial idea, and in particular its proclamation as an ersatz religion, is a false path . . . whose disastrous fruits will not be long in coming." As evidence of Hitler's totalitarian claims and those of National Socialism, which also included the field of religion, Pacelli mentioned the Hitler Youth song cited above in his memorandum.[8]

In summary, the anonymous expert concluded that because the totalitarianism of the Catholic Church that was necessary for salvation was diametrically opposed to the false totalitarianism of National Socialism, conclusion of the Reichskonkordat did not constitute recognition of the regime. It was necessary, he continued, to draw a clear dogmatic line between the Catholic Church and National Socialism, and between the magisterium's rejection of Nazi ideology and the politically and tactically motivated pact with the regime for the purposes of ensuring the apostolate and pastoral care given the totalizing political coordination enforced by the Nazi regime. It should be noted that the memorandum expressed the fear that silence on the part of the Holy See with regard to Nazi racial doctrine might be interpreted by the general public and rank-and-file Catholics as acceptance of this ideology according to the old principle, "Remaining silent they consent." In order to prevent such confusion, and to make it clear to the faithful that the Reichskonkordat did not in fact imply Church acceptance of the Nazi worldview, the expert demanded in no uncertain terms "a pronouncement or written statement on the part of the Holy Father," in which the "differences between German National Socialism and Christianity" were clearly delineated.

The pope did not at first make such a public statement. It would take four years for Pius XI to issue his 1937 encyclical *Mit brennender Sorge,* in which he enunciated the irreconcilability of National Socialism and Catholicism. This delayed reaction has always been attributed to the different personalities and political conceptions of Ratti and Pacelli. Just how Pacelli viewed the fundamental relationship between pure doctrine and political feasibility may be gleaned from an episode during the time of his Berlin nunciature, involving the role of Catholics in the ecumenical movement in Germany during the 1920s.

Pure Doctrine or Political Opportunism? Pacelli and the Ecumenical Movement in Germany

Joint religious services between Catholics and Protestants, ecumenical prayers for peace, a unitary translation of Holy Scripture, or even an ecumenical ministry sanctioned by the Vatican—as it exists today in the Papal Council for the Unity of the Christians—would have been completely unimaginable in the 1920s and 1930s. Theological unity between Lutherans and Catholics over one of the central points of contention of the Reformation, the doctrine of justification, which involves the correct relationship between divine grace and human freedom in redemption, would at the time have been unthinkable. As far as the Roman Curia was concerned, Protestants were nothing more than heretics to be fought. Catholics must be protected from their heresies at all cost. Any contact with Protestant ideas, and in particular all personal contact with Protestants, entailed the risk of infection with the "Protestant virus," jeopardizing eternal salvation. The Roman Inquisition was founded in 1542, not least as a coordinating authority to fight Protestant heresy. For the Roman magisterium, there was only one Church founded by Christ: the Roman Catholic Church with the pope as its visible leader, endowed with infallibility and universal primacy of jurisdiction.

From a Roman perspective, ecumenism was possible, if at all, only as an ecumenism of return, in which Protestants rejected their false path and returned to Catholicism. This fundamental position resulted, among other things, in deep suspicion of mixed marriage between German Catholics and Protestants. Generally, such marriages were to be permitted only when the Protestant partner had previously converted to Catholicism. Rome consistently rejected any form of ecumenism in which Protestant communities were viewed as being on equal footing with the Catholic Church, which would imply a rapprochement or unification of equal partners. As a result, one of the prime missions of the Holy Office was to observe such ecumenical movements, particularly in Luther's home country of Germany, and to initiate drastic countermeasures as required.

In the summer of 1926, Ernesto Ruffini (1888–1967), the consultor of the Holy Office, discharged this "holy mission" when he made the cardinals of the supreme congregation aware of what in his eyes were dangerous ecumenical stirrings in Germany. He had gotten hold of several issues of a journal significantly titled *Una Sancta,* which in his opinion pursued the "unambiguous purpose" of "uniting Catholics and Protestants." The journal was published by the High-Church Ecumenical Association (Hochkirchlich-Ökumenischer Bund), which, as the expert noted acerbically, viewed itself as Catholic, though not Roman Catholic, even though most of the members were Protestant. Ruffini considered this ecumenical movement to be "extremely dangerous" because it damaged the "purity of Catholic faith," owing to the "charming and peaceable manner" in which it promoted its cause, and not least because of the "usurped designation 'Catholic,'" which could easily mislead faithful Catholics. All Catholics, and particularly Catholic priests, should be forbidden to read these writings, and forbidden to coauthor any articles or cooperate in any other way with this journal.[9]

On July 28, 1926, the cardinals of the Holy Office, following Ruffini's lead, decided to instruct the nuncio in Berlin to write a detailed report on the ecumenical movement in Germany, and to forward the relevant publications to Rome. This decision was approved by Pius XI the next day, though the pope was rather astonished that neither Pacelli nor the German bishops had told him about this ecumenical danger, which had apparently existed for some time.[10] On July 30, the cardinal secretary of the Roman Inquisition, Merry del Val, instructed Pacelli to gather precise information about the High-Church Ecumenical Association and inform the Holy Office of its doings, particularly of any involvement by Catholic priests. In addition, the nuncio was to broach this explosive subject with the German bishops.[11]

Pacelli complied with this part of his instruction in a memorandum sent to the German bishops dated September 10, 1926. The bishops, as he wrote, "should enlighten the faithful and the clergy, in particular, and prevent their participation in the movement." In this, Pacelli proved to be an authoritative proponent of pure Catholic doctrine. He was particularly incensed that the Una Sancta movement opposed the clear dogmatic truth that "the Roman Catholic Church is the only true Church founded by Christ," and instead sought the true Church "in a higher 'ecumenical church' that supersedes and improves the Catholic Church and the so-called Christian confessions."[12] With this statement Pacelli, completely in line with the Roman Catholic doctrine enunciated by the Holy Office, not only rejected the notion that non-Catholic Christian communities could constitute a church but quite simply equated the Church of Jesus Christ with the Roman Catholic Church.

The first part of his instruction took considerably longer, but its results were all the more substantial. On November 15, 1926, Pacelli sent a seventy-four-page report to Merry del Val in which he summarized his research on the ecumenical movement in Germany and undertook several preliminary evaluations.[13] Secret copies were made of this report for the cardinals of the Holy Office, which were to form the basis of further deliberations.[14] Pacelli's report began with a brief review of the development of the ecumenical movement in Germany since the end of World War I. The High-Church Association had been formed in Berlin in 1918 but had split in 1924 because of internal disagreements. The result of this split was the High-Church Ecumenical Association, which had since 1925 published *Una Sancta*.

In his report, Pacelli initially downplayed the significance of this movement by emphasizing the extremely low membership—approximately one hundred Protestants and fifteen Catholics. This part of his report could be interpreted as a rationalization for his not having informed Rome earlier about this subject. Surprisingly, however, Pacelli also had to admit that the High-Church Ecumenical Association had some positive aspects. The nuncio stressed in particular its recognition of the priesthood that had been initiated by Jesus Christ and passed down through uninterrupted episcopal succession. Protestants continued to oppose this Catholic understanding of the office, on which depends the validity of celebrating the Last Supper. This difference remained a crucial area of contention preventing ecumenical unity. In addition, the High-Church Ecumenical Association had expressly approved one of the matters dear to Pacelli's heart, namely, the conclusion of a concordat with Bavaria in 1924, in which the Roman guidelines contained in the CIC were to be enshrined in German church law.

Nonetheless, Pacelli's overall evaluation was clearly negative. The ecumenical movement in Germany was attempting to found a new "Protestant-Catholic" Church to replace the Roman Catholic Church. Pacelli also rejected the intention of the Protestant-Catholics to recognize for Una Sancta only the Holy Scripture and Church constitution as they existed during the first centuries before Constantine. This would mean that all medieval and modern developments that characterized Roman Catholicism would be rendered obsolete, including papal infallibility with the universal primacy of jurisdiction, Roman centralism, control over local churches by the Roman Curia and its nunciatures, the unitary Tridentine Latin Mass, mandatory celibacy for priests and members of orders, and the like. He also criticized the movement's intent to adopt Protestant forms such as the Lutheran doctrine of justification, "by grace alone," for the new ecumenical church and the *confessio Augustana* of 1530 as the basis for the church constitution on the same footing with the decisions of the Council of Trent. Pacelli was particularly incensed by the ecumenicists' accusation that the Catholic Church of the late medieval period had, given the numerous injustices that had reigned within it, been largely to blame for the Reformation and the resultant schism. Even though Pacelli approved of the tendencies toward Catholicism that characterized parts of German Protestantism because he took them as further evidence of the superiority of Catholic truth versus Protestant error, he was nonetheless skeptical from a political and strategic perspective. The more Catholic the Protestant confessions and the ecumenical High Church became, the less pressure Protestants would feel to convert to the only true Church. In essence, Pacelli advanced the ancient principle of Catholic ecclesiology, *extra ecclesiam nulla salus*—"There is no salvation outside the Catholic Church."

If for the above-mentioned reasons the ecumenical movement in Germany demanded that the magisterium step in, Catholics—in particular priests—involved in the High-Church Ecumenical Association made such intervention all the more necessary, in Pacelli's view. Pacelli's list of names reads like a Who's Who of censured German Catholic reformists and modernists: in addition to the excommunicated Church historian Joseph Wittig and the apostate Friedrich Heiler (1892–1967), he named among others the left-wing Catholic Ernst Michel (1889–1964), the theologian Arnold Rademacher (1873–1939), and the director of training of the People's Union for Catholic Germany, Heinrich Getzeny (1894–1970), all of whom had run afoul of the Holy Office. Any association in which such supposedly "bad" Catholics were involved had to be the work of the devil. An alliance of this sort required decisive action. Pacelli also pointed out precedents for similar reactions by Rome. For example, in 1864–1865 and again in July 1919, the Supreme Sacred Congregation had condemned a Catholicizing movement within the Anglican Church that was associated with the so-called Oxford Movement of Edward Pusey (1800–1882) and John Henry Newman (1801–1890). It had promoted the collaboration of Catholics in "public and private associations undertaken by Protestants," the purpose of which was unity of the Christian churches.[15] Vatican sources, incidentally, never referred to the Oxford Movement but always to Puseyism in order not to compromise Newman, who later converted and became a cardinal.

Pacelli received a good deal of recognition from the Supreme Sacred Congregation for his research on the ecumenical movement in Germany. In a letter dated December 9, 1926, Merry del Val expressed his "highest satisfaction" with Pacelli in this "exceedingly difficult and delicate matter."[16] In addition, Merry del Val praised Pacelli's September letter to the German bishops as *zelante,* which, from his perspective, was an expression of the highest possible praise. This is surprising at first glance because the word *zelante* generally has rather negative connotations and is usually translated as "zealot." But in the Curia, the term *zelante* is associated with something considerably greater. Two tendencies have become evident in the Roman Curia in general and in the College of Cardinals in particular since the beginning of the early modern era: the *zelanti* and the *politicanti*. The *zelanti*, so called by both their enemies and themselves, were religious hardliners who opposed all political compromise. They were almost fundamentalist in their unconditional assertion of Catholic truth. Dogma, or what they considered to be dogma, could never be watered down or sacrificed at the altar of politics. If need be, the Church and the Curia must accept the negative consequences of this rigidity at the "worldly" level such as in international relations. Not only had the *zelanti* taken up the cause against the Protestant heresy; they had at least since the French Revolution been in complete opposition to anything that even remotely smacked of *liberté, égalité,* and *fraternité*. The general condemnation of liberalism and freedom of conscience as *pestilentissimus error,* particularly in the nineteenth century, was largely the result of their prodding. One of the most important avowed twentieth-century *zelanti* happened to be Merry del Val, who as Pius X's cardinal secretary of state had been made responsible for rooting out modernists in the Catholic Church. Democracy, the emancipation of the Jews, and ecumenism were deeply abhorrent to him. By "honoring" Pacelli as a *zelante,* Merry del Val was acknowledging him as a member of his party of fighters, unflinching in their advocacy of Catholic truth.

The *politicanti,* by contrast, tended to be moderate cardinals and high curial officials who were familiar with modernity and its standards of education, who in spite of their attachment to Catholic norms and beliefs had their eyes fixed on what was politically feasible. They were fundamentally persuaded of the reconcilability of Catholicism and modernity, and they were prepared to accept modern achievements such as freedom of the press, more efficient state administration, and the democratic involvement of the laity at the communal level, even in the Church and in the Vatican itself. The *politicanti* made efforts to negotiate with the states, but also with the proponents of differing opinions within the Church itself, and to work out sustainable compromises. They particularly detested the blind religious zealotry of the *zelanti* because it prevented the Church from enacting needed reforms and adapting to the exigencies of the modern age. Whenever it was in the political interest of the Church, they advocated flexibility in interpreting articles of faith and moral principles, a position for which the *zelanti* frequently accused them of political opportunism. The fact that Merry del Val sized up Pacelli as a *zelante* and not a *politicante,* as supposedly consistent in placing pure doctrine above political tactics, would seem somewhat surprising given the general consensus of Pacelli as a crafty diplomat. The question arises whether Merry del Val characterized Pacelli correctly, possibly in view of his long-term collaboration with Benigni, the hard-line opponent of all things modern in the Office of the Secretary of State. Or had the cardinal secretary of the Roman Inquisition erred, and was Pacelli really a *politicante?* Further developments on the ecumenical front provide an interesting answer to this question.

Initially, Pacelli appeared to confirm Merry del Val's evaluation because, on January 9, 1927, the nuncio informed the Holy Office of Cardinal Bertram's attempt to weaken his letter of the previous year to the German bishops. The chairman of the Fulda Conference of Bishops had asked Franz Xaver Seppelt (1883–1956), Church historian at the Catholic Theological Faculty of the University of Breslau, who since 1925 had also been a canon in Breslau, for an expert opinion of the Una Sancta movement. Pacelli was angered when he learned about the cardinal's secret activities because the effect of Seppelt's votum was "to paralyze the above-cited letter." In contrast to Pacelli, the Church historian had come to the conclusion "that the articles written by the Catholic contributors to *Una Sancta* had not violated the Catholic perspective, and more than that, they supplemented it and supported it objectively; that *Una Sancta* offers circles that would otherwise have no opportunity to learn about matters concerning the Catholic Church the possibility to have its doctrine and all of its institutions explained." In contrast to Pacelli, the Breslau cardinal did not regard the collaboration of Catholic authors in the ecumenical journal as dangerous, and in any case he assumed that it would soon fold because of a lack of subscribers.[17] Because of his denunciation of Bertram's conciliatory stance, Pacelli—at least between the lines—in effect placed the Breslau cardinal in the *politicante* camp, whereas he, by contrast, seemed clearly to belong to the party of the *zelanti.* Merry Del Val immediately informed Pius XI and thanked Pacelli, on January 20, 1927, for his valuable information. The pope, he told Pacelli, was following this "worrisome trend" with great interest.[18]

Clear conclusions were drawn from Pacelli's report in the Holy Office. As a summary report for the cardinals of the congregation put it, Pacelli made it apparent that the ecumenical movement in Germany advanced principles that were "in complete opposition to pure Catholic belief." They negated the primacy of jurisdiction of the Roman pope and his infallibility; they transformed the hierarchical principle; put in question auricular confession; and justified all manner of dissent from dogma. By usurping the title Catholic and ecumenical, this movement posed a great danger for healthy Catholic faith, which must be preserved unabridged. As was customary in the Supreme Sacred Congregation, subsequent to this summary the cardinals and consultors were given a list of questions to be answered in their session. These revolved primarily around the question of whether and how to condemn the ecumenical movement in Germany, and what disciplinary measures should be taken against the Catholic priests involved.[19]

The person entrusted with writing the expert opinion was none other than Ernesto Ruffini, who had set the ball rolling in the first place by denouncing *Una Sancta* the year before. The consultor first gave a broad historical overview of the reactions of the Holy Office to a variety of ecumenical movements in the nineteenth and early twentieth centuries, which he characterized as precedents. Ruffini determined that all ecumenicals, whether in England, Germany, or the United States, always proceeded from "a false heretical assumption that the true Church of Jesus Christ consists in part of the Roman Catholic Church," but in part of other equal Christian churches as well. He had no doubt that the High-Church Ecumenical Association followed this same false principle. For this reason, he considered it "extremely dangerous." "Its foundation consists in fact of principles that plainly contradict the fundamental dogmas of the Church." Here he expressly cited the divisibility of the Church of Jesus Christ into various equal churches, the fundamental fallibility of the Church, and the rejection of the primacy of jurisdiction of the Roman Catholic pope, "because reunification is possible only without it." Because of this, Ruffini believed that it was urgent, "for the well-being of souls and to protect the Holy Faith," for the Church to do everything to prevent further spread of this dangerous tendency, given the "loose mentality of many German Catholics with regard to the correct belief." He therefore advocated an instruction that demonstrated the falseness of these principles on the basis of scripture and tradition, in particular the identity of the Catholic Church with the Church of Jesus Christ.[20]

The consultors of the Holy Office met on February 13 in a so-called *congregatio praeparatoria,* a preparatory session, to discuss the questions contained in the January report based on Ruffini's votum.[21] Apparently, it came to heated arguments and deep differences of opinion. In the end, a majority of eight of the thirteen members of the consulting body who were present decided in favor of a public document banning the ecumenical movement in Germany. One of the consultors, however, held that the German bishops could adequately deal with the matter, and four consultors voted—at least preliminarily—against public condemnation. Opinions were also split on the question of disciplinary measures for the German priests involved. While some held that the priests should be suspended or even excommunicated, others spoke in favor of a more pastoral approach and a brotherly admonition by the respective bishops.

In other words, this preparatory session involved *zelanti* and *politicanti,* the former having been in the majority. Representative of the "zealous" position was the vote cast by the Dominican Ludovico Ferretti (1866–1930), who called the High-Church Ecumenical Association a "schismatic movement" "because it seeks to create a union of the Christian Church without its head. If one is really looking for a head other than the Roman pope, there is no Christian Union because only the pope is *Christ on earth.*"[22] The Redemptorist Joseph Maria Drehmanns (1882–1959) vehemently disagreed with Ferretti. While recognizing the good intentions of the ecumenicals in attempting to win Protestants over to the Catholic Church, he also rejected a public ban for tactical reasons. "The less noise made about this movement the better. . . . An official ban from Rome, regardless of the form it takes, would constitute advertising for them," because it would reinforce the anti-Roman sentiment of many German Protestants, which was even prevalent among some Catholics. Furthermore, the basis for such a condemnation in actual sources was much too thin. Apparently, Pacelli's report did not suffice: "Up to now, we have heard only one representation, and we have no confirmed information about the effect of potential countermeasures"—an argument typical of a *politicante!*[23]

The cardinals of the Holy Office met again on March 9, 1927, to conclude their deliberations. No lesser a figure than Cardinal Secretary of State Merry del Val presented the results, which shows how important he considered the matter to be. If this had been only a German issue, the cardinal wrote, the Church could let the matter rest. However, Merry del Val viewed the High-Church Ecumenical Association as the tip of the iceberg of a worldwide ecumenical organization, part of the worldwide penetration of Protestant thinking into the mindset of countless educated Catholics, and of "dogmatic liberalism and modernism." The campaign conducted by the enemies of the Catholic Church was particularly insidious "because it flirts with a vague feeling of fraternal solidarity and universal reconciliation," but in the process "confuses this doctrinal error with charity." The concept of the revealed and unchangeable dogma of the divine foundation "of the true and only visible and eternal Church of Christ" got lost in this "twaddle about love." And Catholics were increasingly infected by this "plague of religious indifferentism." Any Christian reunification was possible only, so Merry del Val believed, by strict subjugation under the magisterium of the pope and a return to the "only fold" of Christians—the Catholic Church. Any ecumenism that sought to gloss over doctrinal differences was not acceptable. Shuddering, Merry del Val rejected the notion of some ecumenicals, who would grant the pope honorary chairmanship of the Church and place him "at the head of their motley meetings."[24] After a brief and mostly uncontroversial discussion, the cardinals decided unanimously to recommend that the Holy See issue a formal condemnation of the ecumenical movement in Germany.[25]

Once Pius XI approved this decision, the Supreme Sacred Congregation began working on a document to the German bishops, which they finished on April 11, 1927. It banned all Catholics from working in any way with the ecumenical movement, or from contributing to *Una Sancta.* The document listed six heresies that posed a serious danger for the purity of the Catholic faith: first, the rejection of the Roman primacy of jurisdiction; second, the invalidity of numerous doctrinal decisions of the ecumenical councils, the Holy See, and the Roman Curia; third, the view that the Church of Christ had stopped being the one and only Church after the first five centuries of its existence; fourth, the notion that the designation of the true Church of Christ must be defined through a compromise of all Christian communities; fifth, the denial of the apostolic succession of the pope, his role as the vicar of Christ on earth, and therefore his divine legitimacy; and sixth, the claim that the Roman Catholic Church had itself deviated from the true original faith and had sought to cover this up.[26]

Eugenio Pacelli received a copy of this document on April 16, 1927. One would think that the Berlin nuncio would have approved of this unambiguous decision since it was consistent with the conclusions of his report of the previous year. In any case, a *zelante* would have been extremely pleased. But Pacelli's reaction was very different. A few hours after receiving the text, he sent a telegram to Rome, and not to the Holy Office, but to Cardinal Secretary of State Pietro Gasparri, in which he strongly advised against publication of the decree: "In view of the heated feelings and intense polemics current in Germany with regard to the concordat and educational matters, including attacks on the Holy See, it would seem appropriate to me, in all submissiveness, to postpone publication of the letter, and to forward it to the bishops confidentially."[27]

Pacelli found himself in an extremely touchy situation. On the one hand, he had received clear instructions from the Supreme Sacred Congregation, which it was his duty to follow. It would have been impossible for him to oppose this doctrinal decision without risking his post. But on the other hand, he saw publication of this anti-ecumenical and essentially anti-Protestant document as extremely inopportune politically, given that negotiations for a concordat with Prussia were finally moving forward. Such a condemnation would not only upset public opinion but would also have a negative effect on the mostly Protestant negotiators representing the Prussian government and seriously undermine the concordat. Anti-Roman sentiments, which always existed below the surface, would certainly flare up again. But it would have been impossible for a lowly nuncio in Berlin to tell the mighty cardinal secretary of the Holy Office in Rome directly of such considerations, so typical of a *politicante*. There seemed to be no way out of this difficult situation; he could not be *politicante* and *zelante* at the same time. Pacelli decided to weight his argument more on the side of political inopportuneness than on the purity of doctrine—and he found a way to inform the Holy Office, at least unofficially, that his view of the matter was that of a *politicante*.

Pacelli wrote a personal letter—on non-nunciature letterhead—to his friend Giuseppe Pizzardo, with whom he had worked for many years in the Congregation for Extraordinary Ecclesiastical Affairs. As secretary of this political congregation, Pizzardo was also a consultor of the Holy Office. He was to serve Pacelli as a bridge between the political and the dogmatic sections of the Curia. On April 17, Easter Day, Pacelli detailed to Pizzardo the reasons he opposed publication of the decree. The "external reason," that is, the political aspect, was central to him: "You can hardly imagine the attacks against Rome by the Protestant and liberal press as a result of the sharpness of the issue of school law and the concordat." Everything must be done to prevent pouring oil onto the fire and having Rome appear in a bad light. "Internal reasons" included a series of inaccuracies in the text of the decree; the name "High-Church Ecumenical Association" alone was incorrectly rendered in the decree as "High-Ecumenical Church," which, given the typical German "spirit of pedantry," could elicit sharp criticism that would greatly harm "our Holy Church" and not least the Holy Office.[28]

This letter, which lacked any of the trappings of official correspondence, enabled Pizzardo to inform the assessor of the Holy Office, Nicola Canali, unofficially of Pacelli's concerns. Thus, the Supreme Sacred Congregation received no official objections to the decision and therefore had no reason to take up this question in session. This enabled both the obstinate nuncio and Merry del Val and the officials under him to save face. On April 23, 1927, Canali sent a personal letter to Pizzardo, asking him to inform Pacelli "confidentially and completely amicably" of Merry del Val's reactions to his objections to the decree. The assessor dismissed out of hand Pacelli's criticism of supposed inaccuracies in the text. "The Holy Office takes complete responsibility for the above-cited letter and does not believe that there are internal reasons" for considering publication to be inappropriate. However, Canali added that the Suprema would leave it to the Secretariat of State to "assess the external difficulties." In the final analysis, however, the Holy Father, "from the loftiness of his wisdom," would decide the entire matter.[29]

Pacelli, whom Pizzardo had immediately informed of Canali's letter, wrote to Pizzardo on April 28 to clear up "any misunderstandings" that "our dearest Cardinal Merry del Val" might have had. As far as the rejection of his internal reasons was concerned, Pacelli conceded that he might have erred and begged

> humbly for forgiveness that I may have erred in the present case, much as I err daily in the fulfillment of my office, an office that far exceeds my powers, particularly in today's extremely difficult circumstances, and from which for this reason I wish to be freed to withdraw to private life in order that I may exercise the holy services of priesthood. As far as external reasons are concerned, it seemed to a poor writer such as myself, who finds himself in the crossfire of attacks and in the heat of emotions resulting from the various concordats to be prepared and from the future school laws—matters of crucial importance to the future of the Catholic Church in Germany—less appropriate to view the situation as even more dire, namely . . . as the result of a matter that is surely dangerous, but which thank God is still of little importance and pervasiveness, which the most reverend German bishops can take care of themselves without directly involving the Holy See. However, this point of view as well can doubtlessly be better assessed and judged in the serene environment of Rome.[30]

Pacelli prevailed in this matter even though—or precisely because—he had performed a masterpiece of priestly humility. Canali discussed the issue with Pius XI in two audiences, on April 28 and on May 5, 1927. The pope recognized the difficulties that Pacelli had foreseen in publishing the document, although it seemed to him that Pacelli had been "a little too impressed with it."[31] Pius XI ordered that the document not be printed in the *Acta Apostolicae Sedis*. It should be made to seem in public as if the German bishops were proceeding on their own against the ecumenical movement, without an official nudge from Rome.[32] Any public criticism would be directed against them, and the Holy See and Nuncio Pacelli in particular would remain untouched. He may have been an antimodern *zelante,* but his proclivities as a *politicante,* along the lines of Pietro Gasparri, came to the fore. As a result of his subtle intervention, the already difficult political circumstances surrounding negotiation of a concordat with Protestant Prussia were not further prejudiced by an official statement from the Roman magisterium. This did not, however, prevent Pius XI from later condemning ecumenical stirrings in general and explicitly with regard to Germany, particularly as they developed at major ecumenical conferences such as that in Lausanne.

In his advocacy of the primacy of politics over the purity of doctrine, Pacelli had gone to the limits of the possible. He had in a particularly adroit manner managed to attenuate a magisterial instruction from the Holy Office in the interests of his concordat politics. With all his rhetoric of humility and flowery submissiveness, he always remained focused on his political maneuverability as a diplomat of the Holy See in Germany. The arguments of opportunity that he used show clearly that he placed diplomacy ahead of dogma. But in Rome it was in any case a much-favored tactic whenever the Curia sought to cover itself and to keep all its options open to shift responsibility onto the bishops, who were usually made to play a lesser role. Successfully concluding a concordat was more important than maintaining pure doctrine. During the Nazi period, Pacelli and the Holy See would increasingly find themselves balancing doctrine against politics. The key question was whether it was still possible, after concluding a Reichskonkordat with the National Socialists, to deal effectively with the chief Nazi ideologues at the doctrinal and dogmatic level. More specifically, why did Rosenberg's *Myth of the Twentieth Century* land on the Index of Forbidden Books whereas Hitler's *Mein Kampf* did not? What role did the relationship between religion and politics play for Pius XI, his cardinal secretary of state, Eugenio Pacelli, and the other critical players in the Roman Curia in their confrontation with National Socialism? Were they more *zelanti* or more *politicanti?*

Alfred Rosenberg on the Index of Forbidden Books

What options were available to the pope and the Curia for defending the Catholic faith against heretical positions and doctrinal enemies that passed themselves off as political religions? As with all actions involving doctrine, Rome's primary purpose was to protect Catholics from "dangerous" deviations and to immunize them against the devil's insinuations. There were both positive and negative ways of doing this. Since the nineteenth century, the numerous papal encyclicals had served to delineate what was and what was not Catholic doctrine. Each encyclical enunciated the Catholic position on a particular question based on current circumstances, and the faithful were urged to act on these positions in their daily lives. Pius XI decreed a particularly large number of encyclicals. Although these papal doctrinal writings were formulated with a high level of authority, the pope had at his disposal an instrument that was both considerably more solemn and binding than the mere dogmatization of a particular doctrine. An individual statement or doctrine was raised to the level of eternal dogma by the pope when he availed himself of his infallible magisterium and then presented the doctrine to Catholics as a binding article of faith. Anyone who was unable to affirm this article of faith was no longer Catholic. Pius XI, however, made no use of this option during his pontificate; over the entire course of the twentieth century, Rome has elevated only one article of faith to the level of dogma. This occurred in 1950, when Eugenio Pacelli, then Pius XII, defined the dogma of the Assumption of the Blessed Virgin Mary. An anathema that bans contradictory views is always connected with such dogmatization. For example, if the unity of the human race had been elevated to dogma by Pius XI, a solemn condemnation of anti-Semitism and racism would have been enunciated simultaneously. Ratti did not take this path, although he had an encyclical to that effect already prepared. We will come back to that later.

The Holy Office, also known as the Holy Roman and Universal Inquisition, was entrusted with the repressive function of the ecclesiastical magisterium. All forms of deviant religious, social, and political behavior were examined and punished by this office. This was accomplished either by individual judgment of certain persons and groups, or by a decision of principle. The so-called *Syllabus errorum* was one particular form of condemnation of errors, which was used for the first time in 1864, and in a sweeping judgment was used to condemn all "dangerous" tendencies of modernity. Interestingly, thought was given to issuing such a syllabus, that is, a list of errors, in the case of the ideology of National Socialism, too.

The most standard and frequent way of suppressing disagreeable views was book censorship. Following the Reformation, it became crystal clear to Rome that the book was the medium par excellence for spreading dangerous ideas. This was why the Roman Inquisition was founded, in 1542, to exert total control over the book market. Works from all disciplines and sciences would be examined in Rome and banned if necessary. Thus was born the Index of Forbidden Books, the famous (and infamous) blacklist. Not only were Catholics forbidden to read banned books on pain of excommunication, but the possession, manufacture, purchase, or sale of such works entailed a loss of eternal salvation and, in Catholic-dominated areas, social ostracism as well. The Holy Office, which since 1917 had taken over the functions of the Congregation of the Index, founded in 1571, made good use of these well-established procedures. After a denunciation and a preliminary examination by the assessor, at least one consultor was commissioned to write an expert opinion, or votum, which was then duplicated in a confidential printing for the cardinals and consultors of the congregation. After discussion of the votum, the consultors in the preparatory session recommended a resolution, which the cardinals in the actual congregation then took up. Their final decision could end in condemnation, acquittal, postponement, or the need for further expert opinions, and always required the approval of the pope, which the assessor generally received the next day in a private audience. Although the pope usually agreed with the proposed decision, Pius XI in particular frequently made modifications. All the precisely established steps in the procedure are as a rule documented in the Archive of the Roman Congregation of the Faith, so that the process of censorship can usually be reconstructed in minute detail.

According to the Roman Index, last printed in 1948, several important books by Fascist and Nazi authors were in fact banned. One looks in vain, however, for certain other books on the Index of Forbidden Books. Nonetheless, a number of important Italian books with a clear connection to Fascism are to be found. Mario Missiroli's (1886–1974) *Date a Cesare: La politica di Mussolini con documenti inediti* [Render unto Caesar: The politics of

Mussolini with unedited documents] was placed on the Index in 1930, as was the anonymously published *Stato Fascista: Chiesa e Scuola* [Fascist state: Church and school]. In 1934, all works by the philosopher and Mussolini's former minister of culture Giovanni Gentile (1875–1944), and in 1937 the book by Giulio Cogni (1908–1983) bearing the title *Il razzismo* [Racism], were banned. Prohibited Nazi authors included Ernst Bergmann (1881–1945), *Die deutsche Nationalkirche* [The German national church] (1934) and *Die natürliche Geistlehre* [Natural spiritual doctrine] (1937); Raoul Francé (1874–1943), *Von der Arbeit zum Erfolg* [From work to success] (1937); Burghard Assmus (1855–1950), *Enthüllungen über die Sittenverderbnis in den Klöstern* [Exposure of moral turpitude in the monasteries] (1937); and finally Alfred Rosenberg, *The Myth of the Twentieth Century* (1934), and his subsequent reaction to the prohibition and the Church refutations, *An die Dunkelmänner unserer Zeit* [To the obscurantists of our time] (1935). The prohibition on Rosenberg's work was without a doubt the most important in this group.

Until the archives were opened in 2003, we knew only that books had been banned; we were left to speculate as to the background and motives for their prohibition. Unfortunately, the archive of the Inquisition proved a great disappointment in Rosenberg's case because uncharacteristically the pertinent files contained neither letters of denunciation nor expert opinions. As a result, speculation continues to be rife about whether the denunciation came from German bishops, the Jesuits and their allies, or the Roman Curia itself.[33] Nor can we conclusively verify the claim by Bishop Alois Hudal, who as rector of the Santa Maria dell'Anima German national foundation in Rome was also a consultor of the Holy Office at the time, that he himself had written the expert opinion on Rosenberg's book. Hudal's diaries, from which this information comes, have generally been considered unreliable by researchers, particularly in relation to National Socialism and Fascism because he himself was regarded as a Nazi sympathizer. The documents currently available seem to indicate that no action was at first considered to prohibit Rosenberg's *Myth*. Rather, it appears that Rosenberg was, so to speak, caught up in the Bergmann affair and condemned along with him as another proponent of National Socialist ideology.

Hudal, who did write the expert opinion on Ernst Bergmann's *Deutsche Nationalkirche*, suggested in his votum that this book should be viewed not in isolation but as an example of dangerous Nazi ideologues, whom he distinguished from "good" National Socialists like Adolf Hitler.[34] Taking up Hudal's suggestion, the consultors were clear and decisive in their decision of January 29, 1934. Bergmann's book was cited as an example of "exaggerated nationalism," a "return to paganism," and a complete "absorption of the individual by the absolutism of the state." The consultors viewed National Socialism as a "true and genuine heresy" that was even more dangerous than modernism. And they spoke out against an isolated prohibition of *Deutsche Nationalkirche* and demanded that other books cited by Hudal, namely, *Der falsche Gott* [The false god] and *Handbuch der Judenfrage* [Manual of the Jewish question] by Theodor Fritsch (1852–1933), *Erlösung von Jesu Christo* [The redemption of Jesus Christ] by Mathilde Ludendorff (1877–1966), *Germanische Weltdeutung* [Germanic interpretation of the world] by Bernhard Kummer (1897–1962), the *Völkische Beobachter* newspaper, and particularly Rosenberg's *Myth,* be included on the prohibited list.[35]

The trial took on a strange dynamic of its own. Although Bergmann's book was the only title on the agenda, the cardinals condemned Rosenberg's *Myth* along with it in their session on February 7, 1934.[36] Strangely, however, they disregarded the other accused titles. Interestingly, an anonymous article about Rosenberg's book titled "Un libro di odiose falsità per la gioventù tedesca" [A book full of vicious falsehoods for German youth] appeared in *L'Osservatore Romano* on the same day that the Congregation of the Holy Office was to meet. The cardinals, all of whom subscribed to the official Vatican newspaper, would have read the article.[37] Rosenberg's *Myth,* of which a minimum of 73,000 copies had already been sold, represented a paramount danger for young people, according to the article. In a most blasphemous manner and from a radically materialistic perspective, Rosenberg was attempting to create a new racial creed and with it a new worldview. His book was deeply anti-Christian and anti-Catholic. This was clear from the mere fact that Rosenberg portrayed the Jew Jesus as the illegitimate son of a Roman soldier. Each page of the book was full of "defamatory, blasphemous monstrosities." Rosenberg dragged almost all Christian dogmas, personalities, and religious practices through the mud—it was a work full of fanaticism and racial and religious hate. Naturally, the anonymous writer emphasized, Adolf Hitler could not be held responsible for this "error in human judgment" on the part of Rosenberg and his cohorts because, after all, the Reich chancellor had made it clear on numerous occasions that the Third Reich was to be built on a foundation of positive Christianity. This pattern of argumentation in fact points to Hudal as the likely author of the article because it was his declared intent to distinguish the "good" National Socialists surrounding Adolf Hit-

The book banners took aim at Alfred Rosenberg's *Myth of the Twentieth Century,* published in 1930, in which he espoused a "new religion of the blood." His book was placed on the Index of Forbidden Books—Adolf Hitler's *Mein Kampf* was not. Rosenberg is at left.

(The Granger Collection, New York)

ler from the "bad" racist ideologues in league with Rosenberg, who were promoting National Socialism as a new religion.

In any case, the cardinals of the Holy Office seemed to have taken the anonymous article, which in form resembled a votum, as an alternative basis for the missing report for their condemnation of the work of "Hitler's chief ideologue," as the German publisher Ernst Piper later called Rosenberg. In this respect, Hudal was probably telling the truth in his memoirs when he claimed to be the author of the expert opinion in Rosenberg's case. The decree of the Holy Office with its prohibition of *The Myth of the Twentieth Century* was signed by the notary of the Congregation on February 9.[38] It appeared in *L'Osservatore Romano* on February 14, 1934, after Pacelli had looked it over and the pope had given his approval.[39] In its statement of reasons, the decree noted that "the book scorns all doctrines of the Catholic Church, and even the foundations of Christian religion and rejects them completely. It crusades for the necessity of founding a new religion or a new Germanic church and proclaims the principle: 'May a new faith awaken today—the Myth of the Blood, the belief that the divine being of mankind generally is to be defended with the blood. The faith embodied by the fullest realization that the Nordic blood constitutes that mystery which has supplanted and overwhelmed the old sacraments.'"

The files divulge no evidence of steps taken by Pacelli to prevent Rosenberg's book from being indexed, although the note of his audience with Pius XI, on February 10, 1934, once again expresses his doubt that such a decision would prove politically opportune, given the ongoing renegotiations for the Reichskonkordat. It also remains unclear why some of the other books by Nazi authors that Hudal listed, particularly Fritsch's *Handbuch der Judenfrage*, were not placed on the Index. Here, Hudal probably believed that he perceived Pacelli's moderating influence—the cardinal secretary of state would have wanted to prevent an all-out attack on National Socialist authors. In his diaries, Hudal speaks in this connection of "the spiderwebs of diplomatic calculation" at the Curia.[40] As he explained elsewhere in his "life confession," he meant none other than the Secretariat of State and its leader, Cardinal Secretary of State Eugenio Pacelli. In some respects, the Secretariat of State was more influential than the Supreme Congregation of the Holy Office, according to Hudal, "because the decisions are mainly influenced by the political considerations of the moment." "The Secretariat of State also reviews the doctrines worked out by the Holy Office, the supreme office of the faith and morals . . . in terms of their current political feasibility and opportuneness for publication in order to avoid all difficulties with the states. As a result, something that is absolutely correct in and of itself may be condemned as inopportune, which day after tomorrow, when the political landscape has changed, will be represented by that office as its own opinion."[41] At least in terms of the Rosenberg case, Hudal seems to have sized up Pacelli as a *politicante,* as one might expect given his official position as head of the Curia. However, he was unable to produce any convincing evidence that Pacelli had acted as a brake with regard to indexing other major Nazi players. The case of Adolf Hitler is illustrative.

The Roman Guardians of the Faith Set Their Sights on Hitler's *Mein Kampf*

Bishop Hudal was not satisfied that Bergmann and Rosenberg alone would grace the Index. He was aiming at a comprehensive doctrinal statement against the ideological wing of National Socialism that sought to replace Christianity with an Aryan religion. By so doing, he hoped to strengthen what to his mind was the conservative nationalist group around Hitler and Rudolph Hess. "We must avoid attacking Hitler himself, the NS, or Germany, either in our publicity, in speeches, or in declarations!!!" was how Hudal characterized this strategy in a paper titled "Several Points of Information for the Vatican! 'Tactics Are What Matter.'"[42] Because of this, it would be better to "attack *individually* those responsible for the pagan or antireligious developments in Germany!!" As examples he cited Joseph Goebbels, Rosenberg, and Baldur von Schirach.

Hudal knew, however, that he could achieve this goal only with the help of the pope. In October 1934, he therefore used the opportunity of a private audience with Pius XI to submit a proposal in which he recommended the solemn condemnation of three fundamental errors of the times in the form of an encyclical or a new syllabus: "1. The totalitarian concept of the state, which suppresses the personal worth of the individual; 2. The radical concept of race, which dissolves the unity of the human race; 3. Radical nationalism with its abandonment of natural right as a consequence of the exclusive validity of the positive right decreed by nation and state." Pius XI was apparently quite impressed and prepared to have the Holy Office examine these questions. In retrospect, Hudal noted that "perhaps the German people and Austria would have been spared a great deal if these errors, which were to bring such calamity to Europe, had been decreed anathema in 1934." If Hudal is to be believed, the Holy Office immediately empowered a committee "to elaborate the theses of racial doctrine, radical nationalism, and state authority to be condemned in the syllabus."[43]

Unfortunately, the Roman Inquisition never published such a syllabus. This could mean that Hudal simply invented the initiative he described in his *Roman Diaries* in order to portray himself as a stalwart opponent of National Socialism. He would have had reason enough: he was forced to defend himself against intense criticism after the war, when he was accused of Nazi sympathies. In addition, he was suspected of having helped Nazi leaders escape to Latin America with the help of Vatican passports. However, sources found in the Archive of the Congregation of the Faith clearly support Hudal's statements. The holdings *"Rerum variarum"* bearing the signature "1934 No. 29," which consists of four fascicles and twenty individual documents, carry the title "Germany—whether racism, naturalism, totalitarianism, Communism should or should not be condemned by a solemn papal act?" Not least the location indicates that the primary target had (at least originally) been Germany, that is, National Socialism, even though the files also deal with Fascism and Communism.

After his papal audience, Hudal sent a letter on October 7, 1934, to the cardinal secretary of the Holy Office, Donato Sbarretti (1856–1939), in which he emphasized the dangers of the modern doctrines of race and blood in Germany and Austria.[44] He noted that history, culture, art, and religion were "viewed solely from the perspective of race and blood" under National Socialism. Hudal saw this as a particular danger for young people, who were being seduced into a non-Christian, Nordic, and Aryan religiosity, without original sin and redemption, and with no sense of morality or asceticism. The natural religion of National Socialism, focused as it was on the here and now, stood in clear contradiction to Christian doctrine. "It is therefore a sham claim that National Socialism is merely a political party," he wrote, "that is based on a positive Christianity." Rather, it is "a theory that overturns the foundations of Christian religion and is all the more dangerous because it is proclaimed in a time of extreme nationalism, which in and of itself is already a heresy." Hudal painted the darkest picture possible of the consequences of neopaganism and urged the Holy Office to conduct an investigation into the foundations of National Socialist ideology: "The prohibition by the Holy Office of books by Rosenberg and Bergmann was certainly a first step, but it seems inadequate to me given a movement that is all the more dangerous since the other two false doctrines of nationalism and the totalitarian state go along with and support it." In this respect, Hudal's diaries proved to be reliable. The letter to Cardinal Sbarretti of October 7, 1934, which he printed in German, is to be found in a precise Italian translation in the files of the Holy Office.

The cardinals of the Holy Office took up Hudal's recommendation in their session of October 25, 1934, which was chaired by Pius XI. The Holy Father himself ordered an internal study of the *delicata questione,* and after consultation with Jesuit General Wlodimir Ledóchowski instructed Professors Franz Hürth (1880–1963) and Johann Baptist Rabeneck (1874–1950), both teaching at the Gregoriana in Rome, to write an expert opinion on the Nazi doctrine of blood and race.[45] It is interesting that two German Jesuits who were not consultors of the Holy Office were entrusted with this matter. Because this was an internal discussion of National Socialist ideology, it was logical to use German experts, particularly because of their native fluency in German and a precise knowledge of the works in question. But why did the pope not choose Hudal himself as the consultor? Did Pius XI not think him sufficiently reliable? Or did he want German-speaking moral theologians and dogmatists from the Society of Jesus, who were well trained to examine critically the concept of humankind and societal models in modern totalitarian ideologies? Interestingly, Pius XI would also draw on Jesuit expertise in 1938 to prepare the antiracism encyclical, which was never issued. And Hudal fell from grace with the pope by 1936 at the latest. It may be that Pius XI had become so distrustful of him by 1934 that he ignored the rector of the Anima when delegating the responsibility for the report. Or perhaps he also wanted *Mein Kampf* to be examined, a move that Hudal had already rejected.

By mid-March 1935, the congregation had two detailed expert opinions. Hürth, the moral theologian, listed the most important errors of Nazi ideology in his votum: the doctrines of blood and race; the authoritarianism of the state; and biologism—and he came to the conclusion that the National Socialist theory of race was in fundamental contradiction to the Christian view of humankind.[46] The first human beings, according to Hürth, summarizing the biblical creation story, had been created by God. All human beings therefore descended from Adam and Eve. As a result, all peoples were fundamentally equal before God. A master race that ruled over others could not exist according to Catholic doctrine. God sought the salvation of all human beings because Jesus Christ the Redeemer had died on the cross for all. There were no Jews and Greeks, no more slaves and free men, as Hürth formulated it, drawing on St. Paul's Epistle to the Galatians.

At the same time, Ledóchowski submitted another, unsigned votum, which had probably been written by Rabeneck. This opinion caused something of a sensation: Rabeneck dealt almost exclusively with Hitler's *Mein Kampf,* and he wanted the führer's magnum opus to form the basis for a solemn condemnation of the errors of the time. He not only wanted *Mein Kampf* placed on the Index; he also sought a solemn condemnation of the precepts of Hitler's work, which would be significantly more binding. The outcome of this engagement on the part of the Holy Office with Nazi ideology, initiated by Hudal, was the diametric opposite of Hudal's original intent, which had been to condemn the Nazi ideologues and protect Hitler as the purveyor of "good" National Socialism.

In the votum, National Socialist racial doctrine was distilled, mainly from Hitler's *Mein Kampf,* into thirty-seven propositions, which were summarized in Latin.[47] As is customary in the Holy Office, these propositions were meant to outline the most dangerous theories of a work. Whenever a consultor formulated such a proposition, the work was understood to contradict Catholic doctrine, and it therefore had to be condemned by the magisterium. Detailed notes that not only referenced the twenty or so pertinent passages from *Mein Kampf* but also cited from other works by National Socialist authors like Rosenberg, Bergmann, and Wilhelm Frick, were presented in German to help the consultors and cardinals of the Holy Office to follow the argumentation or derivation of the propositions.[48] Rabeneck also provided an Italian translation of these passages because only a few members of the Supreme Sacred Congregation knew German. Three examples may serve to illustrate how Rabeneck proceeded.

The consultor summarized the first proposition of Hitlerian and Nazi doctrine as follows: "From day to day, a certain new way of viewing nature and human matters ('worldview') is being spread with fanatical zeal, which has as its fundamental principle the composition of the blood and natural disposition by which a race is determined." As proof of this statement, the Jesuit reproduced a section from the chapter from *Mein Kampf* titled "Organization of a Party":

> Therefore, I saw my own task especially in extracting those nuclear ideas from the extensive and unshaped substance of a general world view and remolding them into more or less dogmatic forms which in their clear delimitation are adapted for holding solidly together those men who swear allegiance to them. In other words: *From the basic ideas of a general folkish world conception the National Socialist German Workers' Party takes over the essential fundamental traits, and from them, with due consideration of practical reality, the times, and the available human material as well as its weaknesses, forms a political creed which in turn by the strict organizational integration of large human masses thus made possible, creates the precondition for the victorious struggle of this world view.*[49]

Rabeneck's fifth proposition read, "Therefore, there is no single and equal nature of all human beings, but rather the entire human race is subdivided into races by nature itself." As evidence for this condemnable statement, he cited Hitler's remarks on the term *völkisch* (sometimes rendered "folkish"). Hitler generally conceded that the state "has nothing to do with racial considerations." Nonetheless, "a denial of the difference between the various races with regard to their general culture-creating forces must necessarily extend this greatest of all errors to the judgment of the individual. The assumption of the equality of the races then becomes a basis for a similar way of viewing peoples and finally individual men."[50]

In the eighth proposition, the censor dealt with the erroneous doctrine of the "Aryan race": "Because Nature has endowed the Aryan race with an excellent disposition of the body and blood, and therefore of the spirit, it has achieved first place." In the quotation cited, Hitler postulated the "Aryan as culture-founder" to whom "all the human culture, all the results of art, science, and technology" may be "almost exclusively" traced back, because "he alone was the founder of all higher humanity, therefore representing the prototype of all that we understand by the word 'man.'"[51]

Both votums were discussed in detail at the March 21, 1935, session of the Holy Office. Pius XI, who chaired the session, asked the Jesuit general to assign several fathers to resummarize the erroneous principles of Nazi ideology. Ledóchowski then submitted another list, on May 1, containing forty-seven propositions based on the second opinion. Eight of the propositions dealt with nationalism, fifteen with authoritarianism, and twenty-four with the cult of race.[52] After examining the list during the May 2, 1935, session of the Holy Office, Pius XI ordered the consultors to continue to work on the matter according to customary procedures. With this, the actual members of the Supreme Congregation, the consultors, went to work. Nonetheless, it would take almost a year for the cardinals of the Holy Office to revisit this subject.

In his opinion of April 20, 1936, Father Martin Gillet, who was master general of the Dominican order from 1929 to 1946, viewed racism, nationalism, and totalitarianism as little more than "social modernism." This led to deification of the state and to a complete absorption of the individual by the community, which must be condemned, particularly in view of the danger to young people. In essence, these were not merely general pagan errors but decidedly antireligious and anti-Catholic errors, and therefore represented a new cult of idolatry, regardless of whether they manifested in the form of nationalism, Communism, totalitarianism, or racism.[53] Consultor Ruffini, who also played an important role in the dispute over

German ecumenism, came to the conclusion in his votum that ultrana-
tionalism was the defining heresy of the twentieth century, which infected
more or less all peoples, including Catholics and even priests. He felt that
the syllabus that was presented was not sufficiently precise. It conflated
points that clearly violated doctrine with others that could be discussed.
In his opinion, the errors of nationalism could be summarized in three
points: 1. Everything depends on blood; 2. Promotion of one's own race
at any cost; 3. Educating young people to love their own race is the highest good.[54]

Consultor Domenico Tardini, by contrast, asked three fundamental
questions in his opinion.[55] First, should Rome condemn these ideologies
at all? Tardini answered this question with a resounding yes, because racism and totalitarianism destroyed individual freedom, ruined the education of young people, and led to deification of the state. Second, how
should this condemnation be accomplished? He did not believe that a simple book prohibition adequately addressed the seriousness of the errors.
Rather, two more substantial documents should be published: an encyclical by Pius XI solemnly condemning racism, nationalism, and totalitarianism, and a decree by the Holy Office listing and condemning the erroneous propositions individually. As historical models for this approach,
Tardini cited the 1864 *Syllabus errorum* as well as the antimodernist actions
taken by Pius X and the Holy Office in 1907 and 1910. Finally, were the
forty-seven propositions presented perhaps not too explicit, containing
too many scholastic terms, which might limit their reception? Tardini believed that this question had to be answered in the affirmative, and he
therefore urged a few well-ordered and precisely formulated propositions
that were generally comprehensible, and that succinctly summarized the
views that were being condemned. Both documents required extremely
careful preparation, although the sequence of their publication was
unimportant (papal encyclical before syllabus by the Holy Office or the
other way around). Tardini's line of argument makes it clear that the encyclical and the syllabus were to be directed to the community of the
faithful, and not merely to theologians and bishops. Because of this, the
documents needed to be formulated in clear language, without the usual
theological cant, a task that would probably not have been easy for most

of the consultors and cardinals, steeped as they were in the locutions and formulas of neoscholasticism.

Tardini's position largely won the day in the Inquisition in the spring of 1936. In their meeting on April 20, the consultors characterized most of the statements made by the various consultors as valuable foundations for their task, but considered it necessary to continue working on the propositions and to formulate them in language that was generally accessible. To this end, the cardinals impaneled a committee of ten on April 29, 1936, to revise the syllabus, which was to deal with Communism along with Fascism and National Socialism. This committee would meet no fewer than seven times by the end of June.

A forty-four-page draft was printed in July 1936, which contained a three-part general assessment of the totalitarian ideologies of the twentieth century.[56] The first part provided an overview of the principles of Catholic doctrine about the human being as individual and as a social creature; part two developed the true doctrine of race, nation, and the proletariat on the basis of these principles in a manner that assumed the unity of the human race. Part three, finally, listed the individual errors to be condemned in a syllabus and comprised twenty-five propositions: eight on racism, five on hypernationalism, eight on Communism, and four on totalitarianism. The consultors apparently expected criticism for the length and fullness of their document, because they countered this objection at the outset with the argument that many of the shortcomings and uncertainties current among Catholics came about because these "fundamental truths had either not been understood or had been forgotten." As a result, the magisterium had a duty to reinforce them. It should be noted that some in the Holy Office got cold feet thinking about the publication of this text, largely owing to the opportunity argument. Because the consultors feared political difficulties with the governments in Germany and Italy, they wondered whether it might not be more useful to publish only the more basic positive findings contained in the first two parts of the document rather than publish the third, the syllabus with the condemnable propositions from the writings of Mussolini and Hitler.

The congregation therefore decided to continue working on and tightening the list. In October 1936, a reformulated syllabus was issued containing twenty-four propositions involving significant ideological errors. This syllable had four parts.[57] After eight propositions on racism, with references, primarily from Hitler's *Mein Kampf,* and five propositions on hypernationalism and Fascism, mainly from Mussolini's writings, there followed eight propositions on Communism, mainly relating to texts from Lenin and Stalin, and three propositions on totalitarianism, again from Mussolini's writings. Surprisingly, however, the cardinals decided in their session on November 18, 1936, to postpone their final decision about the question of totalitarianism to some unspecified time. The pertinent notation read "dilata sine die." However, a "continuare lo studio" was specified, indicating the intent to continue work on the subject.[58] If the pope wished to address the matter in public, he should limit his statements specifically to the errors inherent in Communism. Fascism and National Socialism were to take a back seat, at least for the moment. In a private audience for the assessor of the Holy Office the following day, Pius XI approved this resolution and let it be known that he in fact intended to proceed against Communism.[59] In accordance with the resolution of November 18, the Holy Office elaborated new propositions, in February and March 1937, dealing in particular with Marx, Lenin, and Stalin. In the March 17, 1937, session, however, the proposed anti-Communist syllabus was also postponed in anticipation of the encyclical *Divini Redemptoris,* to be published two days later, in which Pius XI would in fact speak out against Communism.[60]

In spite of this postponement, however, work continued on the syllabus. The number of propositions on the question of racism and National Socialism was increased from eight to ten. The Latin propositions, which the consultors of the Holy Office had agreed to on April 26, 1937, read as follows:

1. All of the intellectual and moral characteristics of human beings flow as from an exceedingly mighty source from the "blood" in which the capacities of the race are contained.
2. The human races differ one from another in their inherited and unchanging nature to such an extent that the lowest race of humans is

further removed from the highest human race than from the highest species of animal.

3. The power of race and the purity of the "blood" must be preserved and promoted in every manner imaginable, and all means that are useful and effective to this end are reasonable and permissible as such.

4. The primary goal of education is to further develop the capacities of race by ennobling the body so that it becomes strong and well formed, and to inflame the spirit with burning love for one's own race as the highest good.

5. The Christian religion must be subjected to the law of race. Because of this, the doctrine of original sin, redemption by the cross of Christ, and the humility and penance to be practiced must be *rejected* or changed in so far as they alienate the human being from his heroic spirit.

6. The Christian religion must be completely *eliminated* from public life; because of this, all Catholic journals, schools, and associations must be cleared out of the way.

7. The doctrine, constitution, leadership, and cult of the Catholic Church are not such that different peoples, nations, and races would be able, within it, to achieve complete perfection, in accordance with their own natural capacity for life.

8. The concepts of God and religion are defined by nation and race. Religious belief is nothing other than trust in the future fate of one's own people; human immortality exists exclusively in the continuance of one's own people and one's own race.

9. The original source and highest rule of legal order in general is the racial instinct.

10. The "battle for selection" and the "right of the stronger," if successful, grant the victor a priori the right to rule.[61]

According to procedures in the Holy Office, this syllabus in its final form should now have been decided on by the cardinals of the Supreme Congregation and approved by Pius XI. It would thereafter have come into force after publication in the official organ of the Holy See. Such a text, however, is not to be found anywhere in the *Acta Apostolicae Sedis*. What happened? On June 2, 1937, the cardinals of the Inquisition again postponed the syllabus on Communism and racism to an unspecified time.[62] The pope approved this proposed resolution two days later.[63] That is the last file on that subject in the Archive of the Congregation for the Doctrine of the Faith.

But why in the end did the solemn condemnation of racism and of the other errors of the time, and with it a public condemnation of Hitler's *Mein Kampf,* run aground after three years of intensive work in the Holy Office? Following one line of research, one might at first suspect that Cardinal Secretary of State Pacelli forestalled the process for political and tactical reasons. The reports of the sessions of the Inquisition, however, clearly indicate that Pacelli was not even present during the crucial sessions in which the syllabus was discussed—March 17 and June 2, 1937. This means that he was not involved in the discussion—at least not officially— and had no direct effect on the decision in the committee. Of course, this does not rule out indirect influence. In any case, given Pacelli's profile as a *politicante,* he might well have been skeptical of any attempts to condemn the führer and Reich chancellor.

In fact, Alois Hudal claimed that Francesco Marchetti-Selvaggiani (1871–1951), a close ally of Pacelli's, was responsible for putting on the brakes. The first nuncio to the new Republic of Austria had studied with Pacelli and was considered one of the most skilled diplomats in the Curia. Marchetti-Selvaggiani believed an "open battle against the NS to be inopportune because of its repercussions in Italy, whose Fascist Party was becoming ever more dangerously dependent on Berlin."[64] In contrast, however, Cardinal Secretary Sbarretti of the Holy Office had advocated continued work on the propositions on racism. Political considerations played no role in his calculations; he was concerned only with purity of doctrine and consistent opposition to error.[65]

However, the key player in the Roman Inquisition, its actual prefect, was the pope himself. Without his approval no decision made by the Suprema could be enforced. The minutes of the congregation of the cardinals of the Holy Office of June 2, 1937, are revealing on the question of the syllabus. The decision of the cardinals to postpone was approved by Pius XI on June 4 in an audience for the assessor of the Office. It was therefore the pope who, at least formally, put the antiracism syllabus on hold. He added that the current difficult political situation did not permit a syllabus on the errors of racism. The question should be taken up again when the present storms had passed and the Church's political circumstances had quieted down.[66] Here, Pius XI was referring to the increasingly difficult overall position of the Church in Germany and Europe, particularly in Italy and Spain. Or it may have been that the principal reason for his reticence was the enormous effect that the 1937 encyclical *Mit brennender Sorge* had had in Germany. In any case, the files to which we currently have access in the Archive of the Congregation for the Doctrine of the Faith are inconclusive about who might have advised him to place strategic political considerations before the dogmatic line, whether he acted on his own, was simply following the votum of the cardinals of the Holy Office, or whether Pacelli exerted influence in the background. What we do know is that in 1937 the cardinal secretary of state was determined to keep political conflicts with the Fascist regimes to a minimum.

In this connection, one particular statement of Pacelli's from a rare session of the Congregation for Extraordinary Ecclesiastical Affairs, on July 14, 1937, is of particular interest. At issue was the controversial question of whether the Holy See should recognize Franco's Nationalist Spain, thereby continuing to deny recognition to Republican Spain. Cardinal Camillo Laurenti (1861–1938) had raised the concern that support for Franco could give the impression that the Church had made common cause with the "Fascist bloc." Pacelli briefly summarized his opinion at the end of the debate: "It is useful for the Holy See to place itself in the Fascist bloc, which consists largely of Italy and Germany (Japan is far away)." However, the cardinal secretary of state immediately relativized this statement of principle by asking two rhetorical questions: "National Socialist Germany? Which is persecuting the Church?" The answer was quite clear to the Vatican's top diplomat. As useful as it might be for the Holy See to join the Fascist bloc, it would be impossible for tactical reasons: "Even if it were not the intention of the Holy See, it would look as if the Holy See were making a pact with a group that seeks to destroy religion." And there were many among Franco's followers who agreed with National Socialist ideology and deified Hitler. Because of this, Pacelli argued for maintaining the status quo—while keeping all options open. That is, the Holy See should not at present take a position on the Spanish question. Until the situation had become clear, the Church should recognize neither Franco nor the Popular Front.[67] Once the Popular Front government was defeated, the Curia came out on the side of Franco. This stance was consistent with that of "dilata sine die," postponing indefinitely the indexing of Hitler's *Mein Kampf.*

A Typical Roman Compromise?

The Inquisition had little trouble placing Rosenberg's *Myth of the Twentieth Century* on the Index on February 5, 1934. Hitler's *Mein Kampf,* by contrast, was the subject of intense debate in the Holy Office between 1934 and 1937—not merely about whether to prohibit the book, but about whether to use it as the basis for a solemn syllabus. Despite this extraordinary attention it was never indexed, which is at least consistent with the notion that the Roman Curia at the time placed diplomacy ahead of dogma. Obviously, one of the chief ideologues of National Socialism could be placed on the Index even after conclusion of the Reichskonkordat, something that could not be done to a head of state who had (seemingly) come to power by legal means and with whom one had just signed an agreement binding under international law. After all, Hitler had been duly named Reich chancellor because of the Enabling Act, which the Catholic Center Party had helped to pass. The ideological opponent and führer of a political ersatz religion had become a legal head of state. According to Catholic opinion, the Church was duty-bound to recognize him as such.

The pertinent passage from St. Paul's Epistle to the Romans reads, "Let every person be subordinate to the higher authorities, for there is no authority except from God, and those that exist have been established by God. Therefore, whoever resists authority opposes what God has appointed, and those who oppose it will bring judgment upon themselves" (Romans 13:1–2). According to the principles underlying Catholic political science, Rome's hands were tied when it came to initiating action against Hitler and his book. This did not, however, mean that the Vatican could not take up the contents of *Mein Kampf* and counterpose it to "healthy" Catholic doctrine. Of course, this would have to be done anonymously; that is, the magisterium could not publicly admit that the positions it was examining were taken from *Mein Kampf.* And in fact Pius XI decided on a two-pronged indirect attack on Hitler's positions.

On March 14, 1937, the pope issued his famous encyclical against National Socialism, *Mit brennender Sorge.* In July 1936, while the Holy Office was considering which propositions on racism and National Socialism the magisterium was to condemn, Pacelli indicated to Bishop Franz Rudolf Bornewasser (1866–1951) of Trier during his stay in Rome that the pope was considering a "pastorale" based on comprehensive documentation of "violations of the concordat" by the Nazi state.[68] As a result, the German bishops, at their conference in Fulda, on August 18, 1936, requested a statement by the pope about the situation in Germany.[69] The background for this decision was the anti-Catholic incidents occurring in the Reich. These had been preceded by a first wave of so-called immorality trials and the failed renegotiations for the Reichskonkordat, as a result of which the Vatican had few remaining illusions about the Church's political situation in Germany. The German bishops gathered for an extraordinary plenary session in Fulda on January 12–13, 1937. Immediately thereafter, Cardinals Adolf Bertram, Michael Faulhaber, and Karl Joseph Schulte, and Bishops Clemens August Count von Galen and Konrad Count von Preysing traveled to Rome at the invitation of the pope for deliberations. On Friday evening, January 15, Pacelli received Bertram and Faulhaber for informal preliminary discussions, and Faulhaber offered to forward the speech he had made in Fulda about the situation in Germany as a basis for discussion. At the meeting of the bishops on Saturday, January 16, Pacelli disclosed several points about which Pius XI had wanted more information. The bishops expressed the conviction that "for the Church it is currently a matter of life and death. They are directly aiming at its destruction."[70] The representatives of the German episcopate considered a personal letter by the pope to Hitler to be insufficient; instead, they proposed a papal encyclical, a statement of doctrine. Pacelli was skeptical. He wanted to prevent any involvement of the magisterium that might be viewed as taking sides, which would have imperiled the independence of the Holy See. He was only willing to advocate for an encyclical opposing National Socialism because developments in the Spanish Civil War had made it possible simultaneously to condemn Bolshevism and its expansion in Europe. Only a policy of symmetric condemnation could preserve Rome's nonpartisanship. In spite of his reservations, he asked Faulhaber for some key points that might be used in such a pastoral letter.

The audience with Pius XI took place on Sunday morning at the bedside of the ailing pope. At a subsequent luncheon that Pacelli gave for the bishops, he reiterated the consequences that a pastoral letter would have in Germany. On the evening of Monday, January 18, the cardinal secretary of state specified his intentions more precisely and asked Faulhaber to draft an encyclical. Faulhaber secretly wrote a draft, handwritten in German, over the next three nights, which he submitted to Pacelli on January 21. "Nobody knows about this draft. That is why I wrote it at night, so that no typist should know about it," Faulhaber noted.[71] The only person in Rome to whom Pacelli confided was Jesuit General Ledóchowski, who had dealt with the preliminary work of the Holy Office. Further work on the draft was personally supervised by the secretary of state. Over the following weeks, Faulhaber's draft was transformed into a papal encyclical, which was proclaimed from all German pulpits on March 21, 1937. Taken completely by surprise by *Mit brennender Sorge,* the Nazis resumed their campaign against the Church. Only a few days earlier they had been acclaiming *Divini Redemptoris,* the pope's condemnation of Communism.

Pacelli largely elaborated the structure of Faulhaber's draft and its intellectual direction. The text was expanded considerably, particularly in the first part, which dealt with Nazi violations. This was Pacelli's main area of expertise. He had been a signatory to the concordat, and so he felt particularly aggrieved by the "violations of the agreement" that were addressed by *Mit brennender Sorge.* The second, more theological part, contrasted true Catholic doctrine and nationalistic and racist reinterpretations. Here, we can make out similarities between work on the syllabus and work on the encyclical, which is hardly surprising because Pacelli, as secretary of state, was a member of the Supreme Sacred Congregation and was therefore kept up to date about the topics being worked on. Last but not least, he received the private printings of all opinions and other documents. It is likely that he used these models in editing the text of the encyclical.

For example, one section of the encyclical, which Pacelli clearly wrote himself because Faulhaber wrote nothing of the sort, states:

> The Church founded by the Redeemer is one, the same for all races and all nations. Beneath her dome, as beneath the vault of heaven, there is but one place and one country for all nations and tongues; there is room for the development of every quality, advantage, task, and vocation which God the Creator and Savior has allotted to individuals as well as to ethnical communities. The Church's maternal heart is big enough to see in the God-appointed development of such individual characteristics and gifts, rather the richness of diversity than a mere danger of divergency. She rejoices at the spiritual superiorities among individuals and nations. In their successes she sees with maternal joy and pride fruits of education and progress, which she can only bless and encourage, whenever she can conscientiously do so. But she also knows that to this freedom limits have been set by the majesty of the divine command, which founded and wanted that Church one and indivisible.[72]

This statement represents a clear refutation of the proposition on racism—and therefore of Hitler—by a positive deployment of Catholic doctrine. In his votum of March 17, 1934, Rabeneck had summarized Hitler's position as follows: "And so there is no such thing as a unitary and same nature of all human beings; rather, the entire human race is divided into races by nature itself."

An interesting internal document from the Holy Office, dated April 1937—in other words, a month after publication of the encyclical—allows us to crosscheck the syllabus against the encyclical. It had not escaped the cardinals and consultors of the congregation that *Mit brennender Sorge* contained passages that at least dealt with the same material as their own planned syllabus. As a result, on April 1 they commissioned a synopsis that would compare the propositions on racism, hypernationalism, and totalitarianism with statements contained in the encyclical.[73] It used the positive statements of doctrine in the encyclical that at least indirectly rejected particular National Socialist views to derive propositions that summarized the false Nazi positions.

For example, the encyclical reads, "Whoever exalts race, or the people, or the State, or a particular form of State . . . to the highest norm of all values, also the religious ones, and divinizes them to an idolatrous level, distorts and perverts an order of the world planned and created by God."[74] From this statement, the Holy Office derived the condemnable proposition, "Everything that benefits the people or the race is morally good or honorable as a result of that alone." By this process, the third proposition of the syllabus stood refuted by *Mit brennender Sorge*. Furthermore, the encyclical stated that parents "have a primary right to the education of their children in the spirit of their true Faith, and according to its prescriptions."[75] In the synopsis of April 1937, this sentence was simply reversed and formulated in the negative to represent the erroneous Nazi position. The fourth proposition in the syllabus, which was based on *Mein Kampf* and stated as condemnable that the only goal of education was to further improve the race and to develop the body in accordance with one's own race as the highest good, was therefore considered refuted by the encyclical.

The Holy Office viewed the publication of *Mit brennender Sorge* as a clear break of the magisterium with National Socialism and its racial doctrine in the spirit of the Office's own preliminary work on a projected syllabus. This interpretation is supported by a May 1937 statement by Cardinal Secretary of the Holy Office Sbarretti. In contrast to the summer of 1936, when the propositions against racism were held back because of potentially negative reactions on the part of the German and Italian governments, and the Holy Office decided to limit itself to a positive representation of Catholic principles, Sbarretti now felt that after publication of the encyclical, "no further grounds exist to make it appear advisable to exclude the theses on racism."[76] In other words, after *Mit brennender Sorge* had done what the Holy Office had refrained from doing out of respect for the governments in Germany and Italy, that is, denounce racism, there was no further need for the Holy Office to exercise restraint.

At the time, Sbarretti could not have known that Pius XI would, for political reasons, request the Congregation of Studies to continue its work on the antiracism syllabus. Researchers have repeatedly pointed out the close connection between the encyclical and the antiracism syllabus, which appeared on April 13, 1938, as a rescript from the Congregation of Studies to Catholic universities and faculties, and contained eight propositions about racism that contradicted Catholic doctrine.[77] The theologians were requested to subject these propositions to critical analysis, to determine their degree of corruption, and to refute them. Up to now these propositions have been viewed as the result of internal deliberations by the Congregation of Studies, which was responsible for overseeing Catholic education in general and theological studies at universities and seminaries. The new sources in the Archive of the Congregation for the Doctrine of the Faith, however, make clear that these theses may be traced back to the Holy Office's preoccupation with Hitler's *Mein Kampf.* Thus, for example, the second proposition, which dealt with the degree of separation between the various human races and animal species, is worded more or less the same in both documents.

The syllabus of the study congregation had originally been intended only for internal use; the Catholic theologians alone were asked to examine these theses. Nonetheless, the Italian, French, and German press soon got wind of these proceedings and quickly titled the eight theses the "Syllabus against Racism," which significantly was also taken up by the *Nationalsozialistische Monatshefte.* Under the headline, "Pope Organizes Battle against German Racial Doctrine," the party organ edited by Alfred Rosenberg vehemently rejected the Roman allegations—without knowing that the Holy Office had derived these propositions from Hitler's *Mein Kampf.* Not only had the results of German racial research been "distorted," but "'propositions' were insinuated which had never been proposed therein."[78] Thus at least the part of the larger antiracism syllabus that dealt with National Socialist racism made its way into print, though it did not condemn the ideology in the most effective public manner, given that it derived from the work of the Congregation of Studies and not from the considerably more important Suprema, and the actual author of the propositions, Adolf Hitler, was not explicitly named.

Pius XI had decided on a typically Roman compromise between dogma and diplomacy. Accordingly, the dangerous opinions to be found in *Mein Kampf* had been refuted in the syllabus of the Congregation of Studies and contrasted to the true Catholic doctrine in the encyclical *Mit brennender Sorge*. In this respect, the pope met the requirements of pure doctrine. Nonetheless, for political reasons he was not prepared to name names because he was unable and unwilling to attack the führer and Reich chancellor personally. The Catholic mindset of submission to authority may in the final analysis also have prevented the pope from condemning Hitler by name and placing his work on the Index. He may also have been following the advice of Freiburg Archbishop Conrad Gröber, who argued that Pius XI's previous statements "are sufficient proof that our Holy Church has condemned this movement as well-nigh satanic." Gröber held "further censure by the Congregation of the Holy Office" to be counterproductive.[79]

This a priori eliminated a third option for proceeding against the National Socialist dictator, one that had in fact been considered by the Curia—excommunication. The Jesuit Tacchi-Venturi, who served as a liaison between Pius XI and Mussolini, reported in a papal audience on April 10, 1938, that Mussolini was urging the Curia to take more decisive action against Hitler.[80] According to Tacchi-Venturi, Mussolini had during a private discussion on April 7 advised him to wait for a more opportune moment "to take more effective measures" such as excommunication. The führer, according to Mussolini, was no passing phenomenon, and he had achieved much success in Germany. In the final analysis, only war, which no one wanted, could stop him. Mussolini's pleas for more decisive action against Hitler apparently derived from his analysis of the political situation of the Church in Germany after the publication of *Mit brennender Sorge*. To strengthen the common front against Communism, it would be necessary to force Hitler to make peace with the Church.

The apostolic nuncio in Italy, Francesco Borgongini Duca (1884–1954), broached this same topic in a letter to Cardinal Secretary of State Pacelli on May 2, 1938. He reported on a meeting with Italian Secretary of State Galeazzo Ciano (1903–1944), who was also Mussolini's son-in-law, in which Ciano expressed deep regret about the persecution of the Church in Germany. In contrast to Mussolini, Ciano fundamentally appreciated the Curia's restraint with respect to Hitler and the National Socialist regime. Luckily, the Church had "taken no extraordinary actions such as excommunication or the breaking of diplomatic relations."[81]

The reports by Tacchi-Venturi and Borgongini Duca, which are largely in agreement, make it likely that Il Duce was actually considering Church sanctions against Hitler, including the possibility of excommunication. The more diplomatic opinion expressed by his son-in-law, who advised moderation, seems to have been more openly embraced by the Curia. In any case, Mussolini's reasoning had no further consequences. There is no trace in the Vatican archives of any effort to initiate excommunication proceedings against Adolf Hitler. Pronouncing a Reich chancellor and head of state anathema was simply out of the question. Hitler remained a member of the Catholic Church until the day he died. Like the pope, even the devil could be Catholic.

Chronology

1914	*May 27*	The Breslau cathedral chapter postulates Adolf Bertram as prince bishop.
	June 28	Assassination of Archduke Franz Ferdinand in Sarajevo.
	July 28	Austria-Hungary declares war on Serbia.
	August 1	General mobilization in Germany and declaration of war on Russia.
	August 3	Germany declares war on France, followed the next day by Great Britain's entry into the war.
	August 20	Death of Pius X. The conclave takes place during the first weeks of the war. The Italian government guarantees the freedom of the conclave.
	September 3	After several inconclusive ballots, Giacomo della Chiesa is elected pope.
	September 6	In recognition of the war, della Chiesa is crowned not in St. Peter's Cathedral but in the Sistine Chapel. He takes the name Benedict XV.
	October 13	Pietro Gasparri becomes cardinal secretary of state to Benedict XV.
	October 14	Raffaele Merry del Val is named secretary and therefore head of the Holy Office. He keeps this position until his death in 1930.
1916	*January 27*	Founding of the Spartacist League in Berlin.
	May 27	In a speech, U.S. President Woodrow Wilson lays out his ideas for world peace and the right to self-determination for all peoples.
	November	The Office of Secretary of State promulgates a general instruction for Giuseppe Aversa, who will serve as successor to Andreas Frühwirth, as nuncio in Munich.
	November 18	Peace note from Woodrow Wilson.

1917	January 17	Giuseppe Aversa becomes nuncio in Munich.
	March 11	Start of the February Revolution in Russia.
	April 6	The United States declares war on the German Reich.
	April 9	Giuseppe Aversa dies unexpectedly.
	May 17	Benedict XV promulgates the new canon law, written largely by Pietro Gasparri and Eugenio Pacelli, the *Codex Iuris Canonici*.
	May 29	Eugenio Pacelli becomes nuncio in Munich. The general instruction of November 1916 applies to him as well.
	July 19	A resolution initiated by Matthias Erzberger (Center Party) for a peace without annexations is accepted by the Center Party, the German Progress Party, and the SPD.
	August 1	Appeal for peace from Benedict XV. Eugenio Pacelli, who negotiated the terms of the peace initiative in the name of the pope, sees all his efforts end in failure.
	August 24	Michael Faulhaber, bishop of Speyer since 1911, becomes archbishop of Munich and Freysing as a result of nomination by King Ludwig III of Bavaria. His enthronement on September 3 is completely overshadowed by the war.
	November 7	Start of the October Revolution in Russia.
1918	January 8	Woodrow Wilson's Fourteen Point Plan.
	March 3	Treaty of Brest-Litovsk signed between the Central Powers and Russia.
	April 25	Achille Ratti becomes apostolic visitator to Poland and Lithuania.
	July 16	Execution of Czar Nicholas II and his family.
	November 7	Kurt Eisner proclaims the People's Republic of Bavaria, in Munich.
	November 9	Reich Chancellor Max von Baden proclaims the abdication of the kaiser and cedes his office to Friedrich Ebert (SPD). Philipp Scheidemann (SPD) proclaims the Democratic Republic, Karl Liebknecht the Socialist Council Republic. This development was preceded by numerous revolts, among others by sailors (November Revolution).
	November 11	Armistice negotiated.
	November 28	Kaiser Wilhelm II signs his renunciation of the throne.
	December 30	The Communist Party of Germany (KPD) is founded in Berlin
1919	January 19	Election to the constituent National Assembly.
	January 25	The allies agree to found the League of Nations.

	February 6	The Constituent National Assembly meets in Weimar.
	February 13	Government formed by the parties of the "Weimar Coalition": Center Party, German Democratic Party (DDP), and SPD.
	February 21	Bavarian Minister President Kurt Eisner shot, persistent unrest ensues, particularly in Munich.
	March 2–6	Founding congress of the Communist International (Comintern) in Moscow.
	March 23	The former Socialist Benito Mussolini founds the organization "Fasci di combattimento."
	April 7	The Council Republic is proclaimed in Munich.
	April 29	The Munich nunciature is occupied by Communists.
	May 2	Violent end to the Munich Council Republic.
	June 6	Achille Ratti made nuncio in Poland. When he insists that the ban on political propaganda on the part of the clergy be observed, the Polish government has him recalled.
	June 28	Versailles Peace Treaty signed.
	July 31	Adoption of the Weimar constitution.
	November 11	Death of Archbishop Felix Cardinal von Hartmann of Cologne; the chairmanship of the Fulda Conference of Bishops goes to Prince Bishop Adolf Bertram of Breslau.
1920	*January 10*	Versailles Peace Treaty takes effect.
	February 4	The Vatican gives the Bavarian government a draft for a Bavarian concordat. Negotiations last until 1924.
	February 24	Adolf Hitler proclaims the party program of the German Workers Party (DAP, later NSDAP).
	March 13–17	Lüttwitz-Kapp Putsch, followed by a general strike and revolt by the Red Ruhr Army.
	April 16	Eugenio Pacelli named nuncio to the Reich in Berlin. He hands his letter of accreditation to Reich President Friedrich Ebert on June 30.
	June 6	The parties of the Weimar Coalition suffer considerable losses in the first parliamentary elections.
	August 11	First Ecumenical Conference ("World Church Conference") in Geneva. The Roman Catholic Church does not participate.
	November 18	Alberto Vassallo di Torregrossa named Pacelli's successor in Munich. However, he does not take office until 1925 in order to enable Pacelli to complete the negotiations for a concordat with Bavaria.
1921	*June 13*	Benedict XV names Achille Ratti archbishop of Milan and cardinal.

	August 26	Matthias Erzberger murdered.
1922	*January 22*	Death of Benedict XV.
	February 6	Achille Ratti is elected pope on the fourteenth ballot in a conclave lasting four days. The same day, he names Gasparri cardinal secretary of state.
	February 12	Achille Ratti enthroned. He takes the name Pius XI. For the first time since 1870, the customary blessing "Urbi et orbi" is again dispensed from the outer loggia of St. Peter's Cathedral.
	October 27–28	The Italian Fascists begin their march on Rome.
	October 30	Mussolini is made minister president. The Fascist transformation of the state begins.
	December 23	In his first encyclical, *Ubi arcano,* Pius XI coins the term "Catholic Action." All those who have been baptized are to contribute to the spread and renewal of the Kingdom of Christ on earth under strict subordination to the Church hierarchy.
1923	*January 11*	French and Belgian troops march into the Ruhr region; start of the "occupation of the Ruhr."
	March 10	Alfred Rosenberg becomes editor of *Völkische Beobachter.*
	November 8–9	In Munich, the Hitler Putsch fails; Hitler sentenced to five years imprisonment; however, he is released early, in December 1924.
	November 16	Currency reform ends hyperinflation.
1924	*January 21*	Death of Lenin, who in an addendum to his testament insistently warns of Stalin.
	March 29	The concordat with Bavaria is signed and triggers heated public debate.
	June 10	Italian opposition politician Giacomo Matteotti is murdered by close associates of Mussolini. Start of the "Matteotti crisis," by the end of which, in 1925, Mussolini has consolidated his totalitarian regime.
1925	*February 27*	Hitler refounds the NSDAP, in Munich.
	April 26	Paul von Hindenburg is elected Reich president with 48.3 percent of the vote. Wilhelm Marx, candidate of the "Weimar Coalition," is barely defeated with 45.3 percent.
	June 24	The concordat with Bavaria takes effect.
	July 18	The first volume of Hitler's *Mein Kampf* published by Eher-Verlag.
	August 18	Nuncio Pacelli transfers to Berlin.
	October 5–16	The Locarno Conference attempts to normalize relations between the victors and Germany.
1926	*February 24*	Founding of the opus sacerdotale "Amici Israel."

	April 24	Germany and the Soviet Union sign the Berlin Pact.
	November 15	At the behest of the Holy Office, Pacelli writes a report about the ecumenical movement in Germany.
	December 6	The second volume of Hitler's *Mein Kampf* appears.
1927	*April 11*	In a letter to all German bishops, the Holy Office intends to ban all Catholics from participating in the ecumenical movement. Pacelli succeeds in preventing this document from being printed.
1928	*January 2*	Amici Israel petition for a reform of the Good Friday prayer for the Jews.
	January 6	In his encyclical *Mortalium animos,* Pius XI affirms that the Catholic Church is the one and true Church of Christ.
	January 18	The liturgical committee of the Congregation of Rites agrees to a reform in the Good Friday prayer.
	February 15	The parties of the Center-right coalition break off their negotiations about a new Reich educational law after heated argument.
	March 7	The Holy Office rejects a reform of the Good Friday prayer for the Jews.
	March 25	The decree of the Holy Office, in which hatred of Jews and anti-Semitism are condemned, appears.
	March 30	The Italian government bans all non-Fascist youth organizations.
	December 9	Prelate Ludwig Kaas, a confidant of Pacelli's, is elected chairman of the Center Party.
1929	*February 11*	Signing of the Lateran agreements between Italy and the Holy See, consisting of three documents: an agreement under which the Vatican becomes an independent neutral territory under papal sovereignty, a concordat, and a financial agreement. This resolves the "Roman question."
	June 14	The concordat between the Holy See and the Free State of Prussia is signed and takes effect on August 13.
	August 5	Pacelli reports to Vienna Nuncio Enrico Sibilia about a "certain Hitler."
	October 24	Wall Street crash; start of the Great Depression.
	November 18	Pacelli sends his final report, a good hundred pages in length, to Rome summarizing his years in Germany.
	November 29	Pacelli suggests negotiations for a concordat to the government of Baden.
	December 16	Pacelli is made a cardinal and is recalled to Rome.
1930	*February 7*	Eugenio Pacelli becomes Pietro Gasparri's successor as cardinal secretary of state.
	February 14	Cesare Orsenigo named nuncio to Berlin.

	March 29	The first presidential cabinet is named under Reich Chancellor Heinrich Brüning.
	June	Alfred Rosenberg's *Myth of the Twentieth Century* is published.
	July 18	The German parliament (Reichstag) is dissolved.
	September 14	The NSDAP makes significant gains during elections for the fifth German parliament and becomes the second strongest party after the SPD.
	September 30	The General vicariate in Mainz declares Catholicism and National Socialism to be irreconcilable. All German bishops subsequently condemn National Socialism.
	October 5	Reich Chancellor Heinrich Brüning speaks with leading Nazis about their potential collaboration in the government.
1931	*May 30*	Mussolini bans Catholic lay groups. Pius XI protests vigorously against this move.
	October 9	Brüning forms the second cabinet.
	November 10	Paul von Hindenburg and Heinrich Brüning conduct discussions with Hitler.
	December 9	Spain has a new republican constitution that drastically limits the rights of the Church.
1932	*April 10*	Paul von Hindenburg re-elected Reich president.
	May 29–30	Reich President Hindenburg dismisses Brüning; Franz von Papen's presidential cabinet formed.
	June 2	Franz von Papen leaves the Center Party, thereby forestalling his expulsion from the party.
	June 4	The German parliament is dissolved.
	July 20	Franz von Papen unseats the Prussian government and is named Reich commissar for Prussia.
	July 31	The NSDAP becomes the most powerful party in the sixth German Parliament.
	September 9	Konrad von Preysing becomes bishop of Eichstätt.
	September 12	German parliament dissolved after it passes a vote of no confidence in Papen's government.
	October 12	Cardinal Secretary of State Pacelli and the government of Baden sign a concordat, which goes into effect on March 11, 1933.
	November 6	In the elections for the seventh German parliament, the NSDAP suffers electoral losses but remains the strongest party.
	November 17	Franz von Papen's cabinet resigns.
	December 3	Reich President Hindenburg names Kurt von Schleicher the new Reich chancellor.

1933	*January 28*	Schleicher resigns.
	January 30	Adolf Hitler named Reich chancellor; Franz von Papen becomes vice-chancellor.
	February 27	The German Reichstag building is set on fire; the next day, emergency laws are decreed "for the protection of the people and the state."
	March 5	In the eighth parliamentary elections, the NSDAP and the DNVP achieve an absolute majority.
	March 20–21	First concentration camps in Dachau and Sachsenhausen.
	Mid-March	Cardinal Michael von Faulhaber writes a memorandum raising the possibility of retracting the declaration of irreconcilability between Catholicism and National Socialism.
	March 21	"Day of Potsdam"; Hindenburg and Hitler stage a day of national unity.
	March 23	Hitler's government policy statement. The German parliament, including the Center Party, agree to Hitler's "Enabling Act" ("Law to Remedy the Distress of the People and the Nation"), giving Hitler dictatorial powers.
	March 28	The German bishops retract their condemnation of National Socialism.
	April 1	Boycott of Jewish stores, physicians, and lawyers.
	April 7	Jews and opponents of the regime banned from pursuing their professions (Law for the Restoration of the Professional Civil Service).
	April 8	Ludwig Kaas meets with von Papen on the train to Rome. The two discuss negotiations for a concordat with the Reich.
	April 12	Arch-Abbot Raphael Walzer conveys a letter from Edith Stein to Pacelli. Stein entreats the pope to intercede for the persecuted Jews.
	April 20	Pacelli and Pius XI discuss Edith Stein's letter. Pacelli writes to Walzer but never mentions the persecution of the Jews.
	April 24	The Office of the Secretary of State decides that it would be "very delicate" for the pope to protest anti-Semitic acts in Germany.
	May 10	Book burnings in Germany.
	June 1	The Fulda Conference of Bishops meets. All German dioceses, including the Bavarian diocese, are represented for the first time.
	July 5	The Center Party dissolves itself. Germany becomes a one-party state.

	July 18	Clemens August Count von Galen is elected bishop of Münster.
	July 20	The Reichskonkordat is signed.
	September	The Office of the Secretary of State drafts an opinion about the relationship between the Holy See and National Socialism.
	September 21	The Protestant "Pfarrernotbund," which stands in opposition to the "German Christians," is officially formed on September 7, and Martin Niemöller and Dietrich Bonhoeffer soon join. This results in a split in the German Protestant Church.
1934	*January 24*	Alfred Rosenberg is given responsibility for training the NSDAP and its various organizations in Nazi ideology.
	February 14	Rosenberg's *Myth of the Twentieth Century* is placed on the Index of Forbidden Books by the Holy Office.
	April 30	Austria introduces a "corporatist state constitution."
	May 21	The "Associated German Religious Movement" is founded.
	May 29	First synod of the "Confessing Church."
	June 14	First meeting between Hitler and Mussolini in Venice.
	June 30	"Röhm Putsch." A number of prominent Catholics are killed in addition to the leadership of the SA.
	August 2	Death of Paul von Hindenburg. From this time forward, Hitler refers to himself as "führer and Reich chancellor."
	October 25	The Holy Office examines the Nazis' doctrine of blood and race. The expert Johann Baptist Rabeneck investigates Hitler's *Mein Kampf.* The result is a "syllabus" that contains a general reckoning with the ideologies of the twentieth century.
1935	*January 13*	In a plebiscite, 90 percent of the population of the Saar region vote to be reincorporated into the German Reich.
	April 5	Konrad Count von Preysing is elected bishop of Berlin.
	September 15	The anti-Semitic "Nuremberg Laws" (Law for the Protection of German Blood and German Honor; and the Reich Citizenship Law) disenfranchise and discriminate against Jews in Germany.
	October 3	Start of the Italian war against Abyssinia.
1936	*March 7*	German troops march into the demilitarized Rhineland.
	July 17	Start of the Spanish Civil War.
	August 1	Hitler opens the Olympic Games in Berlin.

	September 6	In a sermon at the Xanten pilgrimage, Clemens August von Galen elaborates the right of the Church to resist an unjust regime.
	November 1	Mussolini for the first time talks of a "Berlin-Rome axis." The start of further rapprochement between Germany and Italy.
	November 18	The cardinals of the Holy Office decide to postpone the "syllabus" to a time "undetermined." Nonetheless, they decide to continue examining the issue.
1937	*March 14*	Pius XI condemns National Socialism in his encyclical *Mit brennender Sorge*. The encyclical is read from German pulpits on March 21.
	March 19	The anti-Communist encyclical *Divini Redemptoris* is issued.
	April 26	The "Condor Legion" bombs Guernica.
	June 2	The "syllabus" is definitively postponed. Pius XI confirms this decision of the cardinals on June 4.
	September 25	Mussolini starts a five-day visit in Munich.
	December 13	Pacelli becomes camerlengo of the College of Cardinals.
1938	*March 12–13*	German troops march into Austria; "annexation" of Austria to the German Reich.
	April 10	The question of excommunicating Hitler comes up in an audience with Pius XI.
	April 13	A rescript elaborated by the Study Congregation, with eight theses on racism based on the work on the syllabus conducted by the Holy Office, is sent to Catholic faculties for discussion.
	May 3	Start of Hitler's state visit to Rome. Pius XI withdraws to Castel Gandolfo.
	June 22	Pius XI commissions the Jesuits John La Farge, Gustav Gundlach, and Gustave Desbuquois to draft an encyclical against racism. The "disappeared encyclical" is never published.
	October 1	The German Wehrmacht marches into the Sudeten region after the "Munich Conference."
	November 9–10	Anti-Jewish riots in Germany (Kristallnacht).
	November 17	The Law for the Defense of the Race is decreed in Italy.
1939	*January 10*	Pius XI intervenes with North American cardinals on behalf of Jewish scientists and students.
	January 30	Hitler warns that renewed war will lead to the "destruction of the Jewish race in Europe."

February 10   Death of Pius XI.

February 11   Pius XI had planned to use his speech on the occasion of the tenth anniversary of the conclusion of the Lateran agreements to state his position on Fascism. Pacelli, as camerlengo, has printed copies of the speech destroyed.

March 2   Eugenio Pacelli is elected pope and chooses the name Pius XII.

Notes

Introduction

1. "Nostre Informazioni" [report on the audience of May 15, 1929], in *L'Osservatore Romano*, no. 114 (May 16, 1929), p. 3.

2. "Santa Sede e Nazionalsocialismo: Dottrina e politica," undated [fall 1933]; Archivio Segreto Vaticano, Vatican City (henceforth: ASV), Archivio della Congregazione degli Affari Ecclesiastici Straordinari (henceforth: A.E.S.), Germania, 4 periodo, pos. 643, fasc. 160, fol. 11–15 (r only).

3. Erich Voegelin, *Political Religions*, Toronto Studies in Theology, vol. 23 (Lewiston, N.Y.: Edward Mellen Press, 1986), pp. 2–4.

4. Conrad Gröber, *Handbuch der religiösen Gegenwartsfragen* (Freiburg i. Br.: Herder, 1940), p. 601.

5. *Decrees of the Ecumenical Councils*, ed. Norman P. Tanner, S. J., vol. 1: *Nicaea I to Lateran V* (Washington, D.C.: Georgetown University Press, 1990), p. 230.

6. Engelbert Krebs, article: "Teufel," in *Lexikon für Theologie und Kirche* 10 (1938), pp. 10–17, especially p. 11.

7. Gröber, *Handbuch*, p. 93.

8. *Annuario Pontificio per l'anno 1930* (Vatican City, 1930), p. 29.

9. Speech by Cardinal Riarius Sforza at the First Vatican Council of December 12, 1869, in *Collectio Conciliorum recentiorum Ecclesiae Universae*, ed. Ludovico Petit and Ioanne Baptista Martin (Mansi 53), vol. 17 (Arnhem/Leipzig, 1927), p. 401.

10. Speech by Bishop Bartholomaeus d'Avanzo at the First Vatican Council of June 20, 1870, in *Collectio Conciliorum recentiorum Ecclesiae Universae*, vol. 16 (Mansi 52), pp. 760–767, especially p. 767.

11. August Bernhard Hasler, *How the Pope Became Infallible: Pius IX and the Politics of Persuasion* (Garden City, N.Y.: Doubleday, 1981), p. 48.

12. *Decrees of the Ecumenical Councils*, vol. 2: *Trent to Vatican II*, p. 806.

13. Ibid., pp. 811–816, especially pp. 811, 812, and 816.

14. Cited by Martin Hülskamp, article: "Tiara," in *Lexikon für Theologie und Kirche* 10 (2001), p. 20.

15. "Theologe: Papst Pius XII. wollte Hitler vom Teufel befreien," German Press Agency (DPA) report of January 23, 2002, 3:17 P.M.

16. Dan Brown, *Angels and Demons* (New York: Simon & Schuster, 2000), pp. 192–193.

1. Neutralizing Evil?

1. "Istruzioni per Monsignore Giuseppe Aversa Nunzio Apostolico di Baviera," dated November 1916; ASV, Archivio della Nunziatura di Monaco (henceforth: ANM), vol. 257, fasc. 10, fol. 1–108.

2. "Rundschreiben unseres Heiligsten Vaters Pius X., durch göttliche Vorsehung Papst, über die Lehren der Modernisten vom 8. September 1907, 'Pascendi dominici gregis'" (Freiburg i. Br.: Herder, 1907), p. 83.

3. Eugenio Pacelli, "Im Dienste des Friedens," May 29, 1917, in Pacelli, *Gesammelte Reden, ausgewählt und eingeleitet von Ludwig Kaas* (Berlin: Germania, 1930), pp. 25–27, cf. especially p. 26.

4. Cf. Pacelli to Benigni, dated June 8, 1912; ASV, Fondo Benigni, vol. 36, fol. 45r.

5. Pacelli to Gasparri, dated September 8, 1919; ASV, A.E.S., Germania, 3 periodo, pos. 1665, fasc. 878, fol. 7r–13r, cf. especially fol. 9v.

6. Antonio Scottà, "La conciliazione ufficiosa," *Diario del barone Carlo Monti "incaricato d'affari" del governo italiano presso la Santa Sede (1914–1922) (Storia e attualità 15),* 2 vols. (Vatican City: Libreria Editrice Vaticana, 1997), vol. 1, p. 469.

7. Gasparri to Pacelli, dated May 15, 1917; ASV, ANM, vol. 329, fasc. 1, fol. 37r–v.

8. "Istruzioni per Monsignore Giuseppe Aversa," ASV, ANM, vol. 257, fasc. 10, fol. 1–108.

9. Pacelli to Gasparri, dated June 30, 1917; ASV, A.E.S., Stati Ecclesiastici, 3 periodo, pos. 1317, fasc. 470, fol. 3.

10. Canon 329 §2, in *Codex Iuris Canonici. Pii X Pontificis Maximi iussu digestus Benedicti Papae XV auctoriate promulgatus* (Vatican City, 1917).

11. Eugenio Pacelli, *Die Lage der Kirche in Deutschland 1929,* ed. Hubert Wolf and Klaus Unterburger (Veröffentlichungen der Kommission für Zeitgeschichte A 50) (Paderborn: Schöningh, 2006), pp. 218–223.

12. Ibid., pp. 240–242.

13. Ibid., pp. 248–253.

14. Ibid., p. 229.

15. Pacelli to Vassallo di Torregrossa, dated July 27, 1932; ASV, A.E.S., Baviera, 4 periodo, pos. 185, fasc. 31, fol. 28r–v.

16. Triennial list of the cathedral chapter of Munich and Freising of June 18, 1926; ASV, A.E.S., Baviera, 4 periodo, pos. 165, fasc. 14, fol. 9r–v.

17. Triennial list of the cathedral chapter of Speyer of May 21, 1926; ASV, A.E.S., Baviera, 4 periodo, pos. 165, fasc. 14, fol. 20r–26r.

18. Minutes of the meeting of the Freising Conference of Bishops of September 7–9, 1926; ASV, A.E.S., Baviera, 4 periodo, pos. 165, fasc. 14, fol. 52r–55v, 56r–59v, 60r, 61r.

19. Cf. the corresponding triennial lists; ASV, A.E.S., Baviera, 4 periodo, pos. 165, fasc. 14 and 15.

20. Vassallo di Torregrossa to Pacelli, dated August 16, 1932; ASV, A.E.S., Baviera, 4 periodo, pos. 185, fasc. 31, fol. 36r–37r.

21. Held to Ritter zu Groenesteyn, dated July 16, 1932; ASV, A.E.S., Baviera, 4 periodo, pos. 185, fasc. 31, fol. 32r.

22. Pacelli to Ritter zu Groenesteyn, dated August 30, 1932 (draft); ASV, A.E.S., Baviera, 4 periodo, pos. 185, fasc. 31, fol. 34r.

23. On the Berlin bishop's election of 1933, cf. ASV, A.E.S., Germania, 4 periodo, pos. 648, fasc. 192.

24. On the Berlin bishop's election of 1935, cf. ASV, A.E.S., Germania, 4 periodo, pos. 674, fasc. 234. See also Thomas Brechenmacher, "Teufelspakt, Selbsterhaltung, universale Mission? Leitlinien und Spielräume der Politik des Heiligen Stuhls gegenüber dem nationalsozialistischen Deutschland (1933–1939) im Lichte neu zugänglicher vatikanischer Akten," in *Historische Zeitschrift* 280 (2005), pp. 591–645.

25. Pacelli to Preysing, dated November 27, 1935; ASV, A.E.S., Germania, 4 periodo, pos. 647, fasc. 185, fol. 80r–v.

26. *Die Encyclica Seiner Heiligkeit Papst Pius IX. vom 8. December 1864 und der Syllabus (die Zusammenstellung der 80 hauptsächlichsten Irrthümer unserer Zeit) und die wichtigsten darin angeführten Actenstücke* (Cologne, 1865), pp. 51–74, cf. especially p. 53.

27. Pacelli, *Lage,* p. 109.

28. Ibid., p. 103.

29. Ibid., p. 105.

30. Ibid., p. 139.

31. Ibid., p. 141.

32. Ibid., p. 117.

33. Ibid., p. 111.

34. Ibid., pp. 139 and 141.

35. Ibid., p. 147.

36. Ibid., pp. 173 and 179.

37. Ibid., p. 131.

38. Ibid.

39. Ibid., p. 135.

40. Ibid., p. 137.

41. Julius Bachem, "Wir müssen aus dem Turm heraus," in *Historisch-Politische Blätter,* 137 (1906), pp. 376–386.

42. Pacelli, *Lage*, pp. 163 and 165.

43. Quoted from Karl Bachem, *Vorgeschichte, Geschichte und Politik der Deutschen Zentrumspartei. Zugleich ein Beitrag zur Geschichte der katholischen Bewegung, sowie zur allgemeinen Geschichte des neueren und neuesten Deutschland 1815–1914,* vol. 3 (Cologne: Bachem, 1927), p. 413.

44. Heinrich Brüning, *Memoiren 1918–1934* (Stuttgart: Deutsche Verlangsanstalt, 1970), p. 358.

45. Ibid., p. 135f.

46. Pacelli to the Secretary of State, dated February 20, 1919; ASV, Archivio della Nunziatura di Berlino (henceforth: ANB), vol. 91, fasc. 2, fol. 35r–36v, cf. 36v.

47. Gasparri to Pacelli, dated September 12, 1924; ASV, ANB, vol. 92, fasc. 6, fol. 1r.

48. Pacelli to Gasparri, dated October 22, 1924; ASV, A.E.S., Stati Ecclesiastici, 4 periodo, pos. 359, fasc. 248, fol. 11r–20r, cf. fol. 15r, 16v, 17r, 18r.

49. Gasparri to Pacelli, dated April 29, 1925; ASV, ANB, vol. 92, fasc. 6, fol. 87r.

50. Pacelli to Gasparri, dated May 22, 1925; ASV, A.E.S., Stati Ecclesiastici, 4 periodo, pos. 359, fasc. 248, fol. 24r–25r, cf. fol. 25r.

51. Gasparri to Pacelli, dated May 28, 1925; ASV, ANB, vol. 92, fasc. 6, fol. 95r–96r, cf. fol. 95v–96r.

52. Ibid., fol. 96r.

53. Gasparri to Pacelli, dated September 17, 1925; ASV, ANB, vol. 92, fasc. 6, fol. 145r.

54. Pacelli to Gasparri, dated September 6, 1925; ASV, A.E.S., Stati Ecclesiastici, 4 periodo, pos. 359, fasc. 248, fol. 49r–50v, cf. fol. 50r (copy); ASV, ANB, vol. 92, fasc. 6, fol. 137r–138v, cf. fol. 138r (draft).

55. Pacelli to Gasparri, dated December 9, 1925; ASV, A.E.S., Stati Ecclesiastici, 4 periodo, pos. 359, fasc. 248, fol. 57r–60r (copy); ASV, ANB, vol. 92, fasc. 4, fol. 53r–54r, cf. fol. 54r (draft).

56. Pacelli to Gasparri, dated December 1, 1925; ASV, ANB, vol. 92, fasc. 4, fol. 49r–52r.

57. Pacelli to Pizzardo, dated January 6, 1927; ASV, ANB, vol. 92, fasc. 6, fol. 163r–164r, cf. fol. 163v and 164r.

58. Pacelli, *Lage*, p. 171.

59. "Koalitionsverbreiterung? Stegerwald gegen Spahn," in *Germania*, no. 536, November 17, 1926, p. 1f., cf. p. 1.

60. Pacelli to Pizzardo, dated January 6, 1927; ASV, ANB, vol. 92, fasc. 6, fol. 164r–v.

61. Pacelli, *Lage*, pp. 167 and 169.

62. Ibid., p. 249.

63. Eugenio Pacelli, "Zurück nach Rom, December 10, 1929," in Pacelli, *Gesammelte Reden*, pp. 187–190, cf. especially p. 190.

64. Wolfgang Reinhard, "Historische Anthropologie frühneuzeitlicher Diplomatie: Ein Versuch über Nuntiaturberichte 1592–1622," in Michael Rohrschneider and Arno Strohmeyer, eds., *Wahrnehmungen des Fremden. Differenzerfahrungen von Diplomaten im 16. und 17. Jahrhundert* (Münster: Aschendorff, 2007), p. 67.

65. Pacelli to Gasparri, dated August 25, 1926; ASV, A.E.S., Germania, 3 periodo, pos. 559, fasc. 76, fol. 72r–75v, here cf. fol. 72r–v.

66. Pacelli to Gasparri, dated May 29, 1917; ASV, ANM, vol. 328, fasc. 2, fol. 1r.

67. Pacelli to Gasparri, dated June 30, 1917; ASV, A.E.S., Stati Ecclesiastici, 3 periodo, pos. 1317, fasc. 470-III, fol. 111r–120v, here fol. 111r.

68. Pacelli to Gasparri, dated April 30, 1919; ASV, A.E.S., Baviera, 3 periodo, pos. 62, fasc. 40, fol. 42r–45v, cf. fol. 42v and fol. 45r.

69. Pacelli to Gasparri, dated October 5, 1920; ASV, A.E.S., Germania, 3 periodo, pos. 1706, fasc. 894, fol. 2r–4r, cf. fol. 2v.

70. Pacelli to Gasparri, dated March 29, 1923; ASV, A.E.S., Baviera, 4 periodo, pos. 151, fasc. 2, fol. 68r–69v, cf. fol. 68v.

71. Pacelli to Gasparri, dated April 26, 1924; ASV, A.E.S., Germania, 4 periodo, pos. 546, fasc. 69, fol. 43r–44r, cf. fol. 43r.

72. Pacelli to Gasparri, dated April 30, 1919; ASV, A.E.S., Baviera, 3 periodo, pos. 62, fasc. 40, fol. 42r–45v, cf. fol. 45v.

73. Pacelli to Gasparri, dated April 18, 1919; ASV, A.E.S., Baviera, 3 periodo, pos. 62, fasc. 40, fol. 36r–38v, cf. fol. 36v–37r.

2. Perfidious Jews?

1. Daniel Goldhagen, *A Moral Reckoning: The Role of the Catholic Church in the Holocaust and Its Unfulfilled Duty of Repair* (New York: Knopf, 2002), p. 297n15.

2. "Decree of March 25, 1928," in *Acta Apostolicae Sedis* 20 (1928), p. 103.

3. *The Roman Missal in Latin and English, Arranged for the Use of the Laity to Which Is Added a Collection of Usual Public Prayers,* 3rd ed. (New York: Benziger Brothers, 1925), pp. 493–494.

4. *The Roman Missal in Latin and English, Arranged for the Use of the Laity to Which Is Added a Collection of Usual Public Prayers* (Tournay, Belgium: Society of St. John the Evangelist, Desclée & Co., 1911), pp. 490–491.

5. *The Roman Missal in Latin and English,* 3rd ed., pp. 490–491.

6. Faulhaber to van Leer, dated January 30, 1930, and April 21, 1930; Erzbischöfliches Archiv München (henceforth: EAM), estate (henceforth: ES) Faulhaber 6284.

7. Publicity letter "Pax super Israel" [1926], 3 pages in length; EAM ES Faulhaber 6284.

8. *Pax super Israel,* Rome 1928; Archivio della Congregazione per la Dottrina della Fede, Vatican City (henceforth: ACDF), Sanctum Officium (henceforth: SO), Rerum Variarum (henceforth: RV) 1928, no. 2, fasc. 1, no. 16/2. Cf. also the

summary of the letter that a member of the Holy Office wrote for the deliberations of the congregation; ACDF, SO RV 1928, no. 2, fasc. 2, no. 17.

9. Cf. thereto EAM, ES Faulhaber 4500 and 4501. This link is mentioned in the "Status Operis"; ACDF, SO RV 1928, no. 2, fasc. 1, no. 22.

10. Faulhaber to Asseldonk, dated April 20, 1927; EAM, ES Faulhaber 6284.

11. Latin summary of Faulhaber's Homiletics Course, undated [1927/28]; ACDF, SO RV, no. 2, fasc. 1, no. 23. A copy, registered by the Holy Office on March 13, 1928, is contained in the files.

12. Gariador and Asseldonk to Pius XI, dated January 2, 1928; ACDF, SO RV 1928, no. 2, fasc. 1, no. 2.

13. Sample prayer; ACDF, SO RV 1928, no. 2, fasc. 1, no. 4.

14. "Promemoria explicative," undated [registered by the Holy Office on January 27, 1928]; ACDF, SO RV 1928, no. 2, fasc. 1, no. 6.

15. Gariador and Asseldonk to Pius XI, dated January 2, 1928, with annotation by the secretary of the Congregation of Rites: "Ad R. P. Abb. Ilde. Schuster OSB, Consultorem pro studio et voto"; ACDF, SO RV 1928, no. 2, fasc. 1, no. 2.

16. Marcel Poorthuis and Theo Salemink, *Op zoek naar de blauwe ruiter. Sophie van Leer. Een leven tussen avant-garde, jodendom en christendom (1892–1953)* (Nijmegen, 2000), p. 277; Marcel Poorthuis and Theo Salemink, "Chiliasme, antijudaisme en antisemitisme. Laetus Himmelreich OFM (1886–1957)," *Trajecta*, 9 (2000), p. 58.

17. Promemoria; ACDF, SO RV 1928, no. 2, fasc. 1, no. 5.

18. *Lexicon Totius Latinitatis, consilio et cura Jacobi Facciolati, opera et studio Aegidii Forcellini,* vol. 3 (Schneeberg, 1833), p. 346.

19. Marcus Magistretti, ed., *Manuale Ambrosianum ex codice saec. XI olim in usum canonicae vallis Travalliae in duas partes. Pars altera* (Milan, 1904), p. 194.

20. Schuster to Mariani, dated January 16, 1928; ACDF, SO RV 1928, no. 2, fasc. 1, no. 9. No biographical information could be found on Mariani, secretary of the Congregation of Rites from 1925 to 1929.

21. Instructions from the secretary of the Congregation of Rites to Monsignore Luigi Grammatica, dated January 9, 1928; ACDF, SO RV 1928, no. 2, fasc. 1, no. 6.

22. Giovanni Castoldi to Luigi Grammatica, dated January 16, 1928; ACDF, SO RV 1928, no. 2, fasc. 1, no. 7.

23. "Variazioni," undated [as enclosure 2 sent by the Congregation of Rites to the Holy Office and registered there on January 27, 1928]; ACDF, SO RV 1928, no. 2, fasc. 1, no. 8.

24. Decision of the liturgical committee of the Congregation of Rites, dated January 18, 1928; ACDF, SO RV 1928, no. 2, fasc. 1, no. 3.

25. Mariani to Canali, dated January 25, 1928; ACDF, SO RV 1928, no. 2, fasc. 1, no. 1.

26. Opinion of Sales; ACDF, SO RV 1928, no. 2, fasc. 1, no. 15.

27. Invitation card to the annual meeting [Merry del Val's personal invitation]; ACDF, SO RV 1928, no. 2, fasc. 1, no. 13.

28. One-page typewritten information about the Amici, probably by the assessor, who states that Monsignore Palica had reported about it to the Holy Office; ACDF, SO RV 1928, no. 2, fasc. 1, no. 18.

29. "Brevissimo riassunto di questa prima communicazione periodica del Comitato Centrale degli Amici d'Israele"; ACDF, SO RV 1928, no. 2, fasc. 1, no. 17.

30. "'Amici d'Israele,' Alcune proposizioni erronee o mal sonanti riscontrate nell'Opuscolo dall motto 'Pax super Israel,'" undated; ACDF, SO RV 1928, no. 2, fasc. 1, no. 16/2.

31. Consultors meeting Feria Secunda on February 27, 1928; ACDF, SO RV 1928, no. 2, fasc. 1, no. 19.

32. Votum by Merry del Val for the cardinals' plenary Feria Quarta on March 7, 1928; ACDF, SO RV 1928, no. 2, fasc. 1, no. 20.

33. Minutes of the meeting of the Congregation of Cardinals Feria Quarta, dated March 7, 1928; ACDF, SO RV 1928, no. 2, fasc. 1, no. 21.

34. Minutes of the assessor's audience with Pius XI, dated March 8, 1928; ACDF, SO RV 1928, no. 2, fasc. 1, no. 21 bis.

35. Italian version of the decree for the meeting on March 14, 1928; ACDF, SO RV 1928, no. 2, fasc. 1, no. 25.

36. "Modificazioni al surreferito Schema di Decreto . . . da alcuni Eminentissimi Cardinali"; ACDF, SO RV 1928, no. 2, fasc. 1, no. 27 bis. Translation by Thomas Brechenmacher, *Der Vatikan und die Juden. Geschichte einer unheiligen Beziehung vom 16. Jahrhundert bis zur Gegenwart* (Munich: C. H. Beck, 2005), p. 160.

37. Minutes of Merry del Val's audience with Pius XI, on March 15, 1928; ACDF, SO RV 1928, no. 2, fasc. 1, no. 27.

38. Decree of March 25, 1928, in *Acta Apostolicae Sedis* 20 (1928), p. 103.

39. Minutes of Merry del Val's audience with Pius XI, on March 15, 1928; ACDF, SO RV 1928, no. 2, fasc. 1, no. 27.

40. Minutes of the meeting of the Holy Office and the subsequent audience with Pius XI, dated March 20–21, 1928; ACDF, SO RV 1928, no. 2, fasc. 2, no. 34.

41. Record of Lottini's discussion with Schuster, dated March 16, 1928; ACDF, SO RV 1928, no. 2, fasc. 1, no. 29.

42. Letter of submission handwritten by Schuster to Lottini, dated March 16, 1928; ACDF, SO RV 1928, no. 2, fasc. 1, no. 30.

43. Record of Alfonso Gasparini's discussion with Gariador, dated April 3, 1928; ACDF, SO RV 1928, no. 2, fasc. 2, no. 39.

44. Abbot Gariador's letter of submission, dated April 11, 1928; ACDF, SO RV 1928, no. 2, fasc. 2, no. 41.

45. Record of Asseldonk's discussion with Lottini, dated March 28, 1928; ACDF, SO RV 1928, no. 2, fasc. 2, no. 38.

46. Asseldonk's letter of submission, dated April 12, 1928; ACDF, SO RV 1928, no. 2, fasc. 2, no. 42.

47. Asseldonk's official act of submission in the name of the entire directorship of the Amici Israel, dated April 13, 1928; ACDF, SO RV 1928, no. 2, fasc. 2, no. 43.

48. Decision of the cardinals, dated April 14, 1928, with regard to Asseldonk's two letters; ACDF, SO RV 1928, no. 2, fasc. 2, no. 44.

49. Record of Asseldonk's admonition by Alfonso Gasparini, dated April 17, 1928; ACDF, SO RV 1928, no. 2, fasc. 2, no. 46.

50. Minutes of the meeting of the cardinals of the Holy Office Feria Quarta, dated April 18, 1928; ACDF, SO RV 1928, no. 2, fasc. 2, no. 47.

51. *Jewish World*, April 16, 1928; ACDF, SO RV 1928, no. 2, fasc. 3, no. 48.

52. D. Mondrone, "Il padre Enrico Rosa D.C.D.G. In memoriam patris," *Civiltà Cattolica*, 89, 4 (1938), pp. 481–496.

53. Enrico Rosa, "Il pericolo Giudaico e gli 'Amici d'Israele,'" *Civiltà Cattolica*, 79, 2 (1928), pp. 335–344; ACDF, SO RV 1928, no. 2, fasc. 3, no. 49.

54. Enrico Rosa, "Semitismo e antisemitismo. A propositio del decreto del Sant' Uffizio su 'gli Amici di Israele,'" *L'Avvenire d'Italia*, no. 128, May 30, 1928, p. 2; ACDF, SO RV 1928, no 2, fasc. 3, no. 50.

55. Gustav Gundlach, article: "Antisemitismus," in *Lexikon für Theologie and Kirche* I (1930), col. 504f.

56. Urs Altermatt, *Katholizismus und Antisemitismus. Mentalitäten, Kontinuitäten, Ambivalenzen. Zur Kulturgeschichte der Schweiz 1918–1945* (Frauenfeld: Huber, 1999), p. 51.

57. Ibid., p. 55.

58. Anselm Schott, *Das Meßbuch der heiligen Kirche. Mit liturgischen Erklärungen and kurzen Lebensbeschreibungen der Heiligen*. Neubearbeitet von Mönchen der Erzabtei Beuron (Freiburg i. Br.: Herder, 1937), p. 330.

59. "Declaration of the Congregation of Rites, of June 10, 1948," in *Acta Apostolicae Sedis* 40 (1948), p. 342.

60. *Die Feier der Heiligen Woche* (Beiheft zum Laudate) (Münster, 1956); *Das vollständige Römische Meßbuch lateinisch and deutsch mit allgemeinen and besonderen Einführungen im Anschluß an das Meßbuch von Anselm Schott herausgegeben von Benediktinern der Erzabtei Beuron* (Freiburg i. Br.: Herder, 1956), p. 392.

61. Karl Rahner and Herbert Vorgrimler, *Kleines Konzilskompendium. Sämtliche Texte des Zweiten Vaticanums mit Einführungen and ausführlichem Sachregister* (Freiburg i. Br.: Herder, 1979), p. 351.

62. www.vatican.va/archive/hist_councils/ii_vatican_council/documents/vat-ii_decl_19651028_nostra-aetate_en.html (accessed September 24, 2009).

63. *New Saint Joseph Weekday Missal*, complete ed., vol. I: *Advent to Pentecost* (New York: Catholic Book Publishing Co., 1975), p. 709.

64. "Verzeihen ist Voraussetzung zur Versöhnung. Inständiges Gebet und

besinnliche Stille," in *L'Osservatore Romano,* German ed., no. 11 (March 17, 2000), p. 6.

65. Benedict XVI, apostolic letter "Summorum pontificum," dated July 7, 2007; Verlautbarungen des Apostolischen Stuhles 178 (Bonn, 2007), p. 11.

66. "Nota della Segretaria di Stato," in *L'Osservatore Romano,* no. 31 (February 6, 2008), p. 1.

3. The Pact with the Devil?

1. ASV, A.E.S., Stati Ecclesiastici, 4 periodo, pos. 430, fasc. 340–355.

2. ASV, A.E.S., Stati Ecclesiastici, 4 periodo, pos. 430, fasc. 356–364.

3. François Charles-Roux, *Huit ans au Vatican, 1932–1940* (Paris : Flammarion, 1947), p. 70.

4. Audience of August 11, 1936; ASV, A.E.S., Stati Ecclesiastici, 4 periodo, pos. 430a, fasc. 353, fol. 62r.

5. "La Santa Sede e la situazione religiosa in Spagna," in *L'Osservatore Romano,* no. 186 (August 11, 1936), p. 1.

6. Charles-Roux, *Huit ans,* p. 74.

7. Pacelli to Gasparri, dated November 12, 1923; ASV, ANM, vol. 396, fasc. 7, fol. 5r.

8. Pacelli to Gasparri, dated November 14, 1923; ASV, ANM, vol. 396, fasc. 7, fol. 6r–7v (draft); ASV, A.E.S., Baviera, 4 periodo, pos. 151, fasc. 3, fol 9r–10r (official copy).

9. Pacelli to Gasparri, dated May 1, 1924; ASV, ANM, vol. 396, fasc. 7, fol. 79r–v (draft); ASV, A.E.S., Germania, 4 periodo, pos. 546, fasc. 69, fol. 49r–v (official copy).

10. Pacelli to Sibilia, dated August 5, 1929; ASV, ANB, vol. 94, fasc. 59, fol. 682r–683r.

11. Audience of January 9, 1931; ASV, A.E.S., Stati Ecclesiastici, 4 periodo, pos. 430, fasc. 356, fol. 20r–v.

12. Audience of March 6, 1931; ASV, A.E.S., Stati Ecclesiastici, 4 periodo, pos. 430, fasc. 356, fol. 57r–v.

13. Audience of March 13, 1931; ASV, A.E.S., Stati Ecclesiastici, 4 periodo, pos. 430, fasc. 356, fol. 64r–65v.

14. Cf. as example, audience of June 19, 1931; ASV, A.E.S., Stati Ecclesiastici, 4 periodo, pos. 430, fasc. 357, fol. 9r–10v.

15. Audience of July 10, 1931; ASV, A.E.S., Stati Ecclesiastici, 4 periodo, pos. 430, fasc. 357, fol. 21r–v.

16. Cf. as example, audience of November 11, 1931; ASV, A.E.S., Stati Ecclesiastici, 4 periodo, pos. 430, fasc. 357, fol. 54r–55r.

17. Audience of December 18, 1931; ASV, A.E.S., Stati Ecclesiastici, 4 periodo, pos. 430, fasc. 357, fol. 77r–78r.

18. Audience, undated [early January 1932]; ASV, A.E.S., Stati Ecclesiastici, 4 periodo, pos. 430, fasc. 357, fol. 87r–88r.

19. Audience of April 1, 1932; ASV, A.E.S., Stati Ecclesiastici, 4 periodo, pos. 430, fasc. 358, fol. 2r–3v.

20. Audience of April 29, 1932; ASV, A.E.S., Stati Ecclesiastici, 4 periodo, pos. 430, fasc. 358, fol. 13r–14r.

21. Audience of May 20, 1932; ASV, A.E.S., Stati Ecclesiastici, 4 periodo, pos. 430, fasc. 358, fol. 25r–26v.

22. Audience of June 24, 1932; ASV, A.E.S., Stati Ecclesiastici, 4 periodo, pos. 430, fasc. 358, fol. 42r–v.

23. Audience of September 2, 1932; ASV, A.E.S., Stati Ecclesiastici, 4 periodo, pos. 430, fasc. 358, fol. 72r–73r.

24. Audience of October 21, 1932; ASV, A.E.S., Stati Ecclesiastici, 4 periodo, pos. 430, fasc. 358, fol. 79r–80v.

25. Audience of October 28, 1932; ASV, A.E.S., Stati Ecclesiastici, 4 periodo, pos. 430, fasc. 358, fol. 83r–86v.

26. Audience of November 11, 1932; ASV, A.E.S., Stati Ecclesiastici, 4 periodo, pos. 430, fasc. 358, fol. 96r–99v.

27. Heinrich Brüning, *Memoiren, 1918–1934* (Stuttgart: Deutsche Verlagsanstalt, 1970), p. 358.

28. Cf. Gerhard Besier, in cooperation with Francesca Piombo, *Der Heilige Stuhl und Hitler-Deutschland. Die Faszination des Totalitären* (Munich, 2004), pp. 140–145, 152–162 (English trans. by W. R. Ward, *The Holy See and Hitler's Germany* [New York: Palgrave Macmillan, 2007]); Giovanni Sale, *Hitler, la Santa Sede e gli ebrei, con documenti dell'Archivio Segreto Vaticano* (Milan: Jaca Book, 2004), pp. 275–313. Thomas Brechenmacher is preparing an edition of all Orsenigo's reports in cooperation with DHI Rome and the Commission for Contemporary History; cf. www.dhi-roma.it/denq.html (accessed September 28, 2009).

29. Thomas Brechenmacher, "Teufelspakt, Selbsterhaltung, universale Mission? Leitlinien und Spielräume der Politik des Heiligen Stuhls gegenüber dem nationalsozialistischen Deutschland (1933–1939) im Lichte neu zugänglicher vatikanischer Akten," *Historische Zeitschrift* 280 (2005), pp. 605–607, with much documentation.

30. Orsenigo to Pacelli, dated September 16, 1930; ASV, A.E.S., Germania, 4 periodo, pos. 606, fasc. 117, fol. 18r–19v.

31. Letter from the vicar general of the bishopric of Mainz, Philipp Jakob Meyer, to the leadership of the NSDAP Regional Administrative District of the District of Hessen-Darmstadt concerning the reasons the Catholics were forbidden membership in the party, dated September 30, 1930, in Hubert Gruber, *Katholische Kirche und Nationalsozialismus, 1930–1945. Ein Bericht in Quellen* (Paderborn: Schöningh, 2006), pp. 2–4, cf. especially pp. 2 and 3.

32. Orsenigo to Pacelli, dated October 8, 1930; ASV, A.E.S., Germania, 4 periodo, pos. 621, fasc. 138, fol. 3r–4r.

33. Note from Pizzardo instructing Orsenigo, dated October 13, 1930; ASV, A.E.S., Germania, 4 periodo, pos. 621, fasc. 138, fol. 11r. Cf. Brechenmacher, "Teufelspakt," p. 603.

34. Pizzardo by order of Pacelli to Orsenigo, dated October 13, 1930; ASV, A.E.S., Germania, 4 periodo, pos. 621, fasc. 138, fol. 11r.

35. Orsenigo to Pacelli, dated December 8, 1930; ASV, A.E.S., Germania, 4 periodo, pos. 621, fasc. 138, fol. 19r–20v.

36. Orsenigo to Pacelli, dated December 29, 1930; ASV, A.E.S., Germania, 4 periodo, pos. 604, fasc. 112, fol. 49r.

37. Orsenigo to Pacelli, dated January 27, 1931; ASV, A.E.S., Germania, 4 periodo, pos. 621, fasc. 138, fol. 25r–26r.

38. Report on the negotiations regarding National Socialism of the Diocesan Synod for the Archdiocese of Munich and Freising, dated November 19, 1930, in Gruber, *Kirche,* p. 4f., cf. especially p. 5.

39. Instructions from the Bavarian bishops to the clergy about their stance toward National Socialism, dated February 10, 1931, in Gruber, *Kirche,* pp. 6–8, especially pp. 7 and 8.

40. Vassallo di Torregrossa to Pacelli, dated February 17, 1931; ASV, A.E.S., Germania, 4 periodo, pos. 621, fasc. 138, fol. 27r–v.

41. Declaration of the bishops of the Upper Rhine Church Province about National Socialism, dated March 19, 1931, in Gruber, *Kirche,* pp. 9–11, cf. especially p. 11.

42. Orsenigo to Pacelli, dated March 8, 1931; ASV, A.E.S., Germania, 4 periodo, pos. 621, fasc. 138, fol. 33r–v.

43. Orsenigo to Pacelli, dated October 11, 1931; ASV, A.E.S., Germania, 4 periodo, pos. 604, fasc. 112, fol. 84r–85v.

44. Orsenigo to Pacelli, dated November 21, 1931; ASV, A.E.S., Germania, 4 periodo, pos. 604, fasc. 112, fol. 92r–94r.

45. Orsenigo to Pacelli, dated January 23, 1933; ASV, A.E.S., Germania, 4 periodo, pos. 604, fasc. 113, fol. 41r–42v.

46. Audience of December 19, 1930; ASV, A.E.S., Stati Ecclesiastici, 4 periodo, pos. 430a, fasc. 340, fol. 98r.

47. Audience of April 12, 1931; ASV, A.E.S., Stati Ecclesiastici, 4 periodo, pos. 430a, fasc. 342, fol. 8v–9v.

48. Audience of December 20, 1931; ASV, A.E.S., Stati Ecclesiastici, 4 periodo, pos. 430a, fasc. 344, fol. 47v.

49. Audience of February 3, 1931; ASV, A.E.S., Stati Ecclesiastici, 4 periodo, pos. 430a, fasc. 341, fol. 35r.

50. Göring to Pacelli, dated April 30, 1931; ASV, A.E.S., Germania, 4 periodo, pos. 621, fasc. 138, fol. 38r. Cf. Besier, *Heiliger Stuhl,* pp. 152–156.

51. Pizzardo's memorandum of May 3, 1931; ASV, A.E.S., Germania, 4 periodo, pos. 621, fasc. 138, fol. 40r–v.

52. Audience of July 6, 1931; ASV, A.E.S., Stati Ecclesiastici, 4 periodo, pos. 430a, fasc. 343, fol. 3r–v.

53. Audience of November 15, 1931; ASV, A.E.S., Stati Ecclesiastici, 4 periodo, pos. 430a, fasc. 344, fol. 12r–v.

54. Audience of August 6, 1932; ASV, A.E.S., Stati Ecclesiastici, 4 periodo, pos. 430a, fasc. 346, fol. 36r.

55. Audience of April 17, 1932; ASV, A.E.S., Stati Ecclesiastici, 4 periodo, pos. 430a, fasc. 345, fol. 38r.

56. Audience of April 29, 1932; ASV, A.E.S., Stati Ecclesiastici, 4 periodo, pos. 430a, fasc. 345, fol. 49r.

57. Audience of February 1, 1933; ASV, A.E.S., Stati Ecclesiastici, 4 periodo, pos. 430, fasc. 359, fol. 35r–36r.

58. Announcement by the German bishops about their stance toward National Socialism, dated March 28, 1933, in Gruber, *Kirche*, p. 39f.

59. Klaus Scholder, "Altes und Neues zur Vorgeschichte des Reichskonkordats. Erwiderung auf Konrad Repgen," in Scholder, *Die Kirchen zwischen Republik und Gewaltherrschaft. Gesammelte Aufsätze*, ed. Karl Otmar von Aretin and Gerhard Besier (Berlin: Siedler, 1988), p. 194.

60. Cf. Sale, *Hitler*, pp. 31–62, and Besier, *Heiliger Stuhl*, pp. 169–199. Both, however, had access only to the nuncial reports. Volk in his *Reichskonkordat* made use of a selection of Pacelli's audiences with the pope and with the ambassadors, although he did not cite the precise places of discovery.

61. Audience of February 3, 1933; ASV, A.E.S., Stati Ecclesiastici, 4 periodo, pos. 430, fasc. 359, fol. 37r–39v.

62. Orsenigo to Pacelli, dated February 7, 1933; ASV, A.E.S., Germania, 4 periodo, pos. 643, fasc. 157, fol. 13r–14v.

63. Orsenigo to Pacelli, dated February 16, 1933; ASV, A.E.S., Germania, 4 periodo, pos. 643, fasc. 157, fol. 18r–19v.

64. Orsenigo to Pacelli, dated February 22, 1933; ASV, A.E.S., Germania, 4 periodo, pos. 643, fasc. 157, fol. 62r–63v.

65. Audience of February 10, 1933; ASV, A.E.S., Stati Ecclesiastici, 4 periodo, pos. 430, fasc. 359, fol. 43–46v.

66. Audience of February 24, 1933; ASV, A.E.S., Stati Ecclesiastici, 4 periodo, pos. 430, fasc. 359, fol. 54r–57v.

67. Audience of February 8, 1933; ASV, A.E.S., Stati Ecclesiastici, 4 periodo, pos. 430, fasc. 359, fol. 42r–v.

68. Audience of March 4, 1933; ASV, A.E.S., Stati Ecclesiastici, 4 periodo, pos. 430, fasc. 359, fol. 66r.

69. Audience of March 4, 1933; ASV, A.E.S., Stati Ecclesiastici, 4 periodo, pos. 430a, fasc. 348, fol. 3r. Cf. also Ludwig Volk, *Das Reichskonkordat vom 20. Juli 1933*.

Von den Ansätzen in der Weimarer Republik bis zur Ratifizierung am 10. September 1933 (Veröffentlichungen der Kommission für Zeitgeschichte B 5) (Mainz: Matthias Grünewald-Verlag, 1972), p. 64n24.

70. Charles-Roux to Paul-Boncour, dated March 7, 1933, in Volk, *Reichskonkordat*, p. 65n25.

71. Faulhaber to the Bavarian episcopate, dated March 24, 1933, in Bernhard Stasiewski, ed., *Akten deutscher Bischöfe über die Lage der Kirche 1933–1945*, vol. 1, *1933–1934* (Veröffentlichungen der Kommission für Zeitgeschichte A 5) (Mainz: Matthias Grünewald-Verlag, 1968), pp. 16–18, cf. especially p. 17.

72. Audience of March 4, 1933; ASV, A.E.S., Stati Ecclesiastici, 4 periodo, pos. 430, fasc. 359, fol. 66rv.

73. Orsenigo to Pacelli, dated March 7, 1933; ASV, A.E.S., Germania, 4 periodo, pos. 643, fasc. 157, fol. 21r–22r. About the election, cf. Jürgen Falter, *Hitlers Wähler* (Munich: C.H. Beck, 1991), p. 178f. A thorough analysis of Orsenigo's report is in Brechenmacher, "Teufelspakt," p. 610n49.

74. Orsenigo to Pacelli, dated March 16, 1933; ASV, A.E.S., Germania, 4 periodo, pos. 643, fasc. 159, fol. 69r–70r.

75. Pacelli to Orsenigo, dated March 19, 1933; ASV, A.E.S., Germania, 4 periodo, pos. 643, fasc. 159, fol. 73v.

76. Audience of March 14, 1933; ASV, A.E.S., Stati Ecclesiastici, 4 periodo, pos. 430, fasc. 359, fol. 68r–69v.

77. Audience of March 17, 1933; ASV, A.E.S., Stati Ecclesiastici, 4 periodo, pos. 430a, fasc. 348, fol. 11v.

78. Audience of March 17, 1933; ASV, A.E.S., Stati Ecclesiastici, 4 periodo, pos. 430, fasc. 359, fol. 72r.

79. Audience of March 17, 1933; ASV, A.E.S., Stati Ecclesiastici, 4 periodo, pos. 430, fasc. 359, fol. 70r–71v.

80. Orsenigo to Pacelli, dated March 22, 1933; ASV, A.E.S., Germania, 4 periodo, pos. 643, fasc. 157, fol. 31r–32v.

81. Faulhaber's memorandum [in his own hand], undated [mid-March 1933]; ASV, A.E.S., Germania, 4 periodo, pos. 643, fasc. 159, fol. 119r–121v. Emphasis in original. Volk in *Reichskonkordat*, pp. 221–223, has already published a version based on the stenographic draft, from EAM, ES Faulhaber. However, there was a mix-up in the printing of the first and the second part.

82. Audience of March 27, 1933; ASV, A.E.S., Stati Ecclesiastici, 4 periodo, pos. 430, fasc. 359, fol. 82r.

83. Government declaration by Reich Chancellor Hitler upon introducing the Enabling Act in parliament on March 23, 1933, in Gruber, *Kirche*, p. 34f.

84. Audience of March 25, 1933; ASV, A.E.S., Stati Ecclesiastici, 4 periodo, pos. 430a, fasc. 348, fol. 15r–16v.

85. Audience of March 28, 1933; ASV, A.E.S., Stati Ecclesiastici, 4 periodo, pos. 430, fasc. 359, fol. 82v–83v.

86. Orsenigo to Pacelli, dated March 24, 1933; ASV, A.E.S., Germania, 4 periodo, pos. 645, fasc. 162, fol. 11r–12r. Cf. edition and and translation of this document in Volk, *Akten*, pp. 3–5 (however, without indicating the signature in ASV).

87. Audience of March 28, 1933; ASV, A.E.S., Stati Ecclesiastici, 4 periodo, pos. 430a, fasc. 348, fol. 18r–19r.

88. Orsenigo to Pacelli, dated March 26, 1933; ASV, A.E.S., Germania, 4 periodo, pos. 621, fasc. 139, fol. 77r–78r.

89. Orsenigo to Pacelli, dated March 29, 1933; ASV, A.E.S., Germania, 4 periodo, pos. 621, fasc. 140, fol. 2r–3v.

90. Announcement by the German bishops about their stance toward National Socialism, dated March 28, 1933, in Gruber, *Kirche*, p. 39f.

91. Audience of March 31, 1933; ASV, A.E.S., Stati Ecclesiastici, 4 periodo, pos. 430a, fasc. 348, fol. 20r.

92. Audience of March 31, 1933; ASV, A.E.S., Stati Ecclesiastici, 4 periodo, pos. 430, fasc. 359, fol. 84r–85v.

93. Audience of March 31, 1933; ASV, A.E.S., Stati Ecclesiastici, 4 periodo, pos. 430a, fasc. 348, fol. 20r.

94. Scholder, *Altes*, p. 193.

95. Pacelli to Vassallo di Torregrossa, dated March 29, 1933; ASV, ANM, vol. 418, fasc. 4, fol. 39r.

96. Orsenigo to Pacelli, dated April 2, 1933; ASV, A.E.S., Germania, 4 periodo, pos. 645, fasc. 162, fol. 13r–14v.

97. Orsenigo to Pacelli, dated April 8, 1933; ASV, A.E.S., Germania, 4 periodo, pos. 643, fasc. 157, fol. 70r–71r.

98. ASV, A.E.S., Stati Ecclesiastici, 4 periodo, pos. 430, fasc. 348, passim.

99. Handwritten note by Gasparri, dated June 30, 1933; ASV, A.E.S., Germania, 4 periodo, pos. 645, fasc. 163, fol. 20r. Emphasis in original.

100. Pacelli to Schioppa, dated July 15, 1933; ASV, A.E.S., Germania, 4 periodo, pos. 645, fasc. 166, fol. 71r–73r.

101. Concordat between the Holy See and the German Reich of July 20, 1933, in Volk, *Akten*, pp. 283–294, cf. especially p. 290f.

102. Pacelli to Schioppa, dated July 15, 1933; ASV, A.E.S., Germania, 4 periodo, pos. 645, fasc. 166, fol. 71r–73r. Cf. also edition and translation of the text, though without signature, in Volk, *Akten*, pp. 162–164.

103. Kirkpatrick to Robert Vansittart, dated August 19, 1933, in Volk, *Reichskonkordat*, pp. 250–252. Cf. also audience of August 18, 1933; ASV, A.E.S., Stati Ecclesiastici, 4 periodo, pos. 430, fasc. 360, fol. 37r–v.

104. Ivone Kirkpatrick, *The Inner Circle: Memoirs* (London: Macmillan, 1959), p. 48.

105. Kirkpatrick to Robert Vansittart, dated August 19, 1933, in Volk, *Reichskonkordat*, pp. 250–252, cf. especially p. 251.

4. Molto Delicato?

1. Audience of April 1, 1933; ASV, A.E.S., Stati Ecclesiastici, 4 periodo, pos. 430a, fasc. 348, fol. 21r–v.

2. Konrad Repgen, "Die Außenpolitik der Päpste im Zeitalter der Weltkriege," in Hubert Jedin and Konrad Repgen, eds., *Handbuch der Kirchengeschichte*, vol. 7: *Die Weltkirche im 20. Jahrhundert* (Freiburg i. Br.: Herder, 1979), p. 94. Emphasis in original.

3. Christmas message of Pius XII, dated December 24, 1942, in *Acta Apostolicae Sedis* 35 (1943), pp. 9–24, cf. especially p. 23.

4. Pacelli to Orsenigo, dated April 4, 1933; ASV, A.E.S., Germania, 4 periodo, pos. 643, fasc. 158, fol. 4r.

5. Orsenigo to Pacelli, dated April 8, 1933; ASV, A.E.S., Germania, 4 periodo, pos. 643, fasc. 158, fol. 5.

6. Announcement by Schulte, Klein, and Berning, dated April 9, 1933, in Bernhard Stasiewski, ed., *Akten deutscher Bischöfe über die Lage der Kirche 1933–1945*, vol. 1: *1933–1934* (Veröffentlichungen der Kommission für Zeitgeschichte A 5) (Mainz: Matthias Grünewald-Verlag, 1968), p. 51.

7. Orsenigo to Pacelli, dated April 11, 1933; ASV, A.E.S., Germania, 4 periodo, pos. 643, fasc. 158, fol. 6r–v.

8. Undated and unsigned document [written on the letterhead of the "Segreteria di Stato di Sua Santità, Ufficio Cifra." Document probably relates to the decoding of Orsenigo's report, dated April 11, 1933; ibid.]; ASV, A.E.S., Germania, 4 periodo, pos. 643, fasc. 158, fol. 8.

9. Faulhaber to Pacelli, dated April 10, 1933; ASV, A.E.S., Germania, 4 periodo, pos. 643, fasc. 158, fol. 11r–v.

10. Walzer to Pacelli, dated April 12, 1933; ASV, A.E.S., Germania, 4 periodo, pos. 643, fasc. 158, fol. 15r.

11. Edith Stein to Pope Pius XI, undated [beginning of April 1933]; ASV, A.E.S., Germania, 4 periodo, pos. 643, fasc. 158, fol. 16r, 17r.

12. Audience of April 20, 1933; ASV, A.E.S., Stati Ecclesiastici, 4 periodo, pos. 430a, fasc. 348, fol. 30r–v.

13. Pacelli to Walzer, dated April 20, 1933; ASV, A.E.S., Germania, 4 periodo, pos. 643, fasc. 158, fol. 18r.

14. Roller to Pacelli, dated September 11, 1933; ASV, A.E.S., Germania, 4 periodo, pos. 643, fasc. 158, fol. 62r–63r. No biographical data were found concerning Maximilian Roller.

15. Undated memorandum [1933]; ASV, A.E.S., Germania, 4 periodo, pos. 643, fasc. 158, fol. 49–59 (only r).

16. Arthur Zacharias Schwarz, *Die hebräischen Handschriften der Nationalbibliothek in Wien* (Leipzig, 1925), p. viii.

17. Schwarz to Pacelli, dated April 9, 1933; ASV, A.E.S., Germania, 4 periodo, pos. 643, fasc. 158, fol. 31r.

18. Schwarz to Pius XI, dated April 9, 1933; ASV, A.E.S., Germania, 4 periodo, pos. 643, fasc. 158, fol. 29r, 30r. Emphasis in original.

19. Pizzardo's handwritten note, dated April 26, 1933; ASV, A.E.S., Germania, 4 periodo, pos. 643, fasc. 158, fol. 32r.

20. Margolis to Pius XI [telegram], dated April 22, 1933; ASV, A.E.S., Germania, 4 periodo, pos. 643, fasc. 158, fol. 27r.

21. Scharnagl to Pacelli, dated April 18, 1933; ASV, A.E.S., Germania, 4 periodo, pos. 643, fasc. 157, fol. 86–94 (only r).

22. Pfannenstiel to Vassallo di Torregrossa, dated November 20, 1933; ASV, A.E.S., Germania, 4 periodo, pos. 643, fasc. 158, fol. 73r–v. No biographical data concerning Maria Pfannenstiel and her family have been found.

23. Orsenigo to Pacelli, dated April 28; ASV, A.E.S., Germania, 4 periodo, pos. 643, fasc. 158, fol. 33r–34r.

24. Pacelli to Orsenigo, dated May 19, 1933; ASV, A.E.S., Germania, 4 periodo, pos. 643, fasc. 158, fol. 35r.

25. Orsenigo to Pacelli, dated May 8, 1933; ASV, A.E.S., Germania, 4 periodo, pos. 643, fasc. 157, fol. 107r–108v.

26. Haefner to Pacelli, dated June 29, 1933; ASV, A.E.S., Germania, 4 periodo, pos. 643, fasc. 159, fol. 12–18 (only r).

27. Cf. the article "Das antifaschistische Propaganda-Flugzeug. Die Angelegenheit geklärt," in *Konstanzer Zeitung,* no. 265 (second sheet), dated November 13, 1931, p. 1.

28. Chief public prosecutor of the Berlin Superior Court W.57 to Haefner, dated January 16, 1931; Bundesarchiv Berlin Zc 19261.

29. Michel to Pius XI, dated October 24, 1933; ASV, A.E.S., Germania, 4 periodo, pos. 643, fasc. 158, fol. 64–68 (only r). No biographical data have been found concerning Louis Michel. This could have referred to the concert agent named Michel (1875–1939); however, no indications of his emigration have been found.

30. *Jewish Chronicle,* dated September 1, 1933. An excerpt of the report is in ASV, A.E.S., Germania, 4 periodo, pos. 643, fasc. 158, fol. 48r.

31. Letter from the editor of the *Jewish Chronicle* to Pacelli, dated September 8, 1933; ASV, A.E.S., Germania, 4 periodo, pos. 643, fasc. 158, fol. 47r.

32. Audience of December 18, 1933; ASV, A.E.S., Stati Ecclesiastici, 4 periodo, pos. 430a, fasc. 349, fol. 19r.

33. François Charles-Roux, *Huit ans au Vatican, 1932–1940* (Paris: Flammarion, 1947), p. 62.

34. Pacelli to Pizzardo, dated September 21, 1933; ASV, A.E.S., Baviera, 4 periodo, pos. 190, fasc. 34, without fol. [fol. 17 from beginning, r and v].

35. Audience of November 17, 1933; ASV, A.E.S., Stati Ecclesiastici, 4 periodo, pos. 430, fasc. 360, fol. 29r–31r.

36. Audience of January 5, 1934; ASV, A.E.S., Stati Ecclesiastici, 4 periodo, pos. 430, fasc. 360, fol. 68r–70r.

37. Audience of August 2, 1935; ASV, A.E.S., Stati Ecclesiastici, 4 periodo, pos. 430, fasc. 362, fol. 94r–95r.

38. Audience of March 2, 1934; ASV, A.E.S., Stati Ecclesiastici, 4 periodo, pos. 430a, fasc. 349, fol. 52r.

39. Laghi to Pacelli, dated September 11, 1936; ASV, A.E.S., Stati Ecclesiastici, 4 periodo, pos. 541, fasc. 563, fol. 3r–8r.

40. Gillet to Pacelli, dated September 12, 1938, ASV, A.E.S., Cecoslovacchia, 4 periodo, pos. 144, fasc. 183, fol. 22r–23r.

41. Orsenigo to Pacelli, dated November 15, 1938; ASV, A.E.S., Germania, 4 periodo, pos. 742, fasc. 356, fol. 40r–41v. Title page of the diarium covering the period from September 27 to October 29, 1938, by Tardini; ASV, A.E.S., Stati Ecclesiastici, 4 periodo, pos. 560, fasc. 592, fol. 94.

42. "A propos de L'Antisémitisme. Pèlerinage de la Radio catholique belge," in *La Documentation Catholique,* dated December 5, 1938, p. 1459f., especially p. 1460. Cf. also Emma Fattorini, *Pio XI, Hitler e Mussolini. La solitudine di un papa* (Turin: Einaudi, 2007), p. 181.

43. Tardini's audience with Pius XI, dated October 23, 1938; ASV, A.E.S., Stati Ecclesiastici, 4 periodo, pos. 560, fasc. 592, fol. 123v–126v, cf. especially fol. 124r–v.

44. Antoniutti to Pacelli, dated December 19, 1938; ASV, A.E.S., Stati Ecclesiastici, 4 periodo, pos. 575, fasc. 606, fol. 55r–v.

45. Pius XI to the North American cardinals, dated January 10, 1939; ASV, A.E.S., Stati Ecclesiastici, 4 periodo, pos. 575, fasc. 606, fol. 115r–v.

46. Pietro Scoppola, *La Chiesa e il Facismo. Documenti e interpretazioni* (Rome / Bari: Editori Laterza, 1967), p. 186.

47. "Provvedimenti per la difesa della razza italiana," in *Renzo de Felice, Storia degli ebrei italiani sotto il facismo* (Turin: Einaudi, 1972), pp. 562–566, cf. especially p. 562. Cf. also Gudrun Jäger and Liana Novelli-Glaab, eds., *Judentum und Antisemitismus im modernen Italien: . . . denn in Italien haben sich die Dinge anders abgespielt* (Frankfurter Kulturwissenschaftliche Beiträge 2) (Berlin: Trafo Verlag, 2007).

48. Decennale della Conciliazione, undated [written during the night of January 31 to February 1, 1939]; ASV, A.E.S., Stati Ecclesiastici, 4 periodo, pos. 576, fasc. 607, fol. 1–223. Printout of the speech in Fattorini, *Pio XI,* pp. 240–244.

49. http://www.30giorni.it/us/articolo.asp?id=15291 (accessed September 24, 2009).

50. Gundlach to La Farge, dated May 10, 1933, in Georges Passelecq and Bernard Suchecky, *Die unterschlagene Enzyklika. Der Vatikan und die Judenverfolgung* (Munich: Carl Hanser Verlag, 1997), p. 112; and Anton Rauscher, ed., *Wider den Rassismus. Entwurf einer nicht erschienenen Enzyklika (1938),* Texte aus dem Nachlaß von Gustav Gundlach, SJ (Paderborn: Schöningh, 2001), p. 45.

51. Text of the encyclical in Rauscher, ed., *Rassismus,* pp. 76–167, especially no. 171 on p. 161, no. 182 on p. 166, and no. 183 on p. 167.

52. Robert Leiber, "Pius XII. und die Juden in Rom 1943–1944," in *Stimmen der Zeit* 167 (1960/61), p. 436.

53. Alois C. Hudal, *Römische Tagebücher. Lebensbeichte eines alten Bischofs* (Graz/Stuttgart: Leopold Stocker Verlag, 1976), p. 118.

54. "Hitler verschachert die österreichischen Nazis. Paris 13. Juli 13 (Eigener Report)," in *Volksstimme,* dated July 13, 1933; ASV, A.E.S., Germania, 4 periodo, pos. 643, fasc. 161, fol. 75.

55. Helmuth James Count von Moltke, letter to his wife, Freya, dated September 6, 1941, in Helmuth James von Moltke, *Letters to Freya: 1939–1945,* ed. and trans. Beate Ruhm von Oppen (New York: Knopf, 1990), p. 157.

56. Galen to his mother, dated August 21, 1919; Bistumsarchiv Münster, Sammlung Galen A 4.

57. Orsenigo to Pacelli, dated February 24, 1933; ASV, ANB, vol. 102, fasc. 4 (Galen), fol. 41–46 (only r).

58. Audience of July 8, 1933; ASV, A.E.S., Stati Ecclesiastici, 4 periodo, pos. 430a, fasc. 348, fol. 76r–v.

59. Clemens August von Galen, *Denkschrift über Autorität,* dated February 28, 1933, in Westfälisches Archivamt, Nachlass von Franz von Galen 46.

60. Memorandum of Galen from early March 1936; ASV, A.E.S., Germania, 4 periodo, "Scatole" 46a, fol. 29r (letter by Galen), 30–39 (only r) (memorandum).

61. Galen's sermon in Xanten on September 6, 1936, in Peter Löffler ed., *Bischof Clemens August Graf von Galen. Akten, Briefe und Predigten 1933–1946,* 2 vols. (Veröffentlichungen der Kommission für Zeitgeschichte A 42) (Paderborn: Schöningh, 1996), vol. 1, pp. 439–447.

62. Galen to Berning, dated May 26, 1941, in Löffler, ed., *Galen,* vol. 2, pp. 1460–1463, cf. especially p. 1462.

63. Antonia Leugers, *Gegen eine Mauer bischöflichen Schweigens. Der Ausschuß für Ordensangelegenheiten und seine Widerstandskonzeption 1941 bis 1945* (Frankfurt a. M.: Verlag Josef Knecht, 1996), p. 207f.

64. Galen's sermon, dated August 3, 1941, in Heinrich Portmann, *Cardinal von Galen,* trans. R. L. Sedgwick (London, 1957), pp. 239–246, especially p. 242f.

65. Undated letter from an anonymous Jew to Galen [before September 19, 1941], in Löffler, ed., *Galen,* vol. 2, pp. 901–908, cf. especially p. 901f.

66. M. Pascalina Lehnert, *Ich durfte ihm dienen. Erinnerungen an Papst Pius XII* (Würzburg: Verlag Johann Wilhelm Naumann, 1983), p. 151.

67. Pius XII to Preysing, dated September 30, 1941, in Burkhart Schneider, ed., *Die Briefe Pius' XII. an die deutschen Bischöfe 1939–1944* (Veröffentlichungen der Kommission für Zeitgeschichte A 4) (Mainz: Matthias Grünewald-Verlag, 1966), pp. 154–156.

5. Dogma or Diplomacy?

1. Audience of July 15, 1933; ASV, A.E.S., Stati Eccelesiastici, 4 periodo, pos. 430, fasc. 360, fol. 13r–v.

2. Audience of February 10, 1934; ASV, A.E.S., Stati Ecclesiastici, 4 periodo, pos. 430, fasc. 349, fol. 43r.

3. "Santa Sede e Nazionalsocialismo: Dottrina e Politica," undated [after August 15, 1933]; ASV, A.E.S., Germania, 4 periodo, pos. 643, fasc. 160, fol. 11–15 (only r).

4. Audience of January 25, 1935; ASV, A.E.S., Stati Ecclesiastici, 4 periodo, pos. 430, fasc. 362, fol. 15r–16r.

5. Copy of attachment no. 9 (fol. 118r–v) to Torregrossa's report to Pacelli, dated October 23, 1924, about "Controversia fra la 'Evangelisch-Lutherische Kirche' e la 'Reichskirche.' Preoccupazioni pubbliche" (fol. 98r–101r); ASV, A.E.S., Germania, 4 periodo, pos. 643, fasc. 160, fol. 119r. About the text of the song, see Klaus Scholder, *Die Kirchen zwischen Republik und Gewaltherrschaft. Gesammelte Aufsätze,* ed. Karl Otmar von Aretin and Gerhard Besier (Berlin: Siedler, 1988), vol. 2, p. 143.

6. "Le cause della rivolta e della repressione tedesca. Il bilancio delle giornate sanguinose—Il totalitarismo hitleriano ed i contrasto fra la destra e sinistra—Il costume morale delle milizie d'assalto—La nuova situazione," in *L'Osservatore Romano,* no. 152 (July 4, 1934), p. 1.

7. Pius XI to Schuster, dated April 26, 1931, in *Acta Apostolicae Sedis* 23 (1931), pp. 145–150, especially p. 147f.

8. Memorandum from the Holy See to the German government, dated May 14, 1934, in Dieter Albrecht, *Der Notenwechsel zwischen dem Heiligen Stuhl und der Deutschen Reichsregierung,* vol. 1 (Veröffentlichungen der Kommission für Zeitgeschichte A 1) (Mainz: Matthias Grünewald-Verlag, 1980), pp. 125–164, especially pp. 146f. and 137.

9. Ruffini to the cardinals of the Holy Office, dated July 26, 1926; ACDF, SO RV 1927, no. 28, *Una Sancta.*

10. Meeting of the cardinals Feria Quarta on July 28, 1926, meeting of the cardinals Feria Quinta of July 29, 1926; ACDF, SO RV 1927, no. 28, *Una Sancta.*

11. Merry del Val to Pacelli, dated July 30, 1931 (printed as attachment I to the report of January 1927); ACDF, SO RV 1927, no. 28, *Una Sancta.*

12. Letter from Pacelli to the German bishops, dated September 10, 1926; ACDF, SO RV 1927, no. 28, *Una Sancta.*

13. Pacelli to Merry del Val, dated November 15, 1926; ASV, A.E.S., Germania, 4 periodo, pos. 569, fasc. 84, fol. 7r–29v.

14. Pacelli to Merry del Val, dated November 15, 1926 [secret printing]; ACDF, SO RV 1927, no. 28, *Una Sancta.*

15. Decree of the Holy Office, "De participatione catholicorum societati 'Ad procurandam Christianitatis unitatem,'" in *Acta Apostolicae Sedis* 11 (1919), p. 309.

16. Merry del Val to Pacelli, dated December 9, 1926 (printed as attachment II to the report of January 1927); ACDF, SO RV 1927, no. 28, *Una Sancta*.

17. Pacelli to Merry del Val, dated January 9, 1927; ACDF, SO RV 1927, no. 28, *Una Sancta*.

18. Merry del Val to Pacelli, dated January 20, 1927; ACDF, SO RV 1927, no. 28, *Una Sancta*.

19. "Relazione e Quesiti" of January 1927; ACDF, SO RV 1927, no. 28, *Una Sancta*.

20. Votum of Ruffini of February 14, 1927; ACDF, SO RV 1927, no. 28, *Una Sancta*.

21. Minutes of the Congregatio Praeparatoria Feria Secunda on February 13, 1927; ACDF, SO RV 1927, no. 28, *Una Sancta*.

22. Votum of Ferretti in the consultors meeting Feria Secunda on February 13, 1927; ACDF, SO RV 1927, no. 28, *Una Sancta*. Emphasis in original.

23. Votum by Drehmanns in the consultors meeting Feria Secunda on February 13, 1927; ACDF, SO RV 1927, no. 28, *Una Sancta*.

24. Votum of Merry del Val of February 26, 1927, submitted at the session of the Holy Office Feria Quarta of March 9, 1927; ACDF, SO RV 1927, no. 28, *Una Sancta*.

25. Session of the Holy Office Feria Quarta of March 9, 1927; ACDF, SO RV 1927, no. 28, *Una Sancta*.

26. Draft Feria Quarta of March 16, 1927; ACDF, SO RV 1927, no. 28, *Una Sancta*. Printed in *Archiv für katholisches Kirchenrecht* 107 (1927), pp. 348–350.

27. Pacelli to Gasparri (telegram), dated April 16, 1927; ACDF, SO RV 1927, no. 28, *Una Sancta*.

28. Pacelli to Pizzardo, dated April 17, 1927; ACDF, SO RV 1927, no. 28, *Una Sancta*.

29. Canali to Pizzardo, dated April 23, 1927; ACDF, SO RV 1927, no. 28, *Una Sancta*.

30. Pacelli to Canali, dated April 28, 1927; ACDF SO RV 1927, no. 28, *Una Sancta*.

31. Canali's audience with Pius XI of April 28, 1927; ACDF, SO RV 1927, no. 28, *Una Sancta*.

32. Canali's audience with Pius XI of May 5, 1927; ACDF, SO RV 1927, no. 28, *Una Sancta*.

33. ACDF, SO Censurae Librorum (hereinafter: CL) 4304/1933 (1) for Rosenberg, (2) and (3) for Bergmann, and (4) for Fritsch. On this issue cf. Dominik Burkard, *Häresie und Mythus des 20. Jahrhunderts. Rosenbergs nationalsozialistische*

Weltanschauung vor dem Tribunal der Römischen Inquisition (Römische Inquisition und Indexkongregation 5) (Paderborn: Schöningh, 2005).

34. Hudal's opinion on Bergmann's *Nationalkirche,* dated January 1934; ACDF, SO CL 4304/1933 (2), no. 6/b and 6/c.

35. Minutes of the consultors' meeting of January 29, 1934; ACDF, SO CL 4304/1933 (2), no. 5/1.

36. Session of the cardinals on February 7, 1934; ACDF, SO CL 4304/1933 (1), no. 2 and (2), no. 6 and 6/a.

37. "Un libro di odiose falsità per la gioventù tedesca," in *L'Osservatore Romano,* no. 30 (February 7, 1934), p. 3.

38. Decree of February 9, 1934; ACDF, SO CL 4304/1933 (1), no. 3–3/1.

39. "Suprema Sacra Congregatio Santi Officii," in *L'Osservatore Romano,* no. 36 (February 14, 1934), p. 1.

40. Alois C. Hudal, *Römische Tagebücher. Lebensbeichte eines alten Bischofs* (Graz/Stuttgart: Leopold Stocker Verlag, 1976), p. 145.

41. Ibid., p. 47f.

42. Archive of Santa Maria dell'Anima Rom, papers of Alois Hudal, K 65, fol. 208; cited according to Burkard, *Häresie,* p. 178. Emphasis in original.

43. Hudal, *Tagebücher,* p. 120f.

44. Printed votum of July 1935; ACDF, SO RV 1934, no. 29, fasc. 1, no. 3, fol. 1–5. Copy of Hudal's letter to Cardinal Sbarretti, dated October 7, 1934, and a German version, given to Canali on October 18, 1934, in Hudal, *Tagebücher,* pp. 122–126.

45. Printed votum of July 1935 and memo from Canali about the session on October 25, 1934; ACDF, SO RV 1934, no. 29, fasc. 1, no. 3, fol. 5.

46. Hürth's votum of July 1935; ACDF, SO RV 1934, no. 29, fasc. 1, no. 3, fol. 6–16.

47. Anonymous votum [Johann Baptist Rabeneck] (31 printed pages), dated March 17, 1935; ACDF, SO RV 1934, no. 29, fasc. 1, no. 1.

48. "Notae" to typescript no. 1 (45 pages); ACDF, SO RV 1934, no. 29, fasc. 1, no. 2.

49. Adolf Hitler, *Mein Kampf,* trans. Ralph Manheim (Boston: Houghton Mifflin, 1943), p. 385. Emphasis in original.

50. Ibid., p. 382.

51. Ibid., p. 290.

52. Note from the Assessor of the Holy Office and list of 47 propositions; ACDF, SO RV 1934, no. 29, fasc. 1, no. 3, fol. 16–27.

53. French votum of Gillet of April 1936; ACDF, SO RV 1934, no. 29, fasc. 2, no. 4, fol. 1–3.

54. Ruffini's votum, dated April 20, 1936; ACDF, SO RV 1934, no. 29, fasc. 2, no. 4, fol. 4f.

55. Tardini's votum, dated April 20, 1936; ACDF, SO RV 1934, no. 29, fasc. 2, no. 4, fol. 6–11.

56. "Schema di decreto su razzismo, nazionalismo, comunismo, stato totalitario" (44 printed pages) of July 1936; ACDF, SO RV 1934, no. 29, fasc. 4, no. 12.

57. "Raccolta di testi su razzismo, nazionalismo, comunismo, totalitarismo (proposizioni da condannare)" (41 printed pages) of October 1936; ACDF, SO RV 1934, no. 29, fasc. 4, no. 13.

58. Decree Feria Quarta, dated November 18, 1936; ACDF, SO RV 1934, no. 29, fasc. 4, no. 13 bis.

59. Decree Feria Quinta, papal audience of November 19, 1936; ACDF, SO RV 1934, no. 29, fasc. 4, no. 13 bis.

60. Decree Feria Quarta, dated March 17, 1937; ACDF, SO RV 1934, no. 29, fasc. 4, no. 16 bis.

61. Syllabus of the propositions with preliminary notes (15 pages); ACDF, SO RV 1934, no. 29, fasc. 4, no. 19. Emphasis in original. For an exact list of references from Hitler's *Mein Kampf*, see Hubert Wolf, "Pius XI. und die 'Zeitirrtümer.' Die Initiativen der römischen Inquisition gegen Rassismus und Nationalsozialismus," in *Vierteljahrshefte für Zeitgeschichte*, 53 (2005), pp. 1–42.

62. Decree Feria Quarta, dated June 2, 1937; ACDF, SO RV 1934, no. 29, fasc. 4, no. 19 bis.

63. Papal audience of June 4, 1937; ACDF, SO RV 1934, no. 29, fasc. 4, no. 19 bis.

64. Hudal, *Tagebücher*, p. 121.

65. "Syllabus di proposizioni relative al communismo e al razzismo," of May 1937 (15 printed pages); ACDF, SO RV 1934, no. 29, fasc. 4, no. 19.

66. Papal audience of June 4, 1937; ACDF, SO RV 1934, no. 29, fasc. 4, no. 19 bis.

67. Session of June 14, 1937: Spain, political and religious situation; ASV, A.E.S., Sessioni, anno 1937, without fol.

68. Speyer bishop Ludwig Sebastian's notes of the Plenary Conference of the German Episcopate, Fulda, August 18–20, 1936, in Bernhard Stasiewski, ed., *Akten deutscher Bischöfe über die Lage der Kirche 1933–1945*, vol. 3: *1935–1936* (Veröffentlichungen der Kommission für Zeitgeschichte A 25) (Mainz: Matthias Grünewald-Verlag, 1979), p. 468.

69. Greeting address of the German Episcopate to Pius XI, on August 18, 1936, in Stasiewski, ed., *Akten*, vol. 3, p. 437.

70. Brief report of discussions with the cardinals and bishops then visiting Rome, on January 16, 1937; ASV, A.E.S., Germania, 4 periodo, pos. 719, fasc. 314, fol. 5r–6r.

71. Stenographic draft of Faulhaber's cover letter to Pacelli, dated January 21, 1937, in Ludwig Volk, ed., *Akten Kardinal Michael von Faulhabers 1917–1945*, vol. III:

1935–1945 (Veröffentlichungen der Kommission für Zeitgeschichte A 26) (Mainz: Matthias Grünewald-Verlag, 1978), p. 282.

72. "Mit brennender Sorge," in Dieter Albrecht, ed., *Der Notenwechsel zwischen dem Heiligen Stuhl und der deutschen Reichsregierung* (Veröffentlichungen der Kommission für Zeitgeschichte A 29) (Mainz: Matthias Grünewald-Verlag, 1980), vol. 1, p. 416f.

73. Synopsis (12 printed pages); ACDF, SO RV 1934, no. 29, fasc. 4, no. 18.

74. "Mit brennender Sorge," in Albrecht, ed., *Notenwechsel,* vol. 1, p. 410.

75. Ibid., p. 431.

76. "Syllabus di proposizioni relative al communismo e al razzismo of May 1937" (15 printed pages); ACDF, SO RV 1934, no. 29, fasc. 4, no. 19.

77. Heinz Hürten, *"Kulturkampf. Berichte aus dem Dritten Reich. Paris." Eine Auswahl aus den deutschsprachigen Jahrgängen 1936–1939* (Eichstätter Materialien 3) (Regensburg: Verlag Friedrich Pustet, 1988), pp. 177–181.

78. *Nationalsozialistische Monatshefte,* 9 (1938), p. 822f., especially p. 823.

79. Gröber to Orsenigo, dated February 28, 1933, in Burkard, *Häresie,* p. 247n951.

80. Audience of April 10, 1938; ASV, A.E.S., Germania, 4 periodo, pos. 720, fasc. 329, fol. 31r.

81. Borgongini Duca to Pacelli, dated May 2, 1938; ASV, A.E.S., Germania, 4 periodo, pos. 720, fasc. 329, fol. 25r–v.

Acknowledgments

Eighty years after the Holy See condemned racial anti-Semitism in 1928; seventy-five years after Hitler's seizure of power in 1933; seventy years after Kristallnacht in 1938; fifty years after the death of Pius XII in 1958; and five years after the opening of the German holdings in the Vatican Secret Archives relating to the pontificate of Pius XI in 2003; the year 2008, when the original German version of this book was published—a year of jubilees—seemed an apt time to examine the relationship between the Catholic Church and the Third Reich. This occasion will no doubt continue to see the publication of numerous works, including biographies of Popes Pius XI and Pius XII, and perhaps even a few "general overviews" of the relationship between the Vatican and National Socialism between the years 1933 and 1945. But even now, certain connections have not been clarified with any finality. In particular, we still have little understanding of the popes' stance toward the persecution of the Jews and the Holocaust.

The holdings for the pontificate of Pius XI, from the period 1922 to 1939, comprise more than 100,000 archival units, including boxes, fascicles, and file dossiers, some of which run to 1,000 pages or more. Given this profusion of source material, made newly available in the Vatican Secret Archives since September 2006, it is simply impossible for a historian to present the reader with any sort of general overview of the relationship between the Vatican and National Socialism or even definitive biographies of Pius XI and Pius XII. It will take years, if not decades, of methodical and responsible archival research to develop the understanding that might make such works possible. The goal of the present volume is much more modest. I have selected five general areas of interest and have attempted a historical reconstruction of the "view from

Rome" on Germany between 1917 and 1939. The "representative of Christ on earth" and his colleagues believed themselves to be in a battle against the increasingly dangerous forces of modernity, anticlerical liberalism, Communism, and National Socialism. They viewed the situation in Germany through Roman spectacles, which had their own tint and their own particular focus. For many Catholics, the modern age seemed like a war between the pope and the devil.

My colleagues and I were afforded an unprecedented opportunity to work on the newly accessible sources in Rome, when I was awarded the Leibniz Prize by the Deutsche Forschungsgemeinschaft in 2003. From the preliminary work has emerged, among other things, a research project of the Deutsche Forschungsgemeinschaft, the "Critical Online Edition of the Nuncial Reports of Eugenio Pacelli" (1917 to 1929), and a project on "The Catholic Church and the Totalitarianisms of the Twentieth Century" as part of the Münster Excellence Cluster "Religion and Politics in Pre-modern and Modern Cultures."

The present volume benefited immensely from the numerous discussions occasioned by these projects. It has become clear once again how fruitful and inspiring constructive discussions can be if one is part of a good team of scholars from varied disciplines. It is unlikely that I would have had the privilege of working with such a large and outstanding team if not for the Leibniz Prize and other outside funding, which promoted a variety of research projects. The extraordinary support of my university was no less important in enabling a project that optimally combined research and teaching. Because of this, I wish to express my thanks to the University of Münster.

I also wish to acknowledge my colleagues throughout the world. Work on this topic, which is of general interest to all of us, and our meetings in the Roman archives have resulted in a fountain of questions, if not always answers. These colleagues include, among others, Professors Emma Fattorini, Philippe Chenaux, Matteo Napolitano, Gerald Fogarty, and Thomas Brechenmacher. I also wish to thank Monsignor Alejandro Cifres for his invaluable help in the Archive of the Congregation for the Doctrine of the Faith. And very special thanks to the prefect of the Vatican Secret Archives, Bishop Sergio Pagano, who with the precision and unerring judgment of an archivist of the best school is a role model for all young historians, and who through his own work continues to make clear how important it is to engage personally with the sources.

And now, to all those who contributed directly to the book. First, I would like to thank Assistant Professor Dr. Kirsi Salonen, our point person at the Vatican Secret Archives, for her tireless hunt for sources and her overview of the widely dispersed holdings; Verena Imhorst, my secretary, for her work on the manuscript, and especially for the many handwritten corrections that she entered into the manuscript; Dr. Maria Pia Lorenz-Filograno, foreign language correspondent clerk, for her translations of the often cryptic source notations, which were not always easy; and Elke Surmann, the secretary for Science Communications, for her research and assembly of archival sources and photographs, and for her precise proofreading.

I also wish to thank Assistant Professor Dr. Thomas Bauer, the director of my seminar, who always backed me up; Dr. Klaus Unterburger, my academic assistant, who brought with him his immense erudition and knowledge of the history of twentieth-century theology; Dr. Thies Schulze, who for his profound knowledge of Italian history was of incalculable help in the work on Pacelli's nuncial reports and on the manuscript; Martin Baxmeyer, who in the Excellence Cluster is responsible for the project on the Spanish Civil War, and whose contributions as the "productive anarchist" on our team have become indispensable. Dr. Holger Arning, who is responsible for science communications, monitored the text for comprehensibility and legibility with Argus eyes and the highest level of competence and never avoided a discussion of content.

Without the collaboration of Dr. Barbara Schüler, the head of my office for science communication and science management, this book could never have been written, let alone finished. I want to thank her especially for her outstanding work in coordinating the entire project, and particularly for our many impassioned debates and intense discussions. I would also like to thank Dr. Ulrich Nolte at Verlag C. H. Beck. He always showed patience and asked the intelligent questions that enabled me to further develop the conceptual framework of this book. That he and his assistant, Gisela Muhn-Sorge, are exemplary, and that Beck provides unsurpassed support, need hardly be said.

Finally, I would like to thank Harvard University Press for publishing this book in English, and in particular Kenneth Kronenberg, who assumed the task of translating it. I am grateful to my research assistant Elisabeth-Marie Richter, who monitored and revised the translated manuscript, helping with the delicate terminology.

I dedicate this book in deep gratitude to my parents, Elisabeth and Rupert Wolf, on their Golden Anniversary, May 1, 2008. This year is truly their jubilee year!

Index